Galvano Della Volpe

NLB

Critique of Taste

Translated by Michael Caesar

First published as *Critica del Gusto*
by Feltrinelli, Milan 1960

© Feltrinelli, 1960

This edition first published 1978

© NLB, 1978

NLB, 7 Carlisle Street, London W 1

Printed in Great Britain by
Western Printing Services Ltd
Bristol
bound by
Kemp Hall Bindery,
Oxford

Designed by Ruth Prentice

ISBN 902308 48 3

But the difficulty lies not in understanding that the Greek arts and epic are bound up with certain forms of social development. The difficulty is that they still afford us artistic pleasure and that in a certain respect they count as a norm and as an unattainable model.

Marx   *Grundrisse* (1857)

We all laid, and were bound to lay, the main emphasis on the fact that political, juridical and other ideological representations *are derived* from fundamental economic facts and that this also applied to actions mediated through these representations. We stressed the content and neglected the form, i.e. the ways and means by which these notions come about.

Engels   *Letter to Mehring* (1893)

Contents

8

Translator's Note

This translation is from the third edition of *Critica del Gusto* published by Feltrinelli. Della Volpe's paragraphs and longer sentences have generally been divided, to facilitate the text for English readers. The numeration of sections is the author's; the titles of them are editorial. The main text is complete but for the omission of an analysis of French and German translations of *The Divine Comedy* (Feltrinelli, pp. 106–9), and of poems by Mayakovsky and Slutsky (pp. 42–6, 94–5), for which English translations are lacking. English versions of Greek, German or other poetry have been selected, from among the range available in any given case, for fidelity of translation, in keeping with Della Volpe's own precepts (see Section 16), if necessary even at the price of some archaism of diction – for which allowance must be made.

For the convenience of the reader, the Postscripta on music (Section 20) and the cinema (Section 21), and the Note on Lukács (Appendix 1) have been brought forward from the Notes to the main body of the text. The Notes themselves have been abbreviated by the exclusion of references and discussions which appeared to be of strictly local interest. The lengthy Note on glossematics in Chapter 2 is printed separately at the end of the Appendices. An attempt has been made, where possible, to systematize the Notes and to check and if necessary correct or complete Della Volpe's references. The greater part of this time-consuming work was done by Patrick Camiller, to whom I here take the opportunity of expressing my warm appreciation.

M.C.

Preface

My aim in the present book is to present a systematic exposition of an historical-materialist aesthetic, and by extension, an orderly sociological reading of poetry and art in general. This entails in the first place a radical critique of established aesthetic conceptions, principally if not exclusively those of romanticism and idealism. But it also implies an intention to recover the work of art in all its human fullness. By this I mean the work of art both in its more general epistemological aspects and in its more specialized and technical aspects. The former link it essentially to other human aspirations of a scientific or moral order, while it is the latter which give rise to the problem of the semantic dimension peculiar to art. In pursuing these aims, let me add at once, I have constantly submitted the theoretical theses to be demonstrated and my hypotheses of method to the test of artistic (and therefore historical) critical experiment.

In this way, I have tried for my part to help make good that 'neglect' to which Engels confessed in his own name and that of Marx (*'wir alle . . '*) in the self-criticism he addressed to Mehring in July 1893. He was referring – the passage is quoted in the frontispiece to this volume – to the neglect of the 'formal aspect', or as we would say the logical and epistemological aspect, of 'ideological representations' (in our case, works of art), for a concern with their origin in 'fundamental economic facts' or solid structures – in other words their 'substantive' aspect. The attempt to redress the balance has of course been made before, by such writers as Plekhanov, Gramsci and Lukács – yet nearly always with uneven results. Thus, for example, an examination of the semantic or linguistic side of poetry and of art is one of the main themes of the present inquiry, precisely because it has been lacking hitherto in any materialist aesthetic. It is true that the need for it was felt indirectly by Marx and Engels when they wrote in *The German Ideology*, drawing tacitly on an as yet unchallenged romantic linguistics, that 'language is the immediate actuality of thought'; and it was appreciated implicitly by Gramsci when he defended 'normative grammar' against the idealist linguistics of Bertoni. But that is all. So my predominant use in this study of the essential features of the theory of glossematics is not a matter of chance, nor is it due to any personal inclination of my own for the laborious subtleties of Hjelmslev's 'algebra' of language. The reason is simply that glossematics, the structural linguistics of the Copenhagen school, represents the most coherent and complete development of modern scientific (Saussurian) linguistics, and hence the most general language-theory. My use of it is intended to establish firmly the semantic bases of poetry and literature, before going on to sketch a general aesthetic semiotics.

This book may thus be seen as an attempt at a rationalist and materialist *emendatio* of traditional (bourgeois) taste. In rejecting the late-romantic decadentism and aestheticism of the latter, it is an attempt to defend the realism of poetry. It appears at a critical and contradictory time. On the one hand, a well-known bourgeois novelist can make an emotional attack on Manzoni's Catholic realism, inspired by a desire to discredit the 'modern demand' for 'poetry of propaganda', and in particular socialist realism in art.* On the other hand, there is a no less emotional defence, conducted by Marxist critics not only in Italy, of a strangely distorted poetic of socialist realism. This argues that Engels's recognition of the realism of the reactionary Balzac and Lenin's acknowledgement of the social truth in the writings of the mystical populist Tolstoy were no more than accurate but local 'historical' judgements, rather than particular

---

* For example, in the famous description in *The Betrothed* of the first meeting between Egidio and the nun of Monza, Manzoni's critic underlines with an abstract and onesided relish the following characterization of the seducer's conduct, which according to him is simply a representation of 'sadism' and 'profanatory lust': 'attracted rather than alarmed by the dangers and impiety of the undertaking, one day he ventured to address her' [tr. Archibald Colquhoun, London & New York 1956, p. 145]. He completely ignores, believe it or not, the phrase 'the wretched woman' in 'The wretched woman replied', which is the poetic climax of the passage and at the same time Manzoni's final ethical and religious judgement as a Catholic on the episode. [The 'well-known bourgeois novelist' was Alberto Moravia in his essay 'Alessandro Manzoni o l'ipotesi di un realismo cattolico' (1960), now in *L'uomo come fine e altri saggi*, Milan 1964 – *Tr. note*].

observations of such profundity that they are capable of aesthetic generalization. Such a standpoint suggests the dangerously restrictive conclusion that only with the 'right', progressivist, ideas can realist poetry be written.

Not the least of the tasks that I have set myself in the present study is to demonstrate that such a conclusion not only gives unwitting comfort to the bourgeois aestheticians mentioned above, but it inwardly contradicts the very possibility of constituting a rigorous poetic of socialist realism in the proper sense of the term. The polemical interest alone that these pages may provoke will more than repay the effort they have cost – mine, at any rate, if not the reader's, whom here I sincerely thank.

G. d. V.

The University, Messina, June 1960.

Critique of the Poetic 'Image'

1. Image versus Idea

There is one obstacle that more than any other still hampers the progress of aesthetics and literary criticism: the term 'image' or (poetic) 'imagination', which continues to labour under the burden of aesthetic mysticism left by its romantic past. Thanks to that legacy, while the poetic 'image' may be acknowledged as a symbol or vehicle of truth, the implication always is that this truth is never due to any organic or effective presence in it of intellect or rational discourse or ideas. Ideas, indeed, are still held to be the great enemy of poetry. Nevertheless, the 'veracity' of the 'image' continues to be emphasized, and therewith its cosmic or universal character and its cognitive or 'intuitive' value. The argument has frequently been advanced that there is no way out of this impasse because it derives necessarily from the very nature of poetry. But in fact what we are dealing with is an historical antinomy, whose origins lie in the nature of traditional aesthetic thought, itself romantic and spiritualist (Christian-bourgeois) by definition. Once we have gone beyond this traditional aesthetic, the antinomy itself will be overcome.

The fact remains, however, that our current philosophical criteria are not significantly more advanced than they were, say, when George Moore declared 'ideas' to be 'those pests and parasites of artistic work' and Yeats rejected Ibsen's symbolism because it was too intellectual.[1]

---

1. Frank Kermode, *Romantic Image*, London 1957: ' "Those pests and parasites of artistic work – ideas" (George Moore)' (p. 43); 'The species of image with which he [Wilde] is concerned cannot, of course, stand in any simple relation to merely "intellectual intention". (Both Wilde and Yeats disliked or distrusted the symbolism of Ibsen) . . . This is a perfectly logical anti-intentionalist position, and it is a fundamental one in all Romantic criticism including what is known as the

Even today two critics of the stature of Cleanth Brooks and Robert Penn Warren, to whom in fact we owe some penetrating analyses of the intellectual structure of a number of modern poems, can preface their analysis of the structure of Eliot's *Waste Land* with a methodological note which reads: 'the discussion that follows is to be considered as a means to an *end*: the *imaginative* apprehension of the poem itself'.[2] This is still Coleridge with his miraculous 'imagination' taken over from the German Romantics.[3] Contemporary German aesthetics too teaches an abstract and aestheticist Kantian 'autonomy', as for example in the late Nicolai Hartmann's definition of the 'specificity' of artistic pleasure as 'a contemplative attitude'.[4] As for 'Marxist' aesthetics, what are we to make of a Lukács who tells us that 'art makes us *intuit sensibly*' what science breaks down into 'abstract elements' and conceptual definitions', yet who at the same time finds no contradiction in demanding that the artistic figment be invested with 'typicality' – i.e. intellectuality?[5]

New Criticism of recent years. A corollary of this attitude to intellect (we are dealing with a different but definite order of truth by means of intuition or imagination) is the requirement of concreteness in the work of art' (p. 46).

2. Cleanth Brooks and Robert Penn Warren, *Understanding Poetry* (complete edition), New York 1952, p. 645 [D.V.'s emphases].

3. Coleridge's limits as a follower of Kant and German Romanticism have recently been recognized in Anglo-American criticism: see R. Wellek, *A History of Modern Criticism*, New Haven 1955, vol. II, pp. 151 ff.

4. Nicolai Hartmann, *Aesthetik*, Berlin 1953, for example, pp. 56–57. The wealth and organization of Hartmann's material, however, should be a source of envy to our Italian idealists; his treatment in no way dilutes or impoverishes the complexity of the problems, amongst which he has the merit of tackling that of the means of expression.

5. Georg Lukács, cf. *Writer and Critic*, ed. and tr. A. Kahn, London 1970, p. 77. See his *Prolegomeni a un' Estetica Marxista*, Rome 1957: '*particularity* as an aesthetic category' – 'a technique can be fruitful ... in the artistic sense only if it allows the unfolding of this particularity'. Note also his conclusion, 'a sharp distinction between form and technique', in *Cinema nuovo*, Sept.–Oct. 1958, and my *Verosimile filmico*, Rome 1954, pp. 119 ff.

I should like to add a few words on John Dewey. His anti-metaphysical aesthetic, inspired by the very modern need to reunite art and experience (*Art as Experience*, New York 1934), marks him off sharply, and to his credit, from the authors cited above, with whom I do not wish to confuse him. We should not forget his exemplary, basic critical observation, that 'the odd notion that an artist does not think and a scientific inquirer does nothing else is the result of converting a difference of tempo and emphasis into a difference in kind' (p. 15). It is true that his way of putting the problem is not always rigorous and often has to be taken with caution. His definition, for example, of the 'effective content' as 'the art-object itself' means, as has been pointed out before, the identification of the content of the

Actual artistic (literary) experience, if considered with scientific and epistemological attention and not dogmatically or pseudo-metaphysically, soon begins to tell against aesthetic mysticism. We shall start by taking a few preliminary soundings. I say 'preliminary' because the analysis which follows is only partial and provisional at this stage. It is concerned simply with the immediate import for an appreciation of a poem of the rational meaning implied in its poetic 'images', and it will draw only on the limited material of a few lines or fragments of poetry. But this initial criterion is not an arbitrary one. It is based on that real and objective feature of 'images' which is both primary and permanent, namely that they cannot be separated from their vehicles, *words*; words which, as semantic instruments, are at the same time vehicles of concepts. For it is exactly the question of poetic truth and the nature of that truth – whether it is extra-intellectual or not – that most concerns us here.

So, when Dante writes in his great poem of exile that:

> the Nile springs, as a little stream, from its source there where the great light takes the osier-leaf from the earth,[6]

we have to ask how we can perceive and evaluate the beauty of the last image (the culmination of those that precede it) if we are to take it just as an 'image' without at the same time the explanatory *concept* of the shadow of the leaf being almost obliterated by the perpendicular cast of the sun's rays? As soon as we lose sight of this minimal empirical *notion* ('the most likely interpretation', according to the critics), all we are left with is a *gratuitous non-sense* and a *blurred image*: that is, considered

work of art with the work of art itself and hence a reduction of content to 'form' and an abstract conception of the latter. His limitations can also be seen when – though he is a sworn enemy of all metaphysical aesthetics – he falls back on an unhelpfully generic and abstract criterion like that of 'rhythm'; or, having reduced the problem of the relation between form and content to that between the expressive and the decorative (Dewey is mainly interested in the figurative arts), he ends with a merely quantitative and empirical distinction: 'the difference between the decorative and the expressive is one of emphasis' (p. 126). But a large number of fruitful epistemological observations remain, for example the following conclusion drawn from a comparison between meaning in a work of art and meaning in a signboard: that in the latter case the meaning does not belong 'of its own intrinsic right' to the signboard, while in the former it is the work's 'possession' (p. 83).

6. *Dante's Lyric Poetry*, edited and translated by Kenelm Foster and Patrick Boyde, Oxford 1967, vol. I, poem no. 81 (civ).

rigorously from both an epistemological and an aesthetic point of view, a nothing. Not an image-concept, and therefore not an image or intuition or anything else.

Now, this has got nothing whatsoever to do with making provisional use of a means (the 'explanation') in order to reach an end (the image). What is interesting in the example is that the concomitance of image and concept or intellectual meaning occurs with the most intense problematical urgency in the case of the most purely beautiful image of all, that in which all those preceding it – themselves, need it be said, *image-concepts in so far as they are words in a vocabulary* – culminate. Should we begin to acknowledge that an image is all the more *expressive*, all the more an image, the more it is *meaningful* and rich in sense? And that this could be of some consequence for the question of its truth, because it might suggest that there may be complex scientific and epistemological (though certainly not aestheticist or metaphysical) grounds for the venerable equation 'Beauty = Truth'?

To take another example, it is not difficult to see the extent to which the emotive and poetic effect of Petrarch's lines,

> I pine from place to place,
> the day careworn, weeping in the night,
> never still but as the moon is still.[7]

depends on the logical – epistemological – *inseparability* of a common-or-garden astronomical notion (the moon's state is always changing) from an image-simile (of the agitated lover) which is based on it.

Again, it is not by chance that the most lyrical moment (according to Contini, 'the only truly lyrical moment') of Dante's double-sestina should come in the lines:

> . . . this noble stone will see me lie down in a small stone never to rise until *after time, when* I shall see whether there was ever in the world a lady so beautiful as this cruel lady.[8]

At this point the poem, with its eschatological emphasis, integrates a theological concept (that of the universal judgement at the end of time) so organically and completely with its images that it is only

7. Francesco Petrarca, *Canzoniere* CCXXXVII.
8. Foster and Boyde, op. cit., I, poem no. 79 (cii). Cf. Dante Alighieri, *Rime*, ed. Gianfranco Contini, Turin 1970, p. 164.

through the daring figure of eternity (metaphorical use of temporal terms: 'after', 'when', applied to time itself), based on that theological concept, that we can adequately perceive the enormous force of feeling in them.

Moreover, can we really appreciate what is perhaps Mallarmé's finest line, '*Gloire du long désir, Idées*', without taking into account the precise, albeit naive, platonic sense of the images – in other words the concept of Ideas as transcendent, meta-empirical entities or types, the object of Eros? If we ignore this concept, we lose the 'images' of 'the long desire' and the 'glory' (and all their poetic 'charm'!), and we lose them as *images* because we have lost the *reason* for them and their *sense*, which is anchored in that platonic concept. Which means, as we know, that these 'images' are image-concepts. They are not only that – in due course we shall examine as well their specific semantic aspect. But that is part of what they are: what I should like to call a normal epistemological event, a *logical-intuitive* complex, a concrete concept.[9] Thus, if we ignore the atheist *meaning* of the 'appearance of the truth' in Leopardi's idyll *A Silvia*, we cannot begin to appreciate the moving finale of that sublime poem. For, as De Sanctis saw, Sylvia, who 'has nothing in common with . . . Beatrice or Margareta', 'is pure of all spiritual or supernatural elements': 'neither heaven nor redemption any longer exist'[10].

9. In Mallarmé's case, the Platonic sense of the term 'Ideas' (as entities or types which transcend the world, which are meta-empirical and are the eternal object of Eros) means implicitly that they are *not* ideas of an empiricist or sensationist nature, conceived as earthly products or copies of sensations or experiences. This may help us to a better understanding of the epistemological and aesthetic consequences: namely that without their intimate Platonic meaning (rooted in the Platonic concept of 'ideas'), we cannot appreciate the 'long desire' and the 'glory', for their effective and poetic charm is lost. All that we are left with are vague, obscure images and feelings of the farness of the 'Ideas' to which the 'long' desire alludes. Hence (a paradoxical conclusion for the traditionalist, romantic reader) the more an image is linked to a clear meaning, the more it moves us, takes us over. In short, only the image which *persuades* us, which is image plus meaning or concept, is poetically moving. But notice that thus far we have only the *genus commune* (concrete thought or thought + matter) to which poetry belongs. What we do not yet have is the *differentia specifica*, which is provided by the semantic component (see below, Sections 14 and 17).

10. Francesco De Sanctis, *Giacomo Leopardi*, a cura di W. Binni, Bari 1953, p. 348. De Sanctis's view of *L'Infinito* as 'religious contemplation' (p. 115) seems to us less happy. What in our opinion is expressed in that poem is simply the nullification of human history and the negative satisfaction of losing oneself in a pure and infinite sea of nothingness. This is not enough to generate a positive idea of divine

2. The Poetic Discourse

This first, extremely rapid, survey, in which we have seen the immediate, aesthetic import of the *meanings* or concepts which poetic 'images' objectively imply (i.e. through the words), has led us to a negation of aesthetic mysticism, and enables us to establish some basic elements of the epistemology of art.

We can say straight away that for anyone, Marxists included, to go on talking of knowledge in art as if it were achieved purely through 'images' or 'intuition', and not simultaneously and organically through concepts, can only lead into mysticism and hence dogmatism of the worst sort. What is it that enables us to *know* something – that is to say, perceive something universally valid, if not our ability to penetrate beyond the immediacy of brute matter, which itself has neither form nor expression, and to surmount its chaos and ambiguity? What is it, if not our ability to establish that order and unity which pertains to the universal or conceptual (truth as universality) and is an attribute of the *rational*? Allowing ourselves to abstract for a moment, let us posit these images or intuitions in and for themselves, simply as data presented to the senses, without any conceptual reference. We shall certainly find that they do possess a certain force, an indestructible being of their own (for example, taking the 'great light' of the first passage in its purely sensuous or perceptual, in this case visual, aspect). But we shall also find that once we bring in, as we know we must, their meaning or concept, *by dint of the lexical and grammatical common denominators* 'great', 'light', 'of the sun', not only is their sensuous and material existence as images not negated, it is actually developed and enhanced. The images attain their proper brilliance, their vividness, at the moment and only at the moment when they become *common* in and through those *words* which adequately correspond to them. That is to say, at the moment when they *are expressed*

infinity (a 'raising of the spirit beyond the limits of nature towards the infinite', as De Sanctis puts it), indeed exactly the opposite. But that is a question to be pursued at a more opportune moment. Rather let us recall his brilliant observation on Leopardi's 'Dialogo di un Venditore di Almanacchi e di un Passeggere' in the *Operette Morali*: 'Here there is not simply discourse but drama, the clash of the two *characters* in the clash of *ideas*, even though they seem to be saying the same thing' (p. 703).

or – essentially – when they *communicate*. This is something constantly affirmed by both ordinary and poetic cognitive experience, which to this extent at least are identical.

From this two consequences follow. Firstly, when images have no unitary intellectual sense (the 'sublime meaninglessness' which aesthetic mysticism would have us believe is poetry), there is *something* there, and it is precisely the chaos of brute matter: the images in that case are pre-cognitive, and we are left with the discrete and the manifold, lacking any connection or coherence. But – and this is the second point – in that case they are *not even themselves*, they do not retain force as sensuous or 'lyrical' images. For the being which in the abstract precedes their conceptualization or unification is only what one might call a potential being, compared with the sensuous or material being which unfolds *in synthesis with* the rational. The rational too, if one were to abstract from that synthesis, would be something potential, pre-cognitive and pre-epistemological: an undirected urge towards unity, pure abstract possibility, categorization which does not categorize. Such is the dialectic of matter and reason (dialectic of heterogeneities) as it can be seen with singular clarity, however paradoxical this might sound, in the world of art and in our case poetry.

To illustrate the matter further, let us take Vico's famous thesis of 'poetic characters', according to which Achilles, Ulysses or Orestes are figured 'by imaginative representation' rather than 'by logical abstraction' [*astrazione per generi*] and are therefore 'imaginative universals'. It is striking that when Vico describes these poetic characters as 'certain imaginative universals, dictated naturally by the human mind's innate property of delighting in the *uniform*' and then explains how it is a property of the mind 'to *enlarge* particulars by the imagination' and thus 'to reduce . . . all the deeds of valiant fighters to Achilles and all the devices of clever men to Ulysses',[11] he is forced to contradict himself at his moment of greatest insight. For it is contradictory and absurd on the one hand to recognize man's need for *uniformity* or *unity* or rationality and hence his need for *generalization* or 'enlargement' of particulars, and on the other to assign the satisfaction of this need not to the categories and the process of abstraction by

11. Giambattista Vico, *The New Science*, translated by T. G. Bergin and M. H. Fisch, New York 1948; see in particular Sections 933 and 934.

genera – in short to reason, but precisely to 'imagination' or sense-perception, that is the very synonym of particularity and *multiplicity* (as though the particular could 'enlarge' itself!).

On this point it was Castelvetro, with whom Vico was in direct conflict, who was closer to the truth. Although he relies rather simplistically on scholastic schemas of genera and species, he does make us aware that the universality and hence the poetry of Orestes, Medea and Ulysses must in some way relate to that complex of *abstract qualities* (the anonymous *poioi* of Aristotle) which is the 'species' man, within which they are comprehended.[12] We cannot but conclude that the poetry of Orestes, Medea, Ulysses and Achilles must derive also from their universality, a universality which is simply the possibility and necessity inherent in *types* and *genera* yielded by perceptual – that is empirical – syntheses, governed by the criteria of *categorical abstraction*. For such is that original abstraction proper to the most general genera which are categories, predicates or highest points of view of things – quality, for example, with all that it implies and involves. We are drawn to the conviction, in other words, that 'poetic characters', and in the same way every other figment of poetry, are not those chimerical beasts, the imaginative universals, in which Vico and latter-day Vichians would have us believe. Rather they are dianoetic or discursive universals: normal epistemological events which result, like any other concrete concept or universal, from an abstraction by genera based at one and the same time on the *categorical* nature of things and their *material* or empirical–perceptual being.

Once we have said this, however, we are then bound to rethink the definition of 'form', and therefore 'content', that has become traditional in the modern period. 'Form', it will be seen, is to be identified with thought or concept, and not with the abstract or mystical 'images' (sometimes even image-sounds!) which lack meaning, and are thus *incommunicable* and *inexpressive* – indeed in the last analysis *formless*. 'Content', on the other hand, is to be identified with matter and multiplicity (images). That will be a reversal of the problematic of art inherited from Romanticism. If we did not acknowledge this to be the case, we would have to admit that there really is no sense in talking about 'form' in relation to poetry or art in general. Where there is no

12. Lodovico Castelvetro, *Poetica d'Aristotele Vulgarizzata et Sposta per L.C.*, Basle 1576, pp. 186–7. Cf. G. Della Volpe, *Poetica del Cinquecento*, Bari 1954, especially pp. 84–91.

eidos or *dianoia*, idea or concept (judgement), there is no *form* worthy of the name. There is only chaos, the formlessness of matter and multiplicity. To speak of 'form' in relation to 'imaginative universals' or 'cosmic images' or 'intuitions' (the 'pictures of integral thought' of Shelleyan memory) and the like, following the usage of the Vichian Romantics and the post-Romantics and the decadentists, is – we have already seen – a fallacy. It is like affirming that matter or the particular enlarges, generalizes or formalizes itself.

We must therefore conclude that there is a 'poetic discourse' as there is an historical or a scientific discourse; and that the term 'discourse' is to be taken in a rigorously literal sense – as a rational and intellectual procedure – in the case of poetry as in the others, and without exception. We have to admit, to put it more exactly, that poetry (and art in general) is, just like history and science, *concrete reason* and that *in this it is no different* from history and science in general. They do not differ, that is to say, in their *general* cognitive, epistemological elements of sense-perception (imagination or fantasy) and reason, which they have in common. We must allow ourselves to be persuaded that if there is a sense (as there undoubtedly is) in talking about the sensibility or imagination of an historian or a scientist, the same is no less true in speaking of the rational or discursive nature of poetry. The demand for 'coherence', which everybody agrees is a fundamental requirement in the work of poetry as such, is quite inexplicable if coherence is understood as 'imaginative' coherence, as something instituted *by* the fantasy or imagination rather than *in* the imagination. Coherence and unity (and hence universality) do not exist except for and in *reason*. They are attained only through the rational, from which, as we know, the manifold or purely discrete – that is, fantasy or imagination for itself – acquires a meaning which makes the image *expressive* or, as we say, *telling* (in a literal no less than in a metaphorical sense); and from which it acquires its status as *category*, its *unity*.

So the poet, to be a poet, to give form to his images (albeit in a manner peculiar to him, as we shall see), has to think and reason in the literal sense of the terms. He must come to grips with the truth and reality of things (the 'verisimilar' as an essential element of art, discovered by Aristotle), no less than the historian or the scientist in general. As a poet he must contend with ideologies and events – in short, with experience (including 'historical' experience), even when it is his intention, as in the case of Ariosto or Cervantes, to remove himself from, or to reject, both ideologies and events. It is the complex real dialectic of the work of poetry as such that we must now tackle, a task which follows inevitably from the fact that the poem is no less a discourse than historical or scientific discourse in general.

3. History as Humus

What then has to be established is the *sociological* nature of the poem. The reason is clear. Only if intellectual meanings and articulations (*of what?* of reality that is more or less historical, obviously) go to make up the poem as such does there follow the genuine possibility of founding poetic values on a materialist sociological basis. Only then can Plato's heaven that lies beyond history and the empirical world, and Hegel's realm of the ideal with its *Geister* and 'shadows' and 'spiritual figures', into which poetic values have been hypostatized at least since the German Romantics, be seen for the myth and illusion that they are. Thus, as we determine in the course of our study the meanings or structural values of poetic works (and is not structure, or organizational and compositional order, of itself synonymous with intellectuality?), we shall at the same time be determining the way in which these same works are empirically conditioned by history and society. That will involve the question: do there exist meanings or concepts which are not related, directly or indirectly, to experience of reality – in other words to history?

We may indeed well ask how one could possibly demonstrate the 'full humanity' of the work itself if the sociological character and value of the poem were not demanded by, or better inherent in, its very structural and intellectual substance? For 'humanity' in this sense means both the total human commitment of the individual artist as a being who thinks and feels, imagines and makes moral decisions, and his commitment as a real individual with a certain place in history and membership in a society and civilization. Were this not so, then a realist-materialist aesthetic would be no more than a generous dream.

The essential issue was brought to the surface by no less than Goethe on the one hand and Marx on the other. For it was Goethe who declared that 'the highest lyric is decidedly historical', and that if for instance you tried 'to separate the mythological and historical elements from Pindar's Odes' you would find that 'you had cut away their inner life altogether'[13]; and it was Marx who argued that 'Greek art pre-supposes Greek mythology', that is 'nature and the social forms already elaborated ... by the popular imagination', and concluded that 'the difficulty [for the materialist] lies not in understanding that the Greek [figurative] arts and epic are bound up with certain forms of social development' but rather in the fact that 'they still afford us artistic pleasure and that in a certain respect they count as a norm and as an unattainable model'.[14] Marx's observations show his intuition of the great complexity of the aesthetic problem once the inadequacies of any romantic or idealist approach have been critically ascertained, and it is posed in strictly materialist rather than positivist terms. What his formulation indicates is that the historical and social bonds of a work of art do not condition it mechanically and externally, but must in some way be part of the particular kind of *pleasure* which the work – and not some other object – affords us. They must therefore partake of the very stuff of the work of art as such: in other words of its intellectual and structural substance.

Thus the sort of living sediment, the historical humus whose organic presence in the work of art has properly to be demonstrated by the materialist, is to be traced back to its concrete-rational core. For that, as we have seen, is the sole medium within the work through which we may assume that reality, as a complex of ideologies and facts and institutions of every kind, is articulated.

4. Focal Point

As a first approach to the examination of the social and historical conditioning of the literary work promised above, we shall now undertake a rapid sociological reading of Sophocles' *Antigone*. Before

13. J. W. von Goethe, *Schriften zur Literatur*, Einführung und Textüberwachung von Fritz Strich, Zurich 1950, p. 839.
14. Karl Marx, *Grundrisse*, translated by Martin Nicolaus, Pelican/NLR, London 1973, pp. 110–11.

we do so, however, there is one further point I should like to make. It is that a determination of the *structural* values of any poem, which must be strictly dependent on an ascertainment of its historical and social conditioning (and hence on a wholly functional literary scholarship), will also determine the focal point of the poem. From this point, in concomitance with the semantic peculiarity of poetry to be discussed in due course, will radiate the poetic values of the work: in this case, the 'tragic' values of *Antigone*. For it is this focal point which in every poem sustains the strictly artistic symbolism of the work, that is, its particular and universal signification.

5. Greek Poetry

It was with reference to Greek poetry, and this drama in particular, that Benedetto Croce made the claim that 'poetry does not deal with "problems", but forms images of life in action', and took Hegel to task 'for having been too engrossed in his efforts to resolve the problem of the State and its antinomies to observe in this case a proper respect for the boundaries between poetry and philosophy'.[15] We shall have something to say about Hegel's position in a moment, but the following objections to Croce's seem to us indisputable.

(1) In the absence of certain ethical and religious concepts (among others: *Hubris*, human arrogance; *Sophrosyne*, wisdom as sense of measure, the opposite of hubris; *Nemesis*, divine punishment; *Ananke*, necessity or destiny, as divine plan) and the problems generated by these concepts, neither *Antigone* nor any other Greek tragedy would have any poetic substance at all. To abstract and separate its 'logical unity' from its 'lyrical unity', still the practice of so much aestheticizing criticism in the Crocean manner, is the worst of methods.

(2) As confirmation of the above, we may note that the fulcrum of the tragedy is constituted by a twofold hubris: on the one hand, that of Antigone, the daughter of Oedipus, who disobeys Creon's edict forbidding her brother's burial in the name of a religious law which commands reverence for the dead, and on the other, that of Creon who by immuring Antigone acts as a fitting instrument of those gods

15. Benedetto Croce, *Conversazioni Critiche*, V, Bari 1951, pp. 89 ff.

who intend the destruction of all the house of Labdacus, but never-theless commits an injustice, thus exposing himself to Nemesis. The most poetic moments of the play, all the more lyrical and dramatic the more they express this particular Greek ethos, spring from the twofold hubris at its centre. To give some examples[16]: the under-standing 'wisdom' of Antigone's sister Ismene:

> Therefore I plead compulsion and entreat
> The dead to pardon. I perforce obey
> The powers that be. 'Tis foolishness, I ween,
> To overstep in aught the golden mean [perissá]   (ll. 65–8)
> ...
> Have thine own way then; 'tis a mad endeavour.
> Yet to thy lovers thou art dear as ever   (ll. 98–9);

the logic of Creon, instrument of the gods:

> Yet 'tis no easy matter to discern
> The temper of a man, his mind and will,
> Till he be proved by exercise of power   (ll. 175–7);
> ...
> Now if she [Antigone] thus can flout authority
> Unpunished, I am woman, she the man   (ll. 484–5);

Antigone's arguments to Creon:

> Nor do I deem that thou, a mortal man,
> Could'st by a breath annul and override
> The immutable unwritten laws of Heaven   (ll. 453–5);
> ...
> Ant. Who knows if this world's crimes are virtues there?
> Cr. Not even death can make a foe a friend.
> Ant. My nature is for mutual love, not hate   (ll. 521–3);

the second stasimon of the chorus, on human hope:

> Hope flits about on never-wearying wings;
> Profit to some, to some light loves she brings,
> But no man knoweth how her gifts may turn,

16. Sophocles, *Works*, Vol. I, translated by F. Storr, London and New York 1924.

Till 'neath his feet the treacherous ashes burn.
Sure 'twas a sage inspired that spake this word:

> *If evil good appear*
> *To any, Fate is near;*

And brief the respite from her flaming sword   (ll. 615 ff.);

Creon's logic confuted by his son Haemon:

> *Cr.* The state is his who rules it, so 'tis held.
> *H.* As monarch of a desert thou would'st shine   (ll. 738–9);

the lament of Antigone-Niobe and her terrible reply to the Chorus:

> *Ant.* Nay, but the piteous tale I've heard men tell
> Of Tantalus' doomed child,
> Chained upon Sipylus' high rocky fell,
> That clung like ivy wild,
> Drenched by the pelting rain and whirling snow
> Left there to pine,
> While on her frozen breast the tears aye flow –
> Her fate is mine.
> *Chor.* She [Niobe] was sprung of gods, divine,
> Mortals we of mortal line.
> Like renown with gods to gain
> Recompenses all thy pain.
> Take this solace to thy tomb
> Hers in life and death thy doom.
> *Ant.* Alack, alack! Ye mock me. Is it meet
> Thus to insult me living, to my face?   (ll. 823 ff.);

her final indictment of the gods:

> By friends deserted to a living grave.
> What ordinance of heaven have I transgressed?
> Hereafter can I look to any god
> For succour . . . ?   (ll. 920–3);

the moral drawn by the Chorus and the punished Creon:

> *Chor.* Too late thou seemest to perceive the truth.
> *Cr.* By sorrow schooled. Heavy the hand of God,

Thorny and rough the paths my feet have trod,
Humbled my pride, my pleasure turned to pain;
Poor mortals, how we labour all in vain!   (ll. 1270 ff.);

the Chorus's final warning to Creon:

O pray not, prayers are idle; from the doom
Of fate for mortals refuge there is none   (ll. 1337–8).

(3) The most rigorous classical scholarship has demonstrated that
nothing could be further from Sophocles' mind in *Antigone* than a
conflict between religion and the State. For him as a Greek, the State,
the Polis, is part of the divine order itself, and is not something distinct and opposite as in the modern conception. If this is so, and if it
is also the case that Antigone cannot but embody the spirit of the true
Polis in her religious feeling and action, then we may draw two conclusions. Firstly, Hegel's mistake in his reading of *Antigone*[17] was not,
as Croce alleged, that he posed moral and philosophical problems,
thus transgressing the bounds between poetry and philosophy
(thought!), but that he confused problems of antiquity with problems
of his own day: it was in short an error of scholarship.[18] Secondly, the
profound relationship between Antigone and the Polis reminds us
how extremely *problematical* this play is. If what I have said is correct,
the poet himself (not simply Sophocles the model believer) acknowledges through the interplay of hubris between Creon and Antigone
the religious postulate that misfortune, necessity (*Ananke*), can strike
even the pious and the innocent, even an Antigone. Indeed, that
heaven takes pleasure (the 'game' gods play with men) in converting
human purposes, even noble ones, into destiny, fatality, *Ate*. A fine
example of a play that deals not in problems, but only images of life
in action!

Now, Croce certainly had some justification when he argued,
against positivism, that '*Antigone* criticism has undergone a sort of

17. G. W. F. Hegel, *Aesthetics*, translated by T. M. Knox, Oxford 1975, Vol. II,
pp. 1217 ff.
18. Nevertheless, Hegel's remarkably acute sense of the *poetic* necessity of the
ethos of Sophoclean tragedy and tragedy in general is exemplary even today. It
is not made any less so by its origins in his rationalist concentration on the content, though this in its turn is too abstract and unilateral to cope adequately with
the issues at the core of the problem of art, the relation between Classical and
Romantic, or between the logical and the aesthetic.

"logical metabasis into another genre" ', that is, a transition from the poetic to the historical or philosophical genre. But an aestheticizing spiritualist method of criticism is no answer to positivism, and cannot hope to be. The only valid alternative is a wholly functional criticism based on a combination of semantics and literary-philological scholarship, a criticism totally in function of the *text* as *historical* product. A materialist aesthetic, as will become increasingly clear, provides precisely this criterion of critical and historical judgement, in its turn the best practical attestation of the validity of such an aesthetic. Thanks to this approach, it is possible to weld together, not mechanically but dialectically, the cultural superstructure to which poetry and art in general belong and the social and economic base. One can then *demonstrate*, by bringing out certain poetic-structural complexes (as above and in the following pages), that neither Antigone nor 'Vulcan' nor 'Achilles' etc. would be 'possible' with 'Roberts and Co.' or 'the Crédit Mobilier' or 'powder and lead' (Marx, loc. cit.), precisely because each of them presupposes and contains within its structure as a poetically signifying organism a quite different historical rationale and quite different ideological and cultural (by implication also economic and material) conditions from those of our own times. Which of course implies and confirms what we might call the law of 'long periods', perceived by Engels when he argued that 'the further the particular [cultural] sphere which we are examining [e.g., a given artistic period] is removed from the economic sphere [*sich vom Ökonomischen entfernt*] and approaches that of pure abstract ideology, the more shall we find it exhibiting accidents [and particularities] in its development, the more will its curve run zigzag.' If, however, you plot the *median axis* of this curve, 'you will find that this axis . . . will approach more and more nearly parallel to the axis of economic development the longer the period considered and the wider the field dealt with'.[19] But we shall return to this point.

To revert to Sophocles for the moment, a re-examination of other plays such as *Ajax* and *Oedipus at Colonus* will show that here too the moments of highest 'human' poetry are objectively specific. They cannot exist apart from the ethical and religious ideas mentioned earlier, or from the Greek world-view in general. From *Ajax* we note: (a) The prologue with Athena 'playing' on stage with the hero-

19. Friedrich Engels, letter of 25th Jan. 1894 to W. Borgius, in *Marx-Engels Selected Correspondence*, Moscow 1975, pp. 442–3.

protagonist whom she has sent mad because of his gesture of arrogant pride (hubris). She plays with such cruelty that Odysseus is made to pity the fate of his enemy even more than that of mankind in general. Athena addresses Ajax, all covered in blood from the massacre of a flock of sheep which in his madness he has taken for the Greek captains who have offended him:

> *Athena*: Well, since it is thy pleasure, be it so:
> Lay on, abate no jot of thine intent.
> *Ajax*: I will to work then, and I look to thee
> To be my true ally all times, as now. (*Exit Ajax*)
> *Athena*: Odysseus, see how great the might of gods.
> Could'st thou have found a man more circumspect,
> Or one more prompt for all emergencies?
> *Odysseus*: I know none such, and though he be my foe,
> I still must pity him in his distress,
> Bound hand and foot, to fatal destiny;
> And therein mind my case no less than his.
> Alas! we living mortals, what are we
> But phantoms all or unsubstantial shades?
> *Athena*: Warned by these sights, Odysseus, see that thou
> Utter no boastful word against the gods,
> Nor swell with pride if haply might of arm
> Exalt thee o'er thy fellows, or vast wealth.
> A day can prostrate and a day upraise
> All that is mortal; but the gods approve
> Sobriety and forwardness abhor. (ll. 114–33)[20]

Our friends the aestheticists have read this incomparably poetic and dramatic admonition as simply a prosaic *fabula docet*, thus successfully detaching it from the action of the prologue and everything that follows!

(b) The ambiguous 'deception' by which Ajax calms the fears of his captive-wife after he has returned to his senses and is preparing to commit suicide to save his honour:

> Henceforward I shall know how to yield to Heaven,
> And school myself the Atridae to respect. . . .
> . . . Dread potencies and powers

20. Sophocles, *Works* cit., Vol. II.

Submit to law. Thus winter snow-bestrewn
Gives place to opulent summer . . .
And we, shall we not likewise learn to yield? . . .
For I am going whither I am bound.   (ll. 666–90)

Because this speech involves the universe in the existence and fate of
the protagonist, it has been regarded by most simply as a 'lyrical'
outburst!

(c) The formula with which the Messenger encapsulates Ajax's sin of
pride, that he:

. . . drew on him the dire wrath
Of the goddess – pride too high for mortal man   (ll. 777–8)

reminds us of his comment a little while earlier on those, like Ajax,
who are vain and without sense of measure, that 'born with the
nature of men, they have not their feelings' – a definition of human
feeling thoroughly Greek and historically circumscribed!

For *Oedipus at Colonus*, let this exchange between Ismene and Oedipus
suffice:

Ismene: The gods, who once abased, uplift thee now.
Oedipus: Poor help to raise an old man fallen in youth

(ll. 394–5)[21]

– tremendous lines, the emotion of which furthermore is so *particularly* Greek, and so far removed from being generically or abstractly
human, that Wilamowitz has drawn on them as a notable document
of the Greek conception of the relation between human and divine.[22]

21. Ibid., Vol. I.
22. Ulrich von Wilamowitz-Moellendorf, *Der Glaube der Hellenen*, Basle 1956. Still
on Sophocles, and in particular on the famous poetic cry of Oedipus Rex: 'Why
didst thou harbour me, Cithaeron . . . ?' (*Oedipus Rex*, ed. and vol. cit., l. 1791).
I should like to repeat an observation made by me elsewhere. It is that what in
this cry might seem a 'purely human', *historically undifferentiated* expression of the
well-known dramatic sentiment 'why did things go this way and not another?'
is indeed a statement of that feeling, but precisely in so far as it assumes here an
ancient, Greek, historically particular sense. For it calls into question not blind
chance or human responsibility and guilt, but that fatal plan of the gods whereby
it was predisposed that the infant Oedipus should be exposed in the valley of
Cithaeron, with all the consequences that we know. If, in short, we abstract from
the Greek conception of the relations between the human and the divine, these
words do not give us the profound moral shock which they are yet capable of
arousing, and their particular pathos is obscured.
In a similar way, the poetic line in Hamlet's soliloquy (Act III, sc. 1) which reads

Coming now to the 'rationalist' Euripides, one cannot but recall the following examples:

(1) *The Bacchae*, in which the terrible fate of Pentheus, who will be torn to pieces in the Bacchic revel by his own mother because of his 'impious hubris', is foretold, not only in the first stasimon of the chorus, but even more powerfully later, in the remarkable scene where, setting out on the fateful road to find the Bacchae with the god who has already sent him mad, he suddenly perceives him in animal guise:

> *Pentheus:*   Aha! meseemeth I behold two suns,
> A twofold Thebes, our seven-gated burg!
> A bull thou seem'st that leadeth on before;
> And horns upon thine head have sprouted forth.
> How, *wast* thou brute? – bull art thou verily now.
>
> *Dionysus:*   The god attends us, gracious not ere this,
> Leagued with us now: now seest thou as thou
> shouldst.   (ll. 918–24)[23]

(2) *Hippolytus:* A few extracts taken at random:

> *Nurse:*   ... Sure no goddess Cypris is
> But, if it may be, something more than God,

'Thus conscience does make cowards of us all' signifies undoubtedly (the immediate context makes it clear) that obsessive, 'Hamletic' reflection on the reasons and above all the consequences of any action proposed, which is the major impediment to action itself (see in Act IV, sc. 4, the 'craven scruple / Of thinking too precisely on the event'). It certainly does not signify a Christian, religious consciousness of moral duty (here: not to commit suicide) which Hamlet, as all the commentators are now agreed, does not possess. Even so, the fact remains that Hamlet's 'conscience' would be inconceivable or at any rate inexplicable as a human fact of general interest without that general habit of 'scrupulous' examination, before the tribunal within us, of actions to be undertaken by an individual made theologically responsible, a habit which Christian education has impressed in modern man and which was absent in antiquity. But it is a habit which is a fundamental component of the poetic character of Hamlet and of his poetic truth (Hamlet with all his scruples and obsessions is not a clinical case, as we well know): it is the organic *historical* component of his character. If we ignore this, it is impossible fully to understand and appreciate the poetry of his drama.

23. *Euripides*, translated by Arthur S. Way, Vol. III, London and Cambridge, Mass. 1950.

B

> Who hath ruined her [Phaedra], and me, and all
> this house (ll. 359–61)[24]

or:

> Phaedra: But I shall gladden Cypris my destroyer
> By fleeting out of life on this same day,
> And vanquished so by bitter love shall be (ll. 725–27)

(and cf. fr. 619 of Sophocles' Phaedra: 'this sickness sent by a god');

or:

> Hippolytus [dying in the presence of Artemis]:
> Ah perfume-breath celestial! – mid my pains
> I feel thee, and mine anguish is assuaged.
> Lo in this place the Goddess Artemis!
> Artemis: Yes, hapless one, of Gods best friend to thee.
> Hippolytus: O Queen, seest thou my plight – the stricken one?
> Artemis: I see – but tears are to mine eyes forbid.
> Hippolytus: None now shall hark thine hounds, nor do thee
> service – (ll. 1391–7)

Just these few extracts suffice to make us aware of the peculiarly modern and Christian character of Racine's Phèdre. There, leaving aside the removal of the goddesses Cypris and Artemis, Phaedra is the *protagonist*, individualist and introverted, deep in the moral and morbid analysis of her own human-passion-the-key-to-all-things. Thus, for example, the 'Venus' invoked in her famous cry ('*C'est Vénus tout entière à sa proie attachée*') possesses, in its expressive substance, no more than metaphorical value – Sainte-Beuve was right.[25] All this, although it does not prejudice our artistic pleasure (Pohlenz's view[26]), certainly raises serious questions of appreciation and criticism. as Chateaubriand perceived after his fashion.[27]

Aeschylus, to move one stage back, is masterly in the concatenation of hubris. For our purposes it will be enough to look for a moment at the tragic and poetic position of Agamemnon in the play of the same name, the first part of the Oresteia. This position is misrepresented

24. Ibid., Vol. IV, London and Cambridge, Mass. 1971.
25. C. Sainte-Beuve, 'Racine', in Portraits Littéraires I, Paris 1843.
26. Max Pohlenz, Die griechische Tragödie, Göttingen 1954.
27. François-René de Chateaubriand, Le Génie du Christianisme (1802), II, 3.

and aesthetically falsified if, in line with many critics even today, one ignores the *Ananke* which forces the protagonist to sacrifice Iphygenia and believes instead – anachronistically and anti-artistically – that the misfortune which is to befall Agamemnon 'originates in *his voluntary* decision' (in the words of one illustrious critic) to offer up his daughter. This latter interpretation completely ignores the fact that the text refers explicitly, right from the beginning of the Chorus, to the terrible omen of Artemis' fury at the killing of the pregnant hare by the eagles sent from Zeus to encourage Agamemnon to sail for Troy, and hence to the *need* for propitiation and expiation (by human sacrifice):

> *Chorus:* And when the seer [Calchas], urging Artemis as cause, proclaimed to the chieftains another remedy, more grievous even than the bitter storm, so that the sons of Atreus smote the ground with their staves and stifled not their tears – (ll. 198–202)... But when he [Agamemnon] had donned the yoke of necessity [*anánkas*] ... (ll. 218ff.)[28]

Nor does it do justice to the reader's sense, expressed by Page,[29] that there is no passage in the whole of Greek tragedy equal in pathos and beauty to that central part of the Chorus (ll. 385 ff.) where, with Paris suffering the effects of *Ananke* even more than Menelaus, we are shown the pervasiveness of Necessity:

> *Chorus:* No, he is driven on by perverse Temptation, the over-mastering child of designing Destruction; and remedy is utterly in vain. His evil is not hidden; it shineth forth, a baleful gleam ... Such was even Paris, who came to the house of the sons of Atreus and did dishonour to his hosts' hospitable board by stealing away a wedded wife ... Lo, he sits apart in the anguish of his grief, silent, smitten in his honour but upbraiding not. In his yearning for her who sped beyond the sea, a phantom will seem to be lord of the house. The grace of fair-formed statues is hateful to him; and in the hunger of his eyes all loveliness is de-

28. *Aeschylus*, translated by Herbert Weir Smith, Vol. II, London and Cambridge, Mass. 1957.
29. J. D. Denniston and D. Page (eds.), *Aeschylus : Agamemnon*, Oxford 1957, p. 112

parted . . . For Ares bartereth the bodies of men for gold;
he holdeth his balance in the contest of the spear; and
back from Ilium to their loved ones he sendeth a heavy
dust passed through his burning, a dust bewept with
plenteous tears, in place of more frightening urns well
bestowed with ashes . . . Dangerous is a people's voice
charged with wrath – it hath the office of a curse of public
doom. In anxious fear I wait to hear something shrouded
still in gloom . . . Glory in excess is fraught with peril . . .[30]

Going still further back, the Homeric poems, whose status as historical as well as literary documents is more generally and explicitly
acknowledged (without much thought being given, however, to the
aesthetic problem which this implies), also show how their *poetic*
articulation is constituted by the *concept* – or rather a certain concept –
of Hubris, and the related concept of Nemesis. In passing, one might
illustrate the poetic importance of other data, for instance the religious
spirit current among the Greeks: taking one example among many,
consider the obvious but still objectively particular poetic effect of
Ulysses' attitude on encountering Nausicaa when, shrewdly, he *can*
ask her whether she is a goddess in the literal sense:

I would be suppliant at your knees, O Queen: yet am in doubt
whether you are divine or mortal. If a goddess from high heaven,
then Artemis you must be, the daughter of great Zeus and your
nearest peer in form, stature and parts. But if you are human,

30. To be read, but with caution: H. D. F. Kitto, *Form and Meaning in Drama: A
Study of Six Greek Plays and of Hamlet*, London 1956. Some points are well-made, for
example: 'He [Aeschylus] passes right through this mass of material until he
reaches his inner and unifying reality, the conflict between the two laws of Dike
and Hybris: he is not enthralled by the persons he creates' (p. 210). But there are
also things which are wrong because they are external and inadequate or very
approximate, for example the following purely technical 'reason' which he gives
for the differences between Greek and Elizabethan drama: 'Now, we all know *why*
Greek dramatists did not make the lively and expansive drama which the Eliz-
abethans made: the conditions of their theatre prevented it. They had at the
most three actors, so that the well-populated Elizabethan stage was beyond their
reach' (p. 215). Not to mention the main thesis, that if Greek tragedy is 'religious
drama' (agreed), so is *Hamlet*. Naturally, everything depends in the end on the
concept of 'meaning' with which one starts and how rigorous it is. To be rigorous,
'meaning' and 'ideology' must be identified, whence the organically (not superficially) historical and social character of all meanings, their combined sociological
and artistic value (the polysemic).

child of some dweller on this earth of ours, then thrice blessed
your father and lady mother, thrice blessed your family!

(Book VI, ll. 149 ff.)[31];

or the similar effect of the scene which introduces Circe:

From a loom inside rose a singing voice, of goddess or woman . . .

(Book X, l. 253)

But to return to the principal concepts already mentioned, and to
their functional role within the poetry, see:

(a) *The Iliad*. Here we find both social Hubris, the arrogance of one man
directed against another belonging to the same caste, and Hubris as
the arrogance of men towards the gods, even if it is not yet specified
with that term but known mainly as 'impiety'. As examples of the
first kind, take Book I, ll. 202 ff., where Achilles, on the point of
hurling himself on Agamemnon, reacts to the appearance of Athena,
friend of the Atrides as follows:

Achilles turned in amaze, and by the fire that flashed from her
eyes at once knew that she was Minerva. 'Why are you here', said
he, 'daughter of aegis-bearing Jove? To see the pride [hubris] of
Agamemnon, son of Atreus? Let me tell you – and it shall surely
be – he shall pay for this insolence with his life.'[32];

or the Thersites episode in Book II, ll. 211 ff.; or the Trojans in Book
XIII, ll. 631 ff. 'infected with hubris', the as yet unpunished hubris of
Paris to whom they have given shelter and protection. Examples of
the second kind abound, but let Book XXIV suffice, and in particular
the episode of the outrage committed by Achilles on the corpse of
Hector. The words in which Apollo judges this outrage in the presence
of the Immortals (ll. 33 ff.) are simultaneously poetry and one of the
most ancient documents of Greek ethics, foreshadowing indeed the
problems raised by the ethics of Aristotle:

Cruel are ye, O ye gods, and workers of bane!
. . . Nay, it is the ruthless Achilles . . . that ye are
fain to succour . . . [he who] even as a lion . . .

31. Homer, *The Odyssey*, translated by T. E. Shaw, London 1955.
32. Homer, *The Iliad*, translated by A. T. Murray, London and Cambridge,
Mass. 1925.

goeth forth against the flocks of men to win him
a feast; even so hath Achilles lost all pity,
neither is shame in his heart . . .

(Compare the same god's words inviting Diomedes to 'measure' in Book V, ll. 440–1.) Finally we may recall that the Nemesis which will fall upon Achilles, of which we have some presentiment but which is not represented, is that which determines poetically the close of the poem.

(b) *The Odyssey.* Social hubris predominates: the suitors are like Ulysses princes of Cephallenia and the Ionian islands, not plebeians. But there is some acknowledgement of supreme hubris against the gods, through the sanctions of the after-life against those guilty of it in the inventory of favoured heroes (the sublimity of the shade of Ajax absolutely silent: Book XI, ll. 543 ff.) and the damned. But for the first kind of hubris, which is the ethical leitmotif of the poem, bear in mind Telemachus in Book I, ll. 368 ff. ('O wooers of my mother, insolent and ever-masterful! . . .'), Eumaeus in XIV, Telemachus in XVI, ll. 78 ff., Penelope in XVI, l. 910, Ulysses in XVII, l. 431, and the whole of the second half, and in XVIII ll. 143 ff., Penelope and Laertes in XXI, ll. 63 ff., 351 ff.

Let us proceed now to the lyric poets, including Sappho who need not detain us long. Her restricted range of interests and extreme linearity and simplicity of thought produced, above all, that masterpiece which is the ode to Aphrodite. The poem is pre-eminent, as the criticism of Page has ably shown, because in it 'art and supersition go hand in hand'.[33] But let us consider for a moment the case of Pindar.

Pindar has of late become the unlikely target of certain critics who have turned to aestheticism by way of reaction (as usual) against positivism. Heedless of Goethe's warning, they have tended on the one hand to regard myth, history and thought in the poet as extraneous, non-artistic elements and to fancy a dualism of 'logical unity' and 'aesthetic unity', and on the other to reduce his poetry to 'images' and hence fragments. This has led, taking the error to its logical conclusion, to an implicit reading of Pindar's 'flights', his typical metaphors, as images free from all rational bonds. In reality, of course, these metaphors are typical precisely in that their very bold-

---

33. Denys Page, *Savvho and Alcaeus*, Oxford 1955, p. 18.

ness underlines the nature of metaphor or image in general: that it is a *connecting* or *thinking* of the most *dissimilar* things, a dissimilarity brought under control by reason-intellect and its categories. We hardly need reminding of the first Olympian:

> Best of all things is *water*; but *gold*, like a gleaming fire
> by night, outshines all pride of wealth beside.
> But, my heart, would you chant the glory of *games*,
> Look never beyond the *sun*
> by day for any star shining brighter
> . . .
> nor any contest than Olympia greater to sing.[34]

I invite the reader to try and dissociate the imagery from the ethico-religious concepts and everyday ideas in this conclusive picture of human life in the eighth Pythian ode, without jettisoning the poetry at the same time:

> . . . In brief space mortals'
> delight is exalted, and thus again it drops to the ground,
> shaken by a backward doom.
> We are things of a day. What are we? What are we not? The
>   shadow of a dream
> is man, no more. But when the brightness comes, and God gives it,
> there is a shining of light on men, and their life is sweet. (p. 80)

(See the second Olympian:

> . . . Of things come to pass
> in justice or unjust, not Time the father
> of all can make the end unaccomplished.
> But forgetfulness may come still with happiness.
> Grief, breaking again out of quiet, dies at last, quenched
> under the waxing weight of fair things. (p. 5))

Try, in other words, to abstract the aphorism from the images (whether metaphorical or not) and still preserve the poetry, and see whether it can be done. Likewise for the eleventh Nemean:

> I bless this man for Agesilas, his father,
> for the splendour and linked serenity of his limbs.

34. *The Odes of Pindar*, tr. Richard Lattimore, Chicago 1947, p. 1.

Yet if one, keeping wealth, surpass in beauty likewise
and show his strength by excellence in the games,
Let him yet remember the limbs he appoints are mortal
and that he must put upon him earth, the end of all things.

(p.128)

(See also Schroeder frag. 104:

For friendship's sake I would beseech the Cronides that
a happy time may descend without break on Eolas and his
race. The days of men are eternal, and the body mortal.

meaning, the generations follow endlessly on one another, but individual life comes to an end).

Another example is the eleventh Olympian with its solemn aristocratic celebration of warriors and wise men:

There acclaim him; I warrant you,
Muses, you will visit no gathering cold to strangers
nor lost to lovely things
but deep to the heart in wisdom, and spearmen also. No thing,
    neither devious fox
nor loud lion, may change the nature born in his blood. (p. 35)

Or the second Pythian with its advice to the powerful Hieron to remain faithful to his noble birth and not let himself be deceived, like children fascinated with a monkey (a Pindaric flight!), by envious insinuations:

Learn what you are and be such. See, the ape to children is a
    pretty thing, pretty indeed. (p. 50)

Or the eleventh Pythian with its comment on Hubris (the 'invidious misfortunes' are a concentrated metaphorical formula for the misfortunes dispensed by jealous gods to those who know no limits to their desires):

I am strung to the common virtues; the envious are put aside.
Of these if a man win the uttermost
and, shepherding it in peace, escape the blame
of pride, more beautiful is the ending he makes
in dark death . . . (p. 92)

Or finally the seventh Isthmian with its cautionary re-evocation of
the past glories of Thebes:

> But grace that is grown old
> sleeps, and men are forgetful
> of that which issues not binding the high perfection
> of poetry to bright streams of words. (p. 145)

Confronted with poetry of this stature, the noted English aestheticist
Norwood can find nothing better than to tell us once again that
'morality does not make great poetry, or poetry at all', and that the
'aphorism', the moral statement, is no more a key to Pindar's depiction of the glories of Greece than the stairway by which we enter a
picture-gallery is to Botticelli's 'Birth of Venus' . . .[35]

As for the supposedly extraneous character of myth in Pindar, I
suggest a look at the myths of Iamos and the Dioscuri in the sixth
Olympian and the tenth Nemean in order to feel, in an almost
physical sense, how genuine religious thought, not just the letter but
the spirit of the myth, confers on the poetry an unmistakable strength
and *tone*, indissoluble from it:

> *Ol.* VI:
> while she, putting aside her girdle, crimson dyed,
> and her silver pitcher, under the darkness of low trees
> bore a boy with the heart of divination. The gold-haired god
>   [Apollo]
> made gentle Eleithuia and the Destinies to stand beside her.
> Out of the lovely distress at her loins came Iamos
> straightway into the light, whom she in her grief
> left on the ground. By the god's design two
> green-eyed serpents tended him, with blameless venom
>   distilled of bees . . .
> . . . He [Iamos], assuming in time the bloom
> of delightful youth, gold-chapleted, wading in Alpheus
>   mid-stream, called
> his forefather strong Poseidon, and the archer over god-built
>   Delos
> under the night sky, calming upon his head

35. Gilbert Norwood, *Pindar*, Berkeley and Los Angeles 1945, p. 69.

the care of subjects. Close to his ear his father's voice came
answering, and spoke: 'Arise my son, follow
here in the wake of my voice to the place frequented of all.'

(pp. 16–17)

Nem. X:
and Zeus on Idas crashed the flame of the smoking thunderbolt.
These two burned, forlorn. Men find strife bitter when they
    undertake those who are stronger.
With speed Tyndareus' son ran back to his mighty brother,
and found him not dead, drawing yet some shuddering breath
    of life.
In grief, letting fall hot tears,
he cried aloud: 'Kronion, my father, what release
shall there be from sorrow? Grant death also to me with this
    man, my lord . . .
. . . He spoke, and Zeus came near
and answered: 'You are my son . . .' (p. 127)

Pindar's tone is unmistakable, like that of all great poetry, for
concrete, not abstract, stylistic reasons which are conditioned by and
cannot *in the text itself* be separated from historical and social determi-
nants. In order to demonstrate this, let us compare a famous poem
inspired by Pindar's first Pythian ode, Horace's *Descende caelo* (III, 4). It
is dedicated to wisdom and order as opposed to brute force, and opens
with an appeal to the Muses and to music and a fond remembrance
of the poet's childhood, already placed beneath the sign of heavenly
grace:

Descend from Heav'n, queenly Calliope;
And a long strain, with pipe and thrilling voice,
Or Phoebus' lyre, if such thy choice,
Or cithern, sing for me!
Do ye too [friends] hear her? Or doth fond conceit
Mock me? Methinks I hear, methinks I stray
Through the blest groves, where whispering play
Fair streams and zephyrs sweet.
Me, on Apulian Voltur long ago,
Like bliss befell. Past my nurse Pullia's home
Wand'ring, with play and sleep o'ercome,

The fabled doves did throw
Fresh leaves on me. Strange was to all who keep
High Acheruntia's eyry, Bantium's hills,
Or the rich fields Forentum tills,
How thus a child should sleep
Nor venomed snakes or bears have power to harm;
How I, with sacred bay and myrtle pressed,
Like babe inspired should calmly rest,
Safe through some god-giv'n charm.[36]

The poet goes on to say that he belongs to the Muses in every circumstance of his life, whether in peril or tranquillity:

Your nursling still, dear Muses, safe I climb
The Sabine steeps!...
So long as you stand by me, without fear
Seaward mad Bosphorus I'll dare to face...,

He recounts how in the Pierian grotto the Muses refresh noble Caesar [Augustus] and bestow gentle counsel on whomsoever turns to them; without which brute force collapses under its own weight, as the hapless struggle of the assailants of heaven shows:

We know how Jove swept with the hurtling fire
Of his fell bolts the Titans dire,
Curst mob, clean out of sight, –
Jove, who controls slow Earth, and wind-swept Sea...
One and alone! Yet ev'n he might have feared
That daring horde in brutal strength arrayed,
Confederates who fain had laid
A Pelion high upreared
On dark Olympus. But what could avail
Typhoeus, Mimas, Rhoetus strong in fight
... when 'twas against the shield
Fierce-clanging of Minerva that they swept?
To aid the cause keen Vulcan stept,
Stept Juno, on the field, –
Apollo too, his bow still drawn to aim;

36. Horace, *Complete Works*, edited J. Marshall, London 1937.

Who loves loose tresses in Castalia dear
And Pataran, Delian groves holds dear,
Taking from each a name!

But the gods make power tempered by reason even greater; and the poem ends with the following survey of the eternal punishments meted out to those who transgress the 'gentle counsels', or reason:

Earth on her monstrous children [the Titans] piled, must
   grieve,
Wailing her progeny in hell that drift,
Hurled by Jove's bolt. Hell-fire, though swift
Cannot through Aetna cleave.
On shameless Tityos' breast devouring deep,
A dreadful warder of his guilt remains,
The bird unclean. Three hundred chains
Lustful Pirithous keep.

Let us consider what Eduard Fraenkel calls 'the fundamental difference' between Horace and Pindar in their treatment of this theme.[37] Both begin with music, the gift of the Muses. See the opening lines of the first Pythian:

Golden lyre, held of Apollo in common possession
with the violet-haired Muses; the dance steps, leaders of
festival, heed you;
the singers obey your measures
when, shaken with music, you cast the beat to lead choirs of
   dancers   (Ibid., p. 43)

But 'what is the source of this music in each case? In Pindar's poem it is something established in the customs and the cults of a society to which both the poet and those for whom he wrote belonged. The athletic and other competitions at the festivals at Olympia, Delphi, and elsewhere, and the celebrations by which the victor and his city were honoured, first at the sanctuary itself, then, in a more elaborate form, on his coming home, were all an organic part of the life of the community. The games at the festivals were only one of the occasions which called for musical celebrations ... The institution of these

37. Eduard Fraenkel, *Horace*, Oxford 1957, pp. 273–5.

performances was deeply rooted in the very life, religious and civic, of the society: like the whole of that life it came from the gods. That is why Pindar can start from premises of unchallenged validity and, without an effort, make the transition [*Pyth.* I, 5] from the *mousikón* that is operative in the present performance [in honour of Hieron of Aitna victor in the chariot-race] to the power of harmony that governs the world.'

But 'Horace has no such ground to stand upon, and he was fully conscious of it . . . His poetry, his "music" was not the joint product of an effort of his individuality and of something that was there before he was born, that existed independently of him . . . Horace's *carmina non prius audita* [*Odes* III, i, 2] could never have come into existence except by his own effort . . . For Horace there exist no singers, no festival ceremonies, no tradition on which he can follow . . . This, and not some vain delight in the display of pieces of his own biography [whence the persistent critical opinion that the ode lacks unity because of its excessive 'realism' !], is the reason why he tells us so much about his early childhood and those out-of-the-way places which at that time nourished his imagination and strengthened his mind, why he speaks of dangers overcome and of those favourite retreats where he is allowed to forget the *sescenta negotia* of his life in the noisy capital and is able to listen to the voices of the Camenae. He does not pretend or even wish to be the mouthpiece of a community such as no longer exists; he is determined to remain the man he is, born in a late and distracted age.[38] . . . The bold verb in the first person singular with which the cycle of the Roman Odes begins [III, 1, i: 'Odi profanum volgus . . .'] has its complement in the extensive personal passages of *Descende caelo*. In these passages *there is nothing Pindaric*: they describe the experience which in Horace's own life was the equivalent of Pindar's creed . . . [In the] concluding *diminuendo* . . . by the happiest inspiration Pirithous is made to bring up the rear of those who have sinned against the gods. He too has sinned [having tried to abduct Proserpine from Hell]; on him too a severe punishment is inflicted. But how venial seems his sin: *amatorem* ['lustful'] . . . We find it impossible to

38. It is clear from odes I, 34, *Parcus deorum cultor*, and I, 35, *O diva gratum*, that Zeus and Tyche or Fortune are considered a single identical Power governing the world. 'This conception,' Fraenkel points out, 'was probably familiar to educated persons in Horace's time' (op. cit., p. 253).

connect him with the *immanis turba* [curst mob] of which we heard before. The unfortunate young lover forms a perfect contrast to those monsters . . .'

I believe that the foregoing permits us to see a critical paradigm in the literary and historical relationship between Pindar and Horace (*qua* lyric poet) just described. Precisely because it is valid for these two poets who come from within fairly narrow historical limits, in so far as both belong to the same ancient, pre-Christian era, it suggests itself all the more strongly as a method of approaching poets taken from much more widely separated periods (for example, the relation between Euripides and Racine), and of assessing poetry in general, in the sense outlined. The greater and more authentic the poetry, the more its appreciation requires a *concrete* – that is, *sociological* – account of its style. Such an account is not to be confused either with the critical method of positivism or with the 'realism' of vulgar Marxism: neither of these attains the substance of poetry or for that matter history (not only literary history). This will become clearer as our inquiry proceeds. Leaving the ancient literatures behind us, let us now go on to look at some *exempla* or samples of medieval, modern and contemporary poetry.

6. The Divine Comedy

In the case of the *Divine Comedy* too the reader's capacity to appreciate the poetry and to understand the particular historical nature of its feeling go together. The atmosphere of the opening of the poem, in the first canto of *Inferno*, is that of a dramatic tale: a man, the poet, finds himself in a fearful wood, in a valley; he is threatened by three beasts, who prevent him from climbing a hill; an unexpected helper gets him out. The reader's situation is as follows: either he accepts that Dante is first and foremost using the language of the religious culture and society of his time rather than a personal language of his own, or he does not. If he does, he will be able to participate in the full sense and feeling of the story in all its aspects, particular and universal. If not, his participation will be minimal, his grasp of the poem's expressive values will be generic and abstract, at a merely sensuous level, and he will be deaf to the poetry of this introductory canto (and hence to the poetry of the whole *Comedy*). Only at the expense of self-contradiction can real participation be claimed by those tenacious champions of imaginative "immediacy", who deny the technical and historical character of poetic language – in this particular case, the artistic and poetic import of the *literal* and the *allegorical* in the Middle Ages.

We shall follow the first alternative, to prove its necessity, utility and validity. Let us begin by defining what in the context of medieval religion is 'literal' in Dante's text, before going on to its allegory or symbolism proper. For a start, let us recognize and accept *literal* meanings such as the following: 'wood' (dark, wild, etc.) = the wood of error of this life, the error and sin proper in the Christian sense to this life; 'valley' or 'vale' = 'wood' (cf. our habitual use of 'this vale of tears' meaning 'this life', a kind of dead metaphor, or one not recognized as a metaphor by the believer who uses it); and so on.

The great Dante scholar Michele Barbi has given a clear warning in this respect.[39] 'When critics write on the first canto,' he says, 'and talk about the *fundamental allegory* of the poem (it would be better, if anything, to call it an *initial* figuration), they draw too freely for allegorical significance on what is simply *parabolic* or *tropological* expression, belonging as such to the purely *literal* sense. So when, for example, Dante tells of the *wood* in which he was lost, this is simply a figurative manner of speech to indicate his moral transgression from the right path. When we go on from the figure actually to see this transgression, in the image of the wood, we have still not left the literal dimension nor entered that of allegory; for, as Aquinas says, the literal sense is not the figure in itself but what is figured in it, that is to say its meaning.[40] This is confirmed by the fact that elsewhere, still talking about this same transgression, Dante uses other figures without incongruity, when indeed he does not express it with the baldness of what the rhetoricians call proper speech. See, for example, *Inferno* II, 108 and

39. Michele Barbi, *Problemi Fondamentali per un Nuovo Commento della Divina Commedia* Florence 1956.

40. St Thomas Aquinas, *Summa Theologiae*, translated by Thomas Gilby, Cambridge 1963, I, 1, 10, p. 37: 'The parabolic sense is contained in the literal sense, for words can signify something properly and something figuratively; in the last case the literal sense is not the figure of speech itself, but the object it figures. When Scripture speaks of the arm of God, the literal sense is not that he has a physical limb, but that he has what it signifies, namely the power of doing and making.'

XV, 50, where the image of the *wood* is replaced by that of the *flood* or the *valley*; and *Purgatorio* XXIII, 117, where the poet points out Virgil to Forese and says, without any hint of figurative language, "he turned me from that *life*". Proper and figurative expressions are mingled in the Earthly Paradise scene where Beatrice reproves him for his misdeeds and he himself confesses them. Even more complex figurations, though they are linked in one way or another to the allegorical sense of the poem, belong in themselves to the parabolic language in which Dante is versed, both in conformity with the taste of the period and because of his familiarity with ascetic works and the Scriptures, and they are therefore part of the literal sense. One example is the *three beasts* who bar Dante's path up the "delectable mountain". These are without doubt intrinsic impediments which oppose the liberation of the soul from its moral confusion, and the earliest commentators were right to see them as figuring sin, which is essentially the separation of the soul from the supreme Good by "concupiscentia carnis" [or lust: the leopard], "concupiscentia oculorum" [or avarice: the she-wolf] and "superbia vitae" [or pride: the lion]. These three sum up all that in this world blocks the "path of God" to man.'

But Barbi goes further. 'Even if it is represented through figures (the *wood*, the *three beasts*, *Virgil*, *Beatrice*, *Earthly Paradise*, *Celestial Paradise*), the story is part of the literal sense of the poem. It is a mistake to regard these figures as allegories or, worse, as the fundamental allegory. We only enter the allegorical dimension – and we can call it the *initial* allegory because it is given to us almost entire or at least in its essential outlines in the first two cantos – in so far as the poet sought to adumbrate in his own person the Christian society of the time, with Virgil and Beatrice taking on the significance of imperial and papal authority: the two authorities which, assisted by the arguments of human knowledge [= the wise pagan Virgil] and the teachings of revealed truth [= the blessed Beatrice], should lead men on the paths "of the world" and "of God" respectively to temporal and eternal happiness... Everything in the "letter" of the poem is appropriate to Beatrice as a person "from flesh to spirit risen". In view of his wish to give the poem a meaning which transcends the literal sense, it seems natural that Dante should have wanted to symbolize in Beatrice the knowledge of things divine in the same way as he had called on Virgil to symbolize human wisdom. The symbolism in question is justified, among other considerations, by the fact that, being blessed, she knows things that Virgil, a soul in limbo, and Dante, still soldiering on earth, cannot know ... [However,] when the concepts of allegory are substituted for the poetic invention of the "letter", one can no longer speak of the "most gentle" lady of Florence, nor of her exaltation as the intention of the poem, any more than one can speak of Dante the Florentine citizen or Virgil the poet of Rome or the wood or the earthly or the celestial paradise. We must then speak of humanity which has transgressed, of the need for it to be led back to the providential paths "of the world and God" and to be guided once again to earthly happiness by imperial authority, by the light of reason and philosophy, and to eternal blessedness by the Church, through the teachings of revealed truth and theology.[41] To repeat: the tropological sense, which is part of the "letter", should not be confused with the "allegory" proper; they are linked to one another, to be sure; but they should be kept quite distinct, and regarded as belonging to different levels of thought.'

Barbi's findings, the product of the most rigorous modern Dante scholarship in Italy, can be trusted – along with the lines of inquiry associated with the names of Hegel and Auerbach (see below) and Gramsci's structural-topographical investigations into the Cavalcante episode.[42] We are in complete agreement with them, as far as they go. From the point of view of aesthetics, however, or more precisely literary poetics and the general theory of literature, two points need to be cleared up in order to complete the methodological preliminaries which will enable us to approach the *Comedy* as an artistic organism. The first concerns the precise epistemological and aesthetic sense of those two terms *literal* and *figurative* which constitute the more specific aspect of the historical, medieval language necessarily used by Dante. The second concerns what sort of passage or connection we may expect between this particular *literalness* and the total symbolic or *allegorical* character of the poem. It involves, therefore, the problem of the poem's artistic *unity* – which scholars, if they have not denied

41. Cf. *The Letters of Dante*, translated by Paget Toynbee, Oxford 1966, Epist. X, 15: 'the aim of the whole and of the part is to remove those living in this life from a state of misery, and to bring them to a state of happiness.'

42. Antonio Gramsci, *Letteratura e vita nazionale*, Turin 1950, pp. 34 ff.; cf. *Lettere dal carcere*, Turin 1947, pp. 141 ff.

it like Croce,[43] have ignored, seeing only the distinction between the literal and allegorical senses and their location at two different levels of thought.

On the first point, it should be noted that if the *wood* or the *valley* have a cognitive (and expressive) value for the believer Dante as terms which signify literally *sinful life on earth*, in the same way that Aquinas's *arm of God* is cognitively valid in that it signifies literally God's *power of doing and making*, this is because these terms have the same cognitive function as do for us certain terms like the *brow* of a hill or the *leg* of a table (or indeed, as we have said, *vale of tears* meaning *life* for the sincere Christian believer even of today). These terms are dead metaphors. They are at the zero of consciousness, no longer registered as metaphors or figures, and so taken as literal meanings, even though they continue to function, in terms of their cognitive and practical value, as linkages (intellectuality) of the manifold (images), that is as true metaphors (nobody would think of wiping the brow of a hill). But there is one difference between the two kinds of dead metaphor, a difference of content. The medieval religious type used by Dante and Aquinas is made up of figurative *moral* meanings while the figurative meanings of the latter are material and mundane.

This leads us to a clarification of the second point. For the moral and religious *symbolism* takes shape, structuring and unifying the poem, in so far as it is working primarily on a homogeneous material constituted first and foremost by figurative moral meanings, those 'literal'-figurative meanings or dead metaphors of which we have spoken above. From this derives the *second degree* symbolism which characterizes the symbolic dimension of Dante's poem, its allegory, and which – where it succeeds in unifying or fusing into itself figurative moral meanings and literal meanings (in the proper sense of the term) – constitutes the peculiar artistic greatness of the poet. The proof of the pudding . . . We shall see whether so massive an intellectual construction is worthwhile, in other words whether Dante's poetry requires it in order to be what it is and thus compensates for it.

Let us now return to the introductory canto of *Inferno*, also bearing in mind Canto II which has close links with it. The first thing to be said is that we must be prepared to accept (thanks to the aesthetic inventory just made) as moral meanings the *dark wood* and the *straight*

43. Benedetto Croce, *La Poesia di Dante*, Bari 1921.

way which is lost (the way leading to individual virtue and right order in the affairs of mankind), the *valley* and the *hill* and the *delectable mountain* (the virtuous and well-ordered life which is the foundation of human happiness), and similar terms that occur as the poem proceeds. If we do not, we shall be shutting ourselves away from both the dramatic emotion of the opening (the protagonist's 'fear'), which should hypothetically compensate and explain the abrupt introduction of these figurative elements, and from entry into the edifying vision-revelation which is the poem itself. At the same time, there is no denying that if there is a starting-point to the symbolism, it lies in the depiction of the protagonist as representing the whole of sinful humanity precisely by his wandering in this wood which is the wood of error of this life, and not in just any wood in the material or literal sense (properly so called) into which Dante happens to have stumbled at the age of thirty-five (likewise the valley).

Nevertheless, the *progressive moral meanings* which accompany his entry into *that* wood are not the only or the most important indication of the appearance of symbolism, by which I mean artistic and expressive symbolism, not cold allegory. They are of course strongly suggestive of a certain type of religious and ethical feeling as the following example will show:

> that *wood, savage and harsh and dense,* the thought of which renews my *fear*! (*Inf.* I, 5–6);
> So *bitter* is it that death is hardly more. (*Inf.* I, 7);
> I cannot rightly tell how I entered there, I was so full of *sleep* [of the soul] at that moment when I left the true [=straight] way.
> (*Inf.* I, 10–12);
> But when I had reached the foot of a *hill* at the end of that *valley* which had pierced my heart with *fear* (*Inf.* I, 13–15);
> to look again at the *pass* which never yet let any go *alive*
> (*Inf.* I, 26–7).[44]

But the most important indication is given in *the development of the action* in the encounters that follow. Firstly, those with the three beasts vividly emblematical as they are: the sensual leopard, or lust,

> light and very swift, covered with a spotted hide (*Inf.* I, 32–3);

44. Dante, *The Divine Comedy,* Italian text with translation and comment by John D. Sinclair (3 vols.), revised edition, Oxford 1971.

then the lion of pride,

> holding its head high and furious with hunger so that the air
> seemed in dread of it   (*Inf.* I, 47–8);

and finally, the she-wolf, spectral in its avidity:

> which appeared in its leanness to be charged with all cravings and
> which has already made many live in wretchedness. (*Inf.* I, 49–51);

and which:

> put such heaviness on me by the terror which came forth from
> its looks that I lost *hope of the ascent* [i.e. the hill]   (*Inf.* I, 52–4);
> *the restless beast* . . . coming against me and driving me back step
> by step to where *the sun is silent.*   (*Inf.* I, 58–60).

Then secondly, the encounter with the spirit gifted with pagan
wisdom, that of Virgil coming to his aid:

> Not man; once I was man . . . I was born *sub Julio* . . . in the time
> of the false and lying gods. . . . Art thou then *that Virgil* . . . ?
>   (*Inf.* I, 67–79).

Virgil who, in response to the precise request for help against the
she-wolf in particular:

> See the *beast* for which I turned, save me from her, famous *sage*,
> for she sets the pulses trembling in my veins   (*Inf.* I, 88–90),

gives the following reply:

> Thou must take another road . . . if thou wouldst escape from
> this savage place; for this beast on account of which thou criest
> lets no man pass her way, but *hinders them* till she *takes their life*
>   (*Inf.* I, 91–6).

This reply brings out so expressively the (moral) meaning of the
threat of (spiritual) death – where life is taken simply by impediment
from the hill of virtue, as hope of its ascent languishes – that it rever-
berates not only on all that precedes it (lending particular aesthetic
force to the she-wolf/avarice which here reaches the climax of its
dramatic reality),[45] but also on what immediately follows:

45. A recent commentator, nevertheless, has described the representation of
the she-wolf as 'completely allegorical' and 'interwoven with intellectualistic
elements': *La Divina Commedia*, a cura di Natalino Sapegno, Florence 1968, vol. I, p. 9.

[Virgil:] until the *hound* comes that shall bring her to miserable death . . . he shall hunt her through every city till he has sent her back to Hell whence envy first let her loose,   (*Inf.* I, 101–11),

and right through to the end of the canto, with Virgil's offer to guide Dante 'through an eternal place' (*Inf.* I, 114):

Poet, I entreat thee by that God whom thou knowest not, in order that I may escape *this evil* [the slavery of sin] and worse, lead me where thou hast said, that I may see Saint Peter's gate and those thou makest so sorrowful.   (*Inf.* I, 130–3).

It will not be denied that the *expressive homogeneity* of these encounters also extends to the second canto, which continues the symbolic account of the mystical journey that is the object of the vision. In Virgil's circumstantial announcement of the intervention of the blessed Beatrice:

Seest thou not the *death* which combats him on the *flood* that is not less terrible than the sea?   (*Inf.* II, 107–8),

we are shown that, according to the logic of Christian morality, it is not enough to experience, in Chimenz's words, 'a momentary terror of sin and a flash of reason' in order to undertake the path of redemption: 'this first motion of the soul must be confirmed by a higher light than that of human reason, and by the certainty of heavenly grace.'[46]

In other words, the lines 'but hinders them till she takes their life', are a perfect fusion of the literal or real and the symbolic or allegorical. The episode contains the aggressive action of barring off a path which is proper to a real wolf and a certain consequence of that action. It is a mortal moral blow, but it is so because, in a real and physical sense, it represents impediment to motion, and the impediment is morally lethal because what the journeyer is interdicted is the *place* of salvation, the *hill* of virtuous living, the delectable mountain, and entry is forbidden *not by a wolf like any other* which, though real, might be powerless, but by one 'which appeared in its leanness to be charged

46. Siro A. Chimenz, 'Inferno II', in *Letture Dantesche: Inferno*, a cura di Giovanni Getto, Florence 1955, pp. 27 ff.

with all cravings'. The same fusion holds for what follows from this passage, and for all that part of the *Comedy* which lives.

In conclusion, the following points seem to us sufficiently demonstrated. Firstly, Dante's poetry, like the classical poetry we were considering earlier, is incomprehensible, and therefore inconceivable, apart from the social and cultural *humus* organically present in it with a language which is as quintessentially historical and technical as it is personal. From this derives the specific feeling of the *Comedy*, which strikes us by its *historical* and *human* novelty – we have only to compare that 'death' of the soul on the 'flood' of life with 'death' in Horace, Virgil, Lucretius and the Greeks; and where else could we find that 'fear' of sin in the opening canto, not only in the ancient poets, but in the moderns? – no less than by the novelty of its individual voice – Dante is not Petrarch but neither is he Guido Cavalcanti.

Secondly, the 'machinery of the poem', as Tommaseo called it, the whole technical and moral-allegorical structure,[47] is strictly indispensable and inseparable from the poetry of the *Comedy*, for it confers on the poem its necessary *unity* (of point of view). Without it, the expressive and artistic texture of any individual part or episode would be sacrificed, together with its particular symbolic (or allegorical) universal meaning. So, even with a very popular episode like that of Paolo and Francesca (*Inferno* V), we falsify it aesthetically if we fail to understand that its Christian and Catholic setting endows this particular love-story with an atmosphere that makes it quite distinct not only from the stories inspired by modern, romantic, 'passionate love, (complete with 'heroine') of Desanctisian and Crocean memory, but distinct also from the courtly-love tradition of the Middle Ages (for example the *Espinette amoureuse* of Froissart, despite the notable overlap of expressions such as 'Adont laissames nous le lire'). It is precisely the

47. Including the relationship between figure and fulfilment (*Figur-und-Erfüllung*) which Auerbach has investigated, following a lead from Hegel. This method throws real light on Dante's 'realism', from 'characters' like Ciacco the glutton and Casella and Buonconte to Cacciaguida and the apostle Peter. This 'realism' is simply an extension to the poet's contemporary world of the Judaic–Christian procedure adopted by Paul and the Fathers of the Church, whereby Adam was seen as a 'figure' of Christ, Eve of the Church, and so on, and each event of the Old Testament was conceived as a 'figure' to be brought to 'fulfilment' with the events of the Incarnation of Christ. See Erich Auerbach, *Figura*, Istanbul 1944 (now in *Scenes from the Drama of European Literature*, New York 1959), and *Mimesis*, translated by Willard R. Trask, Princeton 1953. Cf. Hegel, op. cit., especially Vol. II, p. 1104.

structural element, the ethical and religious judgment placing the lovers topographically in the circle of

the carnal sinners, who subject reason to desire   (*Inf.* V, 38–9),

which creates this atmosphere. In order, therefore, to catch the exact tone of Dante's pity we must be sensitive to that complex of historical and intellectual themes noted by the more alert scholars, such as the theory of the 'gentle heart' and 'the ancient shadow of the fatal deity of love looming through the consciousness of the Christian Middle Ages' (Crescini). They all play their part in the compassionate but severe and unalterable judgement not of 'Dante' the pilgrim, but the *poet.*

7. Goethe's Faust

In the case of *Faust*, once again our appreciation of the art of the poem will depend on our capacity to recapture its particular historical feeling. In the case of *Faust*, this involves an ability to define the moral symbolism – modern, not medieval or ancient – of its ending, in other words, to resolve the problem of what exactly is meant by the 'salvation of Faust'. Comprehension of the structural unity of the two parts of *Faust* and therewith adequate articulation of the 'lyric' and 'dramatic' values of the poem are dependent on an answer to that question. Once again we shall be concerned with historical and technical rather than personal or individual language: this time, the language of the philosophical culture and the society of the 'Age of Goethe'. It is the language of naturalist, secular humanism (pantheist, if you will) as it developed from the restless libertarian humanism of the *Sturm und Drang*. Moral aversion to political despotism had become metaphysical aversion to the idea of a divine despot ruling the universe; the conclusions of an anti-despotic and anti-ecclesiastical Enlightenment were now transmuted into the articles of a new 'religiosity', which was lay-pantheistic and idealist in character and no longer lay-deistic or rationalist in the manner of the *Aufklärung*; a sort of mystical coincidence-of-opposites à la Hamann, tempered by a Spinozan *Deus-sive-Natura*. But we must go further if we are to find our way into the poetry of *Faust*, and draw attention to the rigorous and vigorous use which Goethe made of this lay-idealist culture and its language. In Goethe's usage, quite the opposite of Dante's, the theological, moral and religious terms and concepts of the (Catholic) Church are taken purely as metaphors or *figures* of the values proper to the real world – that is the human, secular world; whereas the medieval genius of Dante, as we have seen, puts the vocabulary of daily life such as wood, valley, flood, etc, to use as religious and ethical metaphors, heedless sometimes even of their being metaphors, to be taken as literal-moral meanings. It is significant, for example, that the whole Faust story is bracketed and defined by a 'prologue in heaven' and an 'ascent to heaven'.

Leaving aside for the moment the prologue and the conversation between the 'Lord' and Mephistopheles about the protagonist, let us rehearse some of the more important moments in Dr Faust's story up to his death. Although Part I is often regarded, unilaterally and without further ado, as the 'tragedy of Margareta' by those who insist on seeing it as a separate entity from Part II, we shall find that it contains a presentation of moral and poetic problems that goes beyond Faust's adventure with Gretchen and the seduction, the killing of the child, and the tragic death of the girl herself.

Part I contains the following nodal points:

(1) Faust's profound and tragic disgust with a life lived up to now among abstractions and dead things

> (Why, with a nameless pain oppresst,
> Thy pulse of life doth fail and freeze?
> God fashioned man that he should root
> In living Nature. . . .
> Thou dwellest in a charnel-vault,
> 'Midst mouldering bones of man and brute.')[48]

drives him to evoke *not the devil* (Mephistopheles will appear to him later) but the 'spirit of the Earth'. It is to this spirit that he addresses his religious urge, his pantheistic feeling: the new god presented here by Goethe in a celebrated depiction of Swedenborgian spiritualism.[49]

> *Faust:* Thou boundless Nature, where shall I grasp thee clearly?
> . . .

48. *Goethe's Faust*, translated by Albert Latham, London and New York 1908, Vol. I, p. 27.
49. See H. A. Korff, *Geist der Goethezeit*, Leipzig 1957.

Thou, Spirit of the Earth, to me art higher [than the
Macrocosm];

My powers I feel already higher,
I glow, as if with new-made wine.
Full-steeled to tread the world I feel my mettle,
Earth's woe, Earth's bliss, my soul can not unsettle . . .

Spirit: Panting thou pleadest for my presence,
To look upon my face, . . .
. . . , I appear! –
What mortal dread, thou man of more than mortal essence,
Gets hold on thee? Where now the outcry of thy soul?
The breast, that in itself a world did fashion whole,
And hugged, and cherished? That, with rapture all a-tingle,
Puffed itself up with us that spirits are to mingle? . . .
. . .
Say, is it thou, that by my breath surrounded,
In all life's utmost deeps confounded,
Dost shrink away, a timorous, writhing worm?

Faust: Creature of Flame, thou shalt not daunt me!
'Tis I, 'tis Faust, thy peer I vaunt me!

Spirit: In floods of being, in action's storm,
Up and down I wave,
To and fro I flee,
Birth and the grave,
An infinite sea,
A changeful weaving,
An ardent living;
The ringing loom of Time is my care,
And I weave God's living garment there.

Faust: Though busy Spirit, that rangest unconfined
Round the wide world, how near I feel to thee!

Spirit: Thou'rt like the Spirit thou graspest with thy mind,
Thou'rt not like me!

Faust: Not thee?
Whom then?
I, made in God's own image!
Not even like thee!

(pp. 28–31).

(2) Faust's impulse to suicide, when he is thrust back by the Spirit of the Earth into 'man's uncertain fate', in which:

> The glorious feelings, that erst our soul did quicken,
> Soon in this earthly welter swoon and sicken (p. 36),

and:

> Deep in the heart nests care, a guest unbidden.
> There doth she work her sorrows hidden.
> . . .
> Each blow that falls not dost thou feel. (pp. 36–7);

this impulse is quieted by the sound of the Easter bells, not because of a reawakening of Christian feeling in Faust ('I hear the tale ye tell, but Faith lends no approval': p. 41), but because of the elementary force of an unconscious will to live, which was lacking in Werther but already present in Goethe's Prometheus:

> And yet to your sweet tones, beloved from childhood's prime,
> For this recall to life I am beholden . . . (p. 41)
> . . .
> The vale is abud with the boon of hope (p. 48)
> . . .
> This is the people's very heaven!
> Great and small cry out in glee:
> Here am I man, here man may be! (p. 49)

(and vice-versa his *famulus* Wagner the man of letters, complaining:

> Alone, I should avoid this vulgar scramble,
> For every kind of coarseness is my bane (p. 49)).

(3) The tragic condition of Faust, from which originate the pact (youth and fullness of life in exchange for his soul) and the wager with Mephistopheles (perpetual dissatisfaction), with the importance of these undertakings for the future development of the hero. (a) Having escaped suicide thanks to that desire for life which was lacking in Werther (but having also lost his power of liberation), Faust falls back into the grip of *Weltschmerz*, the torment of 'this cramping earthly life' (p. 72), that harrowing sense of human finitude that may plague a

pantheistic, religious mind; flailing in his own hell, he curses the universe:

> But self-denial! self-denial!
> That is the everlasting song
> In all men's ears that ever rings.
> . . .
> Then could I weep as one of hope forsaken,
> To see the day, which ere its course be done
> Will not fulfil one wish of mine – not one! . . .
> Mars the creations of my fruitful bosom. (pp. 72–3)
> . . .
> Cursed be all baubles that enamour
> With cheating, juggling charm, the soul;
> Or chain it with elusive glamour
> Within this dreary, dungeon-hole!
> Cursed before all the high opinion
> In which the soul itself ensnares!
> . . .
> Cursed be Hope's vision, Faith's delusion,
> And cursed, thrice cursed, be Patience meek! (p. 74)

(b) The profound meaning of the pact-cum-wager which follows with Mephistopheles, 'the Spirit that denies'

> (So thou [Meph.] dost coldly shrive, thou canker,
> The eternal thrill of Life to blight!
> Thy devil's fist in bootless rancour
> Dost clench against Creative Might! pp. 65–6),

and whom Faust's will to life has attracted into his orbit by means of magic, is conveyed at once by the dense interplay of ambiguities in their mutual undertakings:

> *Mephist:* *Here* will I pledge myself to serve thee truly, . . .
> When we meet *yonder*, shalt thou duly
> In a like manner do my hest.
> *Faust:* The Yonder is a trifling matter;
> This world in ruins if thou shatter,
> Why, let the other then arise!
> 'Tis from this world my life its joys doth borrow;

This sun it is that shines upon my sorrow; ...
...
And pray, what wilt thou give, poor Devil?
When could the like of thee rise to the lofty level
To which doth strive the human breast? ...
...
If on the bed of sloth I loll contented ever,
Then with that moment end my race!
Canst thou delude me with thy glozing
Self-pleased, to put my grief away,
Canst thou my soul with pleasures cozen,
Then be that day my life's last day.
That is the wager.
...
When to the moment fleeting past me,
Tarry! I cry, so fair thou art!
...
Then let come doom, with all my heart!
...
And fear not thou that with this bond I'll palter.
The essence of my promise is
To strive with all my might, nor shall I falter
...
All knowledge long hath loathsome been
...
Headlong we'll plunge in the turmoil of Time
...
'Tis action alone attests the man![50]
...
You hear! No dreams of joy am I caressing!
Mephist: Sure testimony we can render:
This Whole but for a God is made.

50. Cf. Faust's interpretation earlier of the opening of St John's Gospel:
'Tis written: *In the beginning was the Word.*
Already I stick, and who shall help afford?
The *word* at such high rate I may not tender;
...
... – from all doubting freed,
Thus write I: *In the beginning was the Deed.* (p.60)

Faust: Nay, but I will!

     . . .

     What am I then, if Fate mine efforts thwart
     The crown of all humanity from earning,
     From which my senses all are ever yearning?

Mephist: To him hath Destiny a spirit given
     That all unbridled, ever forward sweeps,
     And by o'erhasty effort driven,
     The Earth's delights still overleaps

     . . .

     Vainly he'll crave refreshment for his flame.
     Himself unto the Devil had he not made over,
     He'd go to the devil all the same! (pp. 76–84)

In other words, the pact and even more the wager, though Faust himself is unaware of it, are astute pieces of trickery devised by his will to live as an alternative way out of the human hell of *Weltschmerz* to the physical suicide of a Werther, the typical *Sturm und Drang* solution. That other suicide, of the Christian soul, which is the only 'perdition' with which a Mephistopheles can threaten him, does not come into his reckoning at all – indeed Mephistopheles' total and natural incomprehension of Faustian man is already at its height in the way he cannot see into Faust's intentions except through the eyes of the bigot. So Faust's story and its moral take shape from the beginning under the *problematic* sign of an equivalence of *Amor fati* and *Amor vitae* ('Dasein ist Pflicht'). This has to be borne in mind if we are not to lose sight of the poetic whole for the particular episode, e.g. the tragedy of Margareta, for some of the most profound and genuine poetic accents of the work resonate in explicit and organic accord with a general structure and project of which Part I is the problematical and historical foundation.

Given this perspective, it will be seen that Part II is the poetic development and conclusion of the problematic structure outlined in Part I, followed along these principal strands of Faust's later experience:

(1) The reawakening of the will to live in Faust, rejuvenated – after his anguish and self-disgust at Gretchen's death – through contact with nature ('fair country'):

Ariel: What a tumult brings the light!

. . .

Faust: Life's pulses newly-quickened now awaken,
Softly to greet the ethereal twilight leaping;

. . .

Is't Love? Is't Hate? that yonder glowing spindle
In bliss and bale alternating tremendous
About us twines, till we the dazed beholders
To veil our gaze in Earth's fresh mantle wend us.

. . .

The painted rainbow bends its changeful being,
Now lost in the air, now limned with clearest power,
Shedding this fragrant coolness round us fleeing.
Its rays an image of man's efforts render; (Vol. II, pp.13–15)

(2) The great *intellectual* experience of Faust, that of ancient Greece and its myths: his descent to the 'Mothers', personification of Platonic essences, the roots of all created things ('The thrill of awe is still mankind's best lot / And though the world not lets him feel it cheaply / Yet awe-struck, the stupendous feels he deeply' proclaims Faust the Romantic pantheist: p. 78), his first impressions of Peneus peopled by nymphs:

Oh, what a wondrous thrill runs through me!
Come ye as dreams – as memories to me? (p. 127),

Thales' tale of the voluntary sacrifice of Homunculus, chemical man, pure spirit created in Wagner's laboratory, who enters into full life attracted by Nature, love and death, and kills himself against the chariot of marine Cypris, Galatea:

Thales: Homunculus is it, by Proteus beguiled.
The symptoms are those of imperious striving,
A dolorous moan fills my heart with misgiving.
Himself will he shatter upon the bright throne!
A flame and a flash, an effusion, 'tis done. (p. 176),

right through to the union of Faust with Helen restored to life as incarnation of ancient Beauty ('the Form, fairest of all forms': p. 198), a union which is the poetic symbol of poetry understood in the romantic sense as aesthetic (Apollonian) or emotional *contemplativeness:*

> *Faust:* Nor back nor forward, in an hour like this
> The mind doth look; the present –
> *Helen:* Is our bliss. (p. 222),

and to the pantheistic enjoyment of an Arcadian freedom:

> *Faust ·* We stand amazed, and still the question holdeth
> If men, if haply Gods are they?
> So like the herds Apollo was in favour,
> The fairest him resembled quite.
> For where in purest round reigns Nature, ever
> All worlds in one are interknit
> . . .
> And be our bliss Arcadian free! (p. 229):

the upshot being (in agreement with Korff and the best exegetical tradition) a supreme romantic poetic synthesis between Classical and Romantic in the sense of *Weltliteratur* or universal literature already realized by Goethe himself in the *West-östlicher Divan.*

(3) The final and decisive *moral* experiences of Faust. (a) The construction of a certain economic and political dominion:

> *Faust:* No wise! This round of earth, methought,
> Hath scope for great achieving ever.
> Strength do I feel for bold endeavour
> . . .
> At lordship, ownership I aim.
> The deed is all and naught the fame. (p. 258)

(b) Following his remorse for the wretched fate of Philemon and Baucis, a fate for which Faust was indirectly but undeniably responsible through his dispossession of their tiny property:

> *Faust:* The few trees not mine own – they spoil me
> The lordship of the world I have.
> . . .
> With deep, fierce suffering he must
> Enforce himself, that would be just
> . . .
> . . . mine hasty deed I rue. (pp. 308–12),

he successfully resists Care who, visiting him in his extreme old age
and powerless to do anything else, makes him go blind; he explicitly
renounces magic and every sort of superstition:

> Could I . . . stand mere man before thee, Nature! Then
> 'Twere worth the while to be a man with men.
> . . .
> Use superstition soon and late entwines.
> . . .
> Thus are we overawed, we stand alone.
> . . .
> The round of earth enough I know, and barred
> Is unto man the prospect yonderward.
> O fool, who thither turns his blinking glances,
> And of his like above the clouds romances!
> . . .
> Not mute the world is to the man of worth.
> What need hath he to range infinitude?
> . . .
> Unhallowed spectres! . . .
> . . .
> E'en days indifferent transmute ye still
> To a foul web of tangled tribulations.
> 'Tis ill, I know, from demons to be free.
> . . .
> And yet, O Care, though stealthy-great it be,
> Thy might I'll not acknowledge ever!
> . . .
> More deeply-deep Night seemeth to enfold me,
> Yet clear the daylight shines within mine heart.
> I'll hasten to fulfil the plan doth hold me;
> The master's word alone doth weight impart.
> Up from the couch, ye vassals! Every man!
> . . .
> Take tools in hand all! Spade and shovel ply ye!
> What is staked out be straight accomplished by ye!
> . . .
> One mind for thousand hands suffices. (pp. 315–19)

In this opposition of genius or *mind* and hands – the 'hands' or 'operatives' of political economy—we can read the division of labour implied by individualistic or competitive emulation (see Mayakovsky below). (c) Faust dying on his feet, the striving individualist, the (bourgeois) hero of tireless activity, exalted as herald and conscious champion of a (bourgeois) 'community of free beings' called upon to perform great works of production for the well-being of mankind, and finally achieving satisfaction in this vision, the summit and sublimation of his *amor fati* = *amor vitae*:

> Faust: The flood without may bluster to the brim [of the dike].
> And as it nibbles to shoot in amain
> Flock one and all to fill the breach again.
> My will from this design not swerveth,
> The last resolve of human wit,
> For liberty, as life, alone deserveth
> He daily that must conquer it.
> . . .
> With a free people stand on a free soil . . .
> To such a moment past me fleeing,
> Tarry, I'd cry, thou art so fair!
> The traces of mine earthly being
> Not countless aeons can outwear.
> Now, in the presage of such lofty bliss,
> The highest moment I enjoy, e'en this . . .

(He sinks back into the arms of the Lemurs, who lay him on the ground)

> Mephist.: Him can no pleasure sate, no bliss suffice,
> Thus ever after changing forms he springeth.
> Even to this last sorry empty trice,
> Poor wretch, with all his soul he clingeth.
> Me did he sturdily withstand –
> Time triumphs, lies the graybeard in the sand.
> The clock stands still – (p. 322)

Here, the idiotic no less than cynical epitaph which Mephistopheles pronounces over Faust makes it plain that if the latter embodies poetically (symbolizes) the positive, heroic, creative side of modern bourgeois man, Mephisto (*pace* Lukács) embodies and symbolizes only his negative side, all his worst features.[51]

The Epilogue 'in heaven', in which the angels snatch *Faustens Unsterbliches*, 'the immortal part of Faust', from the jaws of the 'colossal hyena' of hell and sing,

> Freed is the noble scion of
> The Spirit-world from evil.
> Him can we save that tireless strove
> Ever to higher level.
> And if Supernal Love did stoop
> To him with predilection,
> Then him shall hail the angelic troop
> With brotherly affection, etc. (p. 336),

complements and completes the Prologue 'in heaven', and specifically what the 'Lord' says to Mephistopheles about Faust:

> *The Lord:* Whilst still man strives, still must he stray.
>
> . . .
>
> From its well-head draw thou this soul astray
>
> . . .
>
> And stand abashed, when thou must needs confess
> That a good man, by his dim impulse driven,
> Of the right way hath ever consciousness.
>
> (*Pt. I*, pp. 22–3)

It is a double completion, one that concerns not only the continuity and the coherence of the immediate meaning of the Prologue and the Epilogue, but also the continuity and coherence of the *symbolic* meaning of both. This is precisely a *non-literal* symbolic (or general) meaning – in other words, it is not based on the letter of the text but on its *metaphorical* value. The 'salvation' of Faustian man, with its echoes of Christian (Catholic) theology, is in fact a contracted (thus precisely metaphorical) expression of a comparison or simile between the *secular* moral values of Faustism, a pantheist–idealist kind of spiritual-

51. Georg Lukács, *Goethe and His Age*, London 1968, pp. 194 ff. On Faust as bourgeois hero, compare the last words of his exaltation and exultation as entrepreneur with the rather similar pronouncement of Ibsen's failed ex-banker John Gabriel Borkman (Act III, sc. 2): 'I have loved . . . the power to create human happiness far and wide about me!'

ism, and the *dogmatic*-spiritualist moral values of that theology. Although it has even greater symbolic moral importance, it is no different in kind from the symbolic and metaphorical use of the Greek myths to signify, as we have seen, the synthesis of Classical and Romantic. As in the earlier case, the general conditions of any metaphorical process are satisfied: *resemblance* (here, a generically spiritualist conception of the world) between *dissimilar* terms (the difference and the distance between a lay, humanistic conception of spiritualism and an ecclesiastical, dogmatic one, with all the divergent social and material conditions underlying that difference). The failure to discern the metaphorical character of this symbolism has in one way or another misled critics like Vischer, Rickert, Böhm, and even Korff. The latter oscillates significantly between a just recognition of the '*artistic* necessity of the religious framework' of the poem, the need for an 'external rapprochement with the mythological presuppositions of the Christian saga of Faust' and the amazing statement that 'this "non-Christian" poem confronts its own non-Christianity with that romantic irony which is its ultimate mystery' – a claim which in any case in effect contradicts the point made shortly before, that the poem 'does not seek to annul it [the Faustian myth] with romantic irony', for 'the Faustian myth too has its inner morality'.[52]

In conclusion, we may add that our technical definition of the final symbolism of *Faust* as symbolism of a metaphorical character (and specifically, according to the grammar of metaphor, as verb-metaphor: 'Den können wir *erlösen*', 'Him can we *save*'), at the same time as showing us the artistic *form* of the work in its final, overall shape, also tells us something about its 'content'. Through the conceptual symbol of the hero's 'salvation', whose associative metaphorical reference to the figures of a perhaps uniquely long and venerable tradition of moral values is a warranty of the validity and objectivity of the Faustian credo, we are given the full measure of the secular 'content' which is inseparable from that form, as a *historical* content. It is a problematical content (think, for example, of the much-discussed immorality of certain actions of our vaunted hero of action: the fate of Margareta and that of Philemon and Baucis for example), but this problematical character is not imputable to the form or art of the poem. On the contrary, Goethe's art has the merit of having raised

52. Korff, op. cit., Vol. IV, pp. 698 and 691.

the problems in the first place and so cast light on the morality of individualist, bourgeois humanism and the modern world in all its complexity – thereby precisely constituting itself as great art, great poetry. No, the problems are imputable, if the word here has any meaning, to history itself, and it is history in turn which will gradually clarify and move towards the solution of such problems in the light of the economics and politics, the morality, science and *art* of socialist humanism. At this point, in truly great poetry, poetry and history are once again inseparable (even if each is *technically* distinct, as we shall see). Thus, there is in the death of Faust a modern secular (bourgeois) pathos, no less *objectively* specific and therefore *poetically* significant than Dante's medieval sense of the supreme illumination of Grace

(Here power failed the high phantasy: *Paradiso* XXXIII, 142),

or the religious feeling of Greece in Sophocles' 'wondrous' death of Oedipus at Colonus:

Wail no more, let sorrow rest,
All is ordered for the best (ll. 1777–9).

8. Eliot and Mayakovsky

Contemporary poetry too reaches its highest peak in those poets who best reflect the society of modern times, or rather, the socie*ties*, of the bourgeois and the socialist worlds; those poets who are richest in thought and moral awareness. Nor could it be otherwise. Eliot, Brecht and Mayakovsky are names that spring to mind as writers who have already given full measure of themselves; others will be mentioned in the course of the argument. Apart from other considerations, our (experimental) inquiry will not for this reason include poets like Yeats, Rilke or Valéry in whom the sense of the past predominates over that of the present. What Kléber Haedens, referring to Valéry, called an 'exemplary banality' of thought[53] presides over their reworking of long-established myths on the topics of love, death, eternity, nature, art and so on, in the traditional cultural patterns of post-romanticism and decadentism (Symbolism). As examples, one might cite the myth of 'narcissism in life and art' of Valéry:

53. Kléber Haedens, *Une Histoire de la littérature française*, Paris 1949, pp. 431–2.

But I, beloved Narcissus, am curious
    Only for my own essence;
All else for me has only a mysterious heart,
    All else is only absence. (*Narcisse* II, ll. 83–6)—

See also the 'spiritual eye' in 'La Jeune Parque' and Alain's fervid commentary; or the Platonic–romantic myth of the inwardness of knowledge (anamnesia) and hence of the 'world's inner space' in Rilke:

Though the reflection in the pond
may often be blurred for us:
know the symbol!

(*Sonnets to Orpheus*, IX, 9–11; and cf. in particular *Duino Elegies*, IX).[54] But with T. S. Eliot, the post-romantic and decadent literary tradition (to which he nevertheless belongs) comes into direct contact with the moral problems of the bourgeois society from which it had sprung, and takes on fresh life. These problems are in particular those of the great crisis of the war and the post-war period (the date of *The Waste Land* is 1922), which had escaped the attention of such various figures as Valéry, Rilke and Yeats.

The spiritualism which Eliot shares with these three and his and their symbolist predecessors assumes in his case a particular form somewhere between Lutheran and Catholic. To see how it acts as a poetic catalyst for the crisis of traditional lay, bourgeois moral values, already on the verge of collapse after the First World War, let us look briefly at some examples of this religious poetic awareness of the crisis. A salient passage from the first section of the *Waste Land* (the arid desert of present-day bourgeois civilization):

Unreal City,
Under the brown fog of a winter dawn,
A crowd flowed over London Bridge, so many,
I had not thought death had undone so many.
Sighs, short and infrequent, were exhaled,
And each man fixed his eyes before his feet.

54. On Rilke, see his most intelligent commentator, Werner Günther, *Weltinnenraum: Die Dichtung R. M. Rilkes*, Berlin 1952; the book takes as its motto Rilke's 'Durch alle Wesen reicht der eine Raum: Weltinnenraum'.

Flowed up the hill and down King William Street,
To where Saint Mary Woolnoth kept the hours
With a dead sound on the final stroke of nine.
There I saw one I knew, and stopped him crying: 'Stetson!
'You were with me in the ships at Mylae!
'That corpse you planted last year in your garden,
'Has it begun to sprout? Will it bloom this year?
'Or has the sudden frost disturbed its bed?
'Oh keep the Dog far hence, that's friend to men,
'Or with nails he'll dig it up again!
'You! hypocrite lecteur! – mon semblable, – mon frère!'

(ll. 60–76).

The essential thing to note here is the way in which Eliot's technique
works – a technique of the metaphorical phrase based for the most
part on cultural allusions and associations with distant historical
events. In the passage quoted: allusions to the Paris of Baudelaire's
Sept vieillards:

Swarming city, city full of dreams, where the ghost accosts the
passer-by in broad daylight!,[55]

to Dante's Limbo, in *Inferno* III, 55–57: '. . . so long a train of people that
I should never have believed death had undone so many'; to the battle
of Mylae won by the Romans in 200 B.C. in the first Punic War, war
of trade and war of conquest *par excellence*; to Psalm 22, verse 20:

Deliver . . . my darling from the power of the dog;

and to the dirge sung by a crazed mother over the body of her son
killed by his brother in Webster's *White Devil*, Act V, scene 4, ll. 110–11:

But keepe the wolfe far thence: that's foe to men,
For with his nailes hee'l dig them up agen.[56];

and to the last line of *Au lecteur* in *Les Fleurs du Mal*, in which Baudelaire
makes the reader co-reponsible for the 'infamous seraglio of our
vices':

' – Hypocrite lecteur, – mon semblable, – mon frère'.

55. Charles Baudelaire, *Selected Verse*, prose translation by Francis Scarfe, London
1961.
56. John Webster, *The White Devil*, edited by C. Hart, Edinburgh 1970.

What should be noted is the part played by this allusive technique in the combination of description and judgement that culminates feelingly in the denunciation of contemporary man[57] for his cruel egoism and hypocrisy; a hypocrite who is ironically advised to keep the scratching dog 'that's friend to men' away from the victim's corpse, that is to hide his crimes – it won't be too difficult for him – from the *humanitarian* conscience of which he is so proud. Underlying the power of this symbolism is representation that is precise and concrete, however complex it may be.

But already in *Gerontion* (1919), the symbolic picture of a hopelessly decaying civilization presented through the thoughts of an old man, we find lines such as the following:

Here I am, an old man in a dry month
. . .
    In the juvescence of the year
Came Christ the tiger.

In depraved May, dogwood and chestnut, flowering judas,
To be eaten, to be divided, to be drunk
Among whispers; by Mr Silvero
With caressing hands, at Limoges
Who walked all night in the next room;
By Kakagawa, bowing among the Titians;
By Madame de Tornquist, in the dark room
Shifting the candles; Fräulein von Kulp
Who turned in the hall, one hand on the door. . . .
. . .
After such knowledge, what forgiveness? Think now
History has many cunning passages, contrived corridors
And issues, deceives with whispering ambitions,
Guides us by vanities. . . .
. . .
                           Think
Neither fear nor courage saves us. Unnatural vices

57. 'Stetson': an ordinary modern English businessman's name, yet it is as though he had fought in the ships of one of the first wars of conquest, for all imperialist wars are one and the same war, and Stetson, whether or not he actually took part in World War I, is the symbol of one who belongs to a rapacious commercial civilization.

Are fathered by our heroism. Virtues
Are forced upon us by our impudent crimes.
These tears are shaken from the wrath-bearing tree.
    The tiger springs in the new year. Us he devours. . . .
. . .
I have lost my passion: why should I need to keep it
Since what is kept must be adulterated?
. . .
. . . De Bailhache, Fresca, Mrs Cammel whirled
Beyond the circuit of the shuddering Bear
In fractured atoms. . . .
. . .
And an old man driven by the Trades
To a sleepy corner.
                    Tenants of the house,
Thoughts of a dry brain in a dry season.

Via Eliot's usual procedure of the phrase-metaphor, two moral meanings prevail in this poem. In the first instance, Eliot exposes the loss of
Christian values in bourgeois society, seen for example in the upper
reaches of so-called 'international café society'. In this social world,
characteristically suggested in the little sketches of the collector of
rare china (Mr Silvero of the caressing hands) the spiritualist Madame
de Tornquist and the rest note how the perversion of sacred love is
given great poetic (metaphorical) relief by the elliptical, oblique
association of the celebration of the sacrament, the love-sacrament,
of holy communion

('To be eaten, to be divided, to be drunk
Among whispers; by Mr Silvero . . .')

both with the pagan fertility-rites of spring (May, therefore, is 'depraved' not only because of its sensual beauty: but spring is also the
season of Easter) and with primitive ritual customs of eating the flesh
and drinking the blood of wild animals in order to acquire their
attributes. These associations, a sort of image-telescope taking the eye
from the nearest to the most distant, explain the 'tiger' which bears
down fearsomely at the end, but from the beginning has been associated with Christ (following the 'moralized' bestiaries of the Middle

Ages), Christ charged with love devouring (cf. *Matthew* ch. 10, v. 34: 'not . . . peace, but a sword', etc.) and giving of himself precisely in the form of bread and wine to be divided, eaten.

Secondly, there is Eliot's mystical devaluation of human history. History is deception, corruption ('adulteration'), and ultimately tears. Note, however, that they are not only tears shed for the monstrous vices fathered by our heroism and the virtues forced upon us by our crimes (war, for example), but, more radically, tears shaken from the Biblical tree of wrath which is the tree of the knowledge of good and evil. Which leads us to the poem in which Eliot expresses his final position, *Four Quartets*, a work of studiedly religious, indeed mystical, inspiration.

In the first of the Quartets, *Burnt Norton*, whose wealth of themes to be developed in the later three is one of the reasons for its pre-eminence in the series, we find the central poetic myth of the rose-garden whose roses 'had the look of flowers that are looked at'. The originality of the poem here lies in the way one of the most moving conventional motifs of human experience – the gardens of our child-hood, those earthly paradises of our innocence, for ever remembered, for ever regretted – is taken as an example of the illusory character of all our human experiences, contained as they are within the limits of temporal distinction, past, present and future. It still has a value, however; but only in so far as it can become a fleeting illumination of something which is 'now and for ever' – in short a symbol of that aspiration to rebirth as spiritual conquest which finds satisfaction only in the eternal 'present' of the mystic, in which all distinctions and oppositions, including those of time, are annulled and the 'stillness' of divine unity, of the Absolute, is enjoyed. Here we see these concepts realized poetically:

> What might have been and what has been
> Point to one end, which is always present.
> Footfalls echo in the memory
> Down the passage which we did not take
> Towards the door we never opened
> Into the rose-garden. My words echo
> Thus, in your mind,
> . . .

                                        Other echoes
Inhabit the garden. Shall we follow?
Quick, said the bird, find them, find them,
Round the corner. Through the first gate,
Into our first world, shall we follow
The deception of the thrush? Into our first world.
  . . .
And the unseen eyebeam crossed, for the roses
Had the look of flowers that are looked at.
There they were as our guests, accepted and accepting.
So we moved, and they, in a formal pattern,
Along the empty alley, into the box circle,
To look down into the drained pool.
Dry the pool, dry concrete, brown edged,
And the pool was filled with water out of sunlight,
And the lotos rose, quietly, quietly,
The surface glittered out of heart of light,
And they were behind us, reflected in the pool.
Then a cloud passed, and the pool was empty.
Go, said the bird, for the leaves were full of children,
Hidden excitedly, containing laughter.
Go, go, go, said the bird: human kind
Cannot bear very much reality.
Time past and time future
What might have been and what has been
Point to one end, which is always present.
  . . .
                                Time past and time future
Allow but a little consciousness.
To be conscious is not to be in time
But only in time can the moment in the rose-garden,
The moment in the arbour where the rain beat,
The moment in the draughty church at smokefall
Be remembered; involved with past and future.
Only through time time is conquered.
  . . .
                                . . . The Word in the desert
Is most attacked by voices of temptation.

The crying shadow in the funeral dance,
The loud lament of the disconsolate chimera.
  The detail of the pattern is movement,
As in the figure of the ten stairs.
Desire itself is movement
Not in itself desirable;
Love is itself unmoving,
Only the cause and end of movement,
Timeless, and undesiring
Except in the aspect of time
Caught in the form of limitation
Between un-being and being.
Sudden in a shaft of sunlight
Even while the dust moves
There rises the hidden laughter
Of children in the foliage
Quick now, here, now, always –
Ridiculous the waste sad time
Stretching before and after.

(cf. *East Coker*, ll. 130 ff., *The Dry Salvages*, ll. 92 ff., and *Little Gidding*, ll. 245–56).

It is sufficient to observe the way in which the poet operates a mystical devaluation of the experience of our first entry into the world through nature (the gardens of our earliest childhood games), reducing it to an example of the illusoriness of our experience in general, as contained and defined by time. Is that garden truly real? he asks himself. Is there any sense in saying that we really went through the door? Do the roses not seem too much like things we have turned over and over in our minds ('And the unseen eyebeam crossed'), too much like fancies, and is not the whole scene, with its lack of authenticity, played out like an intellectual comedy (the echoes, 'accepted and accepting', 'in a formal pattern')? In any case, what is there to prevent the whole garden, children and all, from being a mirage like the optical illusion of the pool filling for an instant in the brightness of the sun? Are not these the tricks that nature and experience play – the tricks of anything that is subject to movement and change, subject to time (the 'detail' of a 'pattern', not the pattern, 'desire', not 'love') and so has no stable being (human kind 'cannot bear very much reality')? No solution remains, then, but to seek refuge in the religious and symbolic value of that childhood garden, to take it as an allusive, fleeting vision (fleeting because it can only be in time, but we are in time) of blessedness and joy everlasting, motionless, perfect and real ('here, now, always – '), and so of a rebirth in eternity: an ascetic spiritual conquest.[58]

Thus, Eliot with his mystical sense of the contemporary crisis of bourgeois society dominates the poetry of that society.[59] He is far in advance not merely of Dylan Thomas (a formalist whose fragmentary world is constructed through a continuous chain-reaction of metaphors alternately surpassing and destroying one another, a sort of belated Rimbaud), but also of Auden, a thoughtful poet sensitive to the fate of bourgeois society, but who is neither as focussed in his ideas nor as technically original as Eliot. He is ahead too of Wallace Stevens, whose aesthetic pantheism bereft of immortality is reminiscent of a modern Lucretius – although *Sunday Morning*, the monologue of a woman debating the pros and cons of Christian religion and coming down against it, is a notable piece, for example:

> She says, 'I am content when wakened birds,
> Before they fly, test the reality

58. See the other *Quartets*, and bear in mind also all the historical material, often evoked indirectly in the text, borrowed by Eliot from the mystics and metaphysicals, from Heraclitus, the Gospel according to St John and Augustine, to Dante (in the *Paradiso*), John of the Cross, etc.

59. On the most controversial points in Eliot's poetry, for example the significance of the 'dog' in *The Waste Land* and the 'rose-garden' in *Burnt Norton*, I am in agreement on the first with Cleanth Brooks, in *T. S. Eliot: A Selected Critique*, edited by Leonard Unger, New York 1948, p. 327, and also with D. E. S. Maxwell, *The Poetry of T. S. Eliot*, London 1952; and on the second, again with Leonard Unger, p. 784. On 'Came Christ the tiger', compare, to see the authentic poetry of this hemistich (in its context):

> Cristo è la fera co lo dolçe odore,
> quelle ke corrono l'anime sante,
> de le quali per vivo amor se pasce

> (Christ is the beast of the sweet scent,
> those who run are the hallowed souls,
> on whom for living love he feasts)

('De la pantera', from the *Bestiario Moralizzato di Gubbio*, in *Poeti del Duecento*, a cura di Gianfranco Contini, Milan–Naples 1960, vol. II, p. 317).

Of misty fields, by their sweet questionings;
But when the birds are gone, and their warm fields
Return no more, where, then, is paradise?',[60]

There is no need even to mention a Spender or a lesser Auden (*After they have tired, Statistics*).

But note should be taken here of the poetry of Eugenio Montale, the sole or greatest Italian poetry of the crisis and thus, by our criterion, the most significant and lasting contemporary bourgeois poet in Italian. The loss of certainty of the real and of any kind of faith, the aridity of pure existence, nature itself decomposed into ironic intellectual allusions, a dry and gelid yet subtly tormenting pathos – such is the moral schema of this genuinely *suffering* poetry. It is the poetry of a world with colours like these:

> Here . . . the colour
> that endures is of the mouse leapt up
> among the rushes, or with its dash of
> poisonous metal the starling which goes
> into the vapours of the bank.
>
> ('Boats on the Marne', *Le Occasioni*).[61]

A poetry expressed in dicta like these:

> Nowadays we can tell you only this,
> what we are *not*, what we do *not* want.
>
> ('Do not ask us . . .', *Ossi di seppia*),

which ends with a 'little testament' that says:

> This that with the night flickers
> in the casing of my thought,
> mother-of-pearl track of snail
> or sanding of trodden glass,

60. Wallace Stevens, *Collected Poems*, London 1955. On Stevens, see for example the perceptive study by R. P. Blackmur, 'Examples of W.S.', in *Form and Value in Modern Poetry*, New York 1957, pp. 183 ff.

61. Eugenio Montale, *Selected Poems*, translated and with an introduction by George Kay, London 1969. The three collections from which the examples are drawn were published as follows: *Ossi di Seppia* ('Cuttle-fish Bones'), Milan 1925; *Le Occasioni* ('Occasions'), Milan 1939; *La Bufera e Altro* ('The Storm and Other'), Milan 1956.

is no light from church or factory
nourished
by red prelate or by black.
Only this rainbow I have
to leave you as a token
of a faith that was battled for,
of a hope that burnt more slowly
than the heavy block in the grate.
Keep its powder in your compact
when, every light extinguished,
the round-dance will grow hellish
and a shadowy Lucifer alight upon a prow
in the Thames, Hudson, the Seine,
shaking his wings of brimstone half-
sawn through with labour, to tell you: time's up.
It is not an heirloom or a charm
that can take the shock of monsoons
on the spider thread of remembering,
but a story lives on in its ashes alone
and persistence is simply extinction.

("Little testament", *La Bufera e altro*)

The last line evokes Eliot's '. . . what is kept must be adulterated'; but
we should always remember the difference between Eliot's religious,
indeed mystical, conclusion and the absolutely and *negatively* atheist
conclusion of Montale.

With Vladimir Mayakovsky, the poet of the socialist revolution of
October 1917, it seems as though the world is born anew. Atheism
itself, the atheism of scientific socialism, is a positive element, a component of the optimism of a new humanism. The poet doubts and
denies the existence of love but only in its traditional bourgeois sense
of a humanitarian, Christian love of the spirit:

Lenin
        tore
            their Pharisee phrases
                            to shreds,
    exposed
            in print

                    their aristocratic nakedness.
But we need
            no longer
                    talkerites' idle charm,
about men being brothers
                    and what freedom's worth –
for we,
        with Marxism fully armed,
are the only
            Bolshevik Party
                    on earth.
                        'Vladimir Ilyich Lenin' (1924)[62]

for it is now reaffirmed and recreated as socialist solidarity:

Proletarians
            come to Communism
                    from the depths beneath –
the depths of mines,
                sickles,
                    and factories.
I
    plunge into Communism
                from the heights of poetry above,
because for me,
            without it,
                    there is no love.
                        'Home!' (1925)[63]

and again:

It may,
        may be,
            some time,
                some day,
                    along a pathway of the
                    Gardens of the Zoo

62. *Vladimir Mayakovsky*, tr. and ed. Herbert Marshall, London 1965.
63. Mayakovsky, ibid.

she too –
    for she loved animals –
            will also the
                    Gardens re-enter
smiling,
        like that photo
                in the desk of my room.
She is beautiful –
            they will for certain resurrect her.
Your
    thirtieth century
            will leave far behind it
flocks of trifles' heart-rending sighs.
...
Resurrect –
        I want to live out my life!
So that love won't be a lackey there
of livelihood,
            wedlock,
                    lust
                        or worse.
Decrying bed,
            forsaking the fireside chair,
so that love shall flood the universe.
So as not to be,
            by sorrow aged made,
begging in the name of some Christ's birth.
So that,
        the very first cry of
                'Comrade!' –
Shall spin into one this very earth.
                    'Of this Love' (1923)[64]

The principles of historical materialism and the theoretical and
practical themes of Marxism and Leninism are articulated poetically,
expressed in metaphor or more often in fulgurating hyperbole (there
is a Pindaric strain in Mayakovsky's socialist realism). At the same time,

64. Mayakovsky, ibid.

it is interesting to note in poems like *To Comrade Nette* how certain Whitmanesque themes, such as the feel for modern technology and the celebration of human labour, take on a quite different and much wider significance in Mayakovsky. The ethos of co-operative socialist emulation leads to an extraordinary strengthening of the individual's powers, for he is integrated into a type of *social* production which transcends him as an individual, but in order to secure the fruits of his labour, whether of the hand or the brain, for the social corpus as a whole. This is just the opposite of what was already expressed characteristically in the bourgeois *Faust*, where, as we have seen, competitive emulation and consequently the division of labour were celebrated in the contrast between the '*genius* of one man', the entrepreneur or 'industrious man' (Smith), which is exactly what Faust represents, and the 'thousand hands' of what Adam Smith still referred to as the 'labouring poor'. Needless to say, the extraordinarily increased dominion of man over nature through work, already celebrated poetically by the bourgeois Faust, is renewed as an unparalleled poetic theme in the socialist Mayakovsky.

To register another difference of poetic tone, compare the crude but human and ultimately optimistic picture of bourgeois moral alienation in *The Woolworth Girl*, which depicts a young girl working in a giant department store in America, with the cameo offered by Eliot in *The Waste Land* of an objectively similar instance of alienated life (the sordid domestic interior of a City typist's 'home'). Eliot's is a pitiless description, which no light brightens save that which might emerge, once 'history' and the whole world have been denied, from an inhuman 'eternity'. In general, it is instructive to compare Eliot's Christian pessimism with Mayakovsky's refusal that 'the day', which 'grief degrades', should be 'trafficked for the love of Christ'.

To conclude, it is not hard to see that Mayakovsky's greatest poetic strength lies in the brilliant way in which he uses metaphorical and hyperbolic connections to achieve a *typification* of the values of the socialist society in which he lived, and of its ideals, institutions and decisive events. There should be nothing surprising in this, if only because we have already noted the concrete *intellectual* nature of metaphorical connections in so far as they link or unify what is multiple and dissimilar (images), in the same way as other literal connections or concepts. For the same reason, we should not be disconcerted by the *tendentious* character of his poetry (his own poetic declared: 'poetry starts where there is a tendency'[65]). It is that which logically constitutes the socialist realism of Mayakovsky's poetry, the evaluative, judging realism of a combatant for a social cause – socialism and communism. Thus the extremely modern Pindarism of his poetry, based on an historically particularized vocabulary which is often indeed technical, as were those of Pindar, Dante and Goethe, is inseparable from its (socialist) realism.

9. *Metaphor as Truth*

Having completed our experimental reading of a series of poetic texts, we can now draw the following conclusions. (1) Poetry, as discourse, derives its truth or cognitive values, like every other kind of discourse, from image-concepts or logical-intuitive complexes: confirmation of which is to be found in the indispensable presence of a *structure* (intellectuality) or *meaning* in every poetic product or 'figment'. (2) Since every meaning points back directly or indirectly to experience and history, and hence to a sociological *quid*, it alone permits a historical–materialist foundation of poetry: whose scientific, anti-dogmatic and anti-metaphysical character makes it in turn the only critically acceptable one. (3) Nevertheless, the specificity and peculiarity of poetry has also to be demonstrated and this can only be done by an analysis of the *semantic* (verbal) component of poetry which we shall come to in due course. This will show us how poetic discourse differs from scientific discourse and so enable us to attach a more precise meaning to certain phrases used above, such as objective and historical feeling (pathos). In the meantime, however, we shall examine certain fundamental categories of literary poetics a little more deeply than when we mentioned them in particular textual analyses: such categories as metaphor and hyperbole, symbol and allegory. This will permit us to develop the concept of literary *truth* as literary *abstraction*, implicit in the notion of literary or poetic discourse.

First, though, it will be helpful to draw one further consequence

65. Mayakovsky, *How are Verses Made?*, tr. G. M. Hyde, London 1970, p. 17.

from the analyses undertaken above. This is a clarification by contrast of the negative phenomenon known as literary *banality* or the *unpoetic,* properly so called. For it should now be obvious that this phenomenon is imputable not, as is the wont of critics, to 'poverty' of 'imagination' or 'images', but to imagination or images which are not sufficiently *structured* or *intellectual* to prevent their being merely random or generic in *meaning.* It can be attributed therefore to their very opaqueness as *images* (see above for the principle of the reciprocal implication of reason and matter or datum and thought). Here again we are leaving aside for the moment the specific and specifying semantic component. Still, even if what we have said is taken to include scientific banality as well, we have glimpsed enough of the substance of literary banality or the unpoetic to suggest a more balanced aesthetic judgement to critics like Cleanth Brooks and Robert Penn Warren who, despite their premise that 'the end' of appreciation is the 'imaginative apprehension' of a poem and that awareness of its structure is only 'a means' to that end, nevertheless conclude of the 'stock response' that 'the good poet seeks to provide in his work the motives or the grounds for the responses of taste of his audience, but the bad poet, like an advertising copywriter, merely appeals to conventional mental attitudes, however crude or generic these may be.'[66] Enough, that is, to warn critics and theorists against the kind of incongruity and contradiction which results from continuing to give (at best) unequal weight to reason and sense-perception or fantasy in the discussion of poetry.

Moving on then to the problem of metaphor,[67] let us turn to the *Rhetoric* of Aristotle, 1405a, 5–10 ff. The classical features of this succinct formulation of the philosophical and epistemological problems of metaphor are distinctly embarrassing and challenging to our latter-day aestheticist assumptions about metaphor. For these are inherited

66. Brooks and Warren, op. cit., p. 571.

67. On metaphor, see: G. Della Volpe, *Poetica del Cinquecento* (for the Classical and Renaissance sources); Edmond Huguet, *Le Langage Figuré au Seizième Siècle,* Paris 1933; Helen Reese Reese, *La Mesnardière's Poëtique* (1639), London–Paris 1937, especially pp. 190 ff.; H. Pongs, *Bild in der Dichtung,* Marburg 1927–39; W. Empson, *The Structure of Complex Words,* London 1951, especially pp. 331 ff. (and with caution, by the same author, *Seven Types of Ambiguity,* New York 1955); C. Brooke-Rose, *A Grammar of Metaphor,* London 1958; H. Seidler, *Allgemeine Stilistik,* Göttingen 1953, especially pp. 162 ff. and 301 ff.; R. Tuve, *Elizabethan and Metaphysical Imagery,* Chicago 1947, passim.

from Vico, Romanticism and Idealism with their bias towards metaphor as an 'imaginative' nexus or construct of pure images (the usual contradiction in terms), something purely expressive: 'certainly a *vividness*', according to one of the last decadent aestheticists, Ezra Pound, founder of Imagism.[68] Yet in the *Rhetoric*, Aristotle says not only that metaphor endows style with 'perspicuity' (intellectual virtue!) even before 'pleasure and a foreign air', but also that it is 'most important . . . both in poetry and in prose'.[69] The point is echoed intelligently by both Cicero and Quintilian. According to Cicero, the phrase 'adolescence the flower of life' is 'a sort of *definition*' of adolescence itself;[70] while Quintilian, again confirming the intellectual and cognitive force or truth-value of metaphor, does not hesitate to affirm of hyperbole (his dictum is all the more valid for normal metaphor) that if it lies, it is 'without any intention to deceive us'.[71] Again Quintilian, this time following Cicero, observes that it is 'from necessity' that one speaks in prose of the 'gem', *gemma*, for a vinebud and of a 'hard' or 'rough' man, etc. because there is 'no literal term'[72] *and for no other reason*, and not because there is 'no genus or species' as will be claimed by Vico, who wants genera and species reserved to 'philosophy'! In other words, that passage in the *Rhetoric*, with its implicit theory of metaphor as intellectual connection, genus or concept, and hence as an instrument appropriate to poetry or non-poetry, puts us today in an awkward position. We cannot deny that metaphor is intellectual (concretely, as we shall see, not abstractly) and so that it belongs as much to 'prose' as it does to poetry. On the other hand, we cannot accept a straightforward identification of poetry and non-poetry, art and non-art, and we have in some way

68. Ezra Pound, *Literary Essays*, London 1954, p. 52. Of Dante's passage 'Era già l'ora che volge il disio' in *Purgatorio* VIII, 1 ff., he says: 'These things have in them that passionate simplicity which is beyond the precision of the intellect' (p. 53). But, allowing for the necessary anti-imagistic reservations, one cannot but agree with his admonition: 'Don't use such an expression as "dim lands *of peace*". It dulls the image. It mixes an abstraction with the concrete. It comes from the writer's not realizing that the natural object is always the *adequate* symbol' (p. 5; Pound's emphases).

69. Aristotle, *The 'Art' of Rhetoric*, tr. J. H. Freese, London and Cambridge, Mass. 1959.

70. Cicero, *Rhetorica ad Herennium*.

71. Quintilian, *Institutio Oratoria*, Book VIII, vi, 74, translated by H. E. Butler, Vol. III, London and Cambridge, Mass. 1959.

72. ibid., VIII, vi, 6.

to distinguish between the poetic or artistic use of metaphor and its non-poetic use. In this respect too we cannot, even if we wished, avoid the problematic modern insistence on the 'autonomy' or specificity of the work of art.

Once again, we shall leave the solution of this problem until we explore the question of the semantic component of poetry. In the meantime, let us consider what is already undeniable in regard to metaphor: its indispensability as a mental, intellectual, cognitive instrument. The lack of adequate proper terms is certainly not enough to explain why it is so indispensable. For every day we actually choose to express ourselves through these broader and deeper linkages between disparate objects represented by metaphorical language, rather than through proper terms whose power of generalization has become weak. I am not referring here only to the innumerable so-called dead or dormant or worn-out metaphors such as the leg of the table or the brow of the hill, or the neck of the bottle or the vale of life,[73] but rather to those which so often structure the subtlest arguments and tightest definitions (think of the most celebrated of those used in philosophy, 'form' and 'content', and all those to be found in this very sentence: 'structure', 'subtle', 'tight', 'used' . . .). Despite the illustrious standing of many such arguments and definitions, their truth-value would be nil if it had to be conceded that metaphor was association *by* images, a game of the fancy, rather than association *of* images. So one might say of metaphor that it is like the air we breathe, without which we would perish as thinkers (and this too is a metaphor, developed as a simile). It has been shown elsewhere that in order for Horace to defend metaphor and Hobbes to attack it, both used metaphor ('serendis verbis', 'ignis fatui').

We have seen then that intellectuality and therefore truth is a feature shared by both poetry and prose, and that one of the means through which it is attained is metaphor, notwithstanding its prestige as the 'queen of poetry'. Thus it is not legitimate to distinguish, in this generic regard of *truth*, poetic from non-poetic metaphor. To see how metaphor is further justified epistemologically, we need once

---

73. In any case it is only from a superficial, psychological point of view that these seem dead; in reality, they are very much alive, as we saw with those used by Dante, in so far as they continue to be functional from the epistemological – hence practical – point of view, or that of truth.

again to go back to the earliest formulation in Aristotle, though of course rethinking the issue in modern terms. In *Rhetoric* 1410b, 10 ff., we are told that metaphor provides us with easy instruction and knowledge 'through the genus' ('when Homer [*Odyssey* XIV, l. 213] calls old age stubble, he teaches and informs us through the genus; for both have lost their bloom') – in other words, in so far as it is a general notion or idea. The same conception is repeated today, after Castelvetro and others by I. A. Richards when he summarizes the principle of metaphor as a 'combination of general aspects'.[74] Again, in the *Poetics* 1459a, 17, Aristotle says that 'the right use of metaphor means an eye for resemblances',[75] that is, that 'metaphors should be drawn from objects which are proper to the object, but not too obvious; just as, for instance, in *philosophy* it needs *sagacity* to grasp the similarity in things that are apart' (see *Rhetoric* 1412a, 5 ff., and compare Richards: 'Thought is metaphoric and proceeds by comparison', p. 94). Given these premises, Aristotle concludes by showing under the heading of Logic in the *Topica* that *similarity* in metaphor, 'for those who use metaphors always do so on account of some similarity' (VI 140a 10), is the same categorical norm as the similarity or sameness which regulates inductive, hypothetical and definitional *reasonings*. To limit ourselves to the latter, we are told that: '(The consideration of similarity) [=sameness] is useful for the assignment of definitions because, if we can see what is identical in each particular case, we shall have no doubt about the genus in which we must place the subject under discussion when we are defining it; for, of the common predicates, that which falls most definitely in the category of essence must be the genus.' (I 108b 1–25).[76] An example of modern recognition of this elementary epistemological law of the 'consideration of similarity', shared by poetic and metaphoric with scientific and philosophical thought, is provided by the late Marc Bloch in some reflections on the

74. I. A. Richards, *The Philosophy of Rhetoric*, New York and London 1936, p. 93. Richards makes the following acute observation on the rationalist poetics of the 18th century: ' "The particulars of resemblance [between tenor and vehicle] are so perspicuously collected" [Dr Johnson], that is a typical 18th-Century conception of the kind of comparison that metaphor should supply, the process of pointing out likenesses – perspicuously collecting particulars of resemblance' (p. 122); think of Voltaire's aversion for Pindar.

75. 'i.e. the power of detecting "identity in difference" ': Aristotle, *The Poetics*, translated by W. Hamilton Fyfe, London 1960, XXII, 17 and p. 90, note (a).

76. Aristotle, *Topica*, translated by E. S. Forster, London 1960.

methodology of history. He proceeds from the observation that '*comparison* underlies practically every scrutiny [of evidence]' to the conclusion that 'such scrutiny moves between these two extremes: the *similarity* which confirms and that which discredits' and that 'in the last analysis the scrutiny of sources is based on an instinctive metaphysic of the *similar* and the *dissimilar*, the *one* and the *many*' (metaphysics of course do not come into it, for the epistemological guarantee is sufficient).[77]

Here too, in the case of metaphor, as in the case of Vico's 'poetic characters' discussed above, we are concerned with empirical (aesthetic) abstractive synthesis by genera or types, conditional on categories, and hence with an *intellectuality* which is not abstract but *concrete*. In short we are concerned with a logical-intuitive complex (that is already implicit in Aristotle's use of the study of the similarity or sameness of dissimilars). This is shown in Aristotle's analysis of the following rather subtle but exemplary instances of metaphor in Homer and Empedocles. An example of transference from genus to species, we are told, is the following: 'Here stands my ship' (*Odyssey* I, 185; XXIV, 308), because 'riding at anchor', *ormein*, is a specific mode of the generic term 'stand' or 'be still', *estanai*, which is used here in its stead. An example of transference from one species to another is 'Drawing off his life with the bronze [of a weapon]' (Empedocles, *Katharmoi*) and 'Severing with the tireless bronze [of a cupping-bowl]' (*ibid.*), where the poet used 'drawing off', *arusai*, for 'severing', *tamein*, and severing for drawing off, both being species of the generic term *aphelein*, 'removing'.[78]

There are a number of comments to be made on this analysis. In the first place, the metaphor of the ship 'standing' works as a metaphor, rather than being an insipid abstraction, on one condition. To wit, that the sort of definition which it represents (as Castelvetro puts it), that is the reference of the species *ormein* back to its genus *estanai*, does not consist of a purely formal nexus of abstracts but rather of a logical-intuitive nexus of the different species (not only *ormein*) with their genus. In other words, it cannot be pure abstract *similarity* or synthesis without analysis, but rather must be synthesis-and-analysis. If we do not grasp this point, we misunderstand the intuitive or

77. Marc Bloch, *Apologie pour l'Histoire ou Métier d'Historien*, Paris 1952, pp. 52 and 55.
78. Cf. Aristotle, *Poetics*, ed. cit., XXI, 7-10.

imaginative element, or vividness, which renders Homer's metaphor expressive. For we can now see that its charge of vividness or intuition or *diversity* is not neutralized but rather, given the principle of heterogeneities implying each other, is developed and intensified by the *relational* force of its specific *connections*, which constitute in concrete terms the concept-genus of 'standing'. This should be clear to any reader who can perceive that the ship *stands* at *anchor* as the cart *stands* on its *wheels* or a man on his *feet*, etc.

A second consideration is the following. What we have said about this first of Aristotle's types of transference (the subtler and more difficult of the two because of its drastic intellectualism) may be applied with greater ease to the second type, where it is more obvious because the effect of transference is assigned to an interchange between specific terms rather than between generic and specific. We should nevertheless be very clear that in this second example the poetic effect is achieved not only by the concreteness of the 'specific', (which is not of course pure specific *ratio* or abstract *essence*: the expressive or intuitive aspect of 'drawing off' and 'severing' cannot be eliminated!) but also and equally by the relevant 'genus' (the 'removing'). It is the genus, with its conditioning categorical values ('action' implying 'being'), which properly constitutes, in this as in every other case, the meaningfulness or universality (validity) of the metaphor from which its expressive or intuitive force can never be separated. It should be noted, indeed, how this second type of transference, where 'drawing off' is used with such poetic effect *instead* of 'severing' and vice versa, presupposes such a complex of similarities and dissimilarities that it obviously cannot be realized except by generalization and abstraction through categories (the 'action' of 'removing') that occurs *simultaneously* with the imagination's activity of specification and concretization. The same logical-intuitive complexity may be discerned, albeit less obviously, in the first kind of metaphor.

But thirdly, it can now be seen that with this concept of metaphor as a relation of similarity and dissimilarity (or logical-intuitive complex), as concrete intellectuality, we are in possession of a philosophical *criterion* of metaphor, one that is genuinely philosophical and undogmatic in that it is experimental and *functional*. It is therefore normative for literary criticism and history, in accordance with the implicit lesson on method contained in Aristotle's procedure: not to detach the *theory* (of metaphor, or tragedy, as the case may be) from the analysis of the poetic *fact* or object to be explained. Thus, in the passage cited, the theory explains the lines from Homer and Empedocles and shows how they are received and appreciated by the reader (using 'appreciation' or 'taste' in a very different sense from the standard modern usage, whether romantic or mystical-aesthetic) in as much as the lines themselves, with their clarity and validity enhanced, confirm and corroborate the truth of the theory in their turn. Only by adopting this criterion do we find an adequate way of seeing metaphor and symbol in poetry without falling into either the one-sidedness of rationalist aesthetics, for which only a flat, abstract 'reasonableness' of metaphor – in other words the greatest possible *similarity* or oneness of its elements – is satisfactory, or the onesidedness of romantic and decadent aesthetics which is interested only in the *pissimilarity* of the elements, hence in the 'imaginative' impact of (mystically cosmic) 'images' or their 'vividness'. If we leave aside the semantic dimension this criterion is the norm of every integral reading of metaphor and symbol in poetry, whereby it is in turn convalidated. We may cite as an example of a satisfactory reading (though it is limited by his psychologism) I. A. Richards' analysis of the famous metaphor in *Hamlet*, 'What should such fellows as I do crawling between earth and heaven?', of which he notes: 'When Hamlet uses the word crawling its force comes not only from whatever resemblances to vermin it brings in but at least equally from the differences that resist and control the influences of their resemblances. The implication there is that man should not so crawl. Thus, talk [merely] about the identification or fusion that a metaphor effects is nearly always misleading and pernicious'.[79]

By making us aware of the *intellectual* aspect (one aspect) of metaphor, this criterion may also help us to avoid some of the gross errors which arise in translation of poetry from a mistaken idea (an *aesthetic* one) of 'concreteness' which leads in practice to shoddiness and gaucheness. An example might be the inveterate habit of translating 'standing' in the Homer example above by 'anchored' (see Bérard even), presumably on the assumption that the former is abstract and the latter concrete, whereas in fact it is literal but flat in comparison with the metaphor of 'standing'. Another case is the rendering of Shakespeare's

79. Richards, op. cit., p. 127.

'Ripeness is all' by 'readiness is all' ('esser pronti è tutto', 'le tout est d'être prêt'; an exception is A. W. Schlegel's 'Reif sein ist alles'), thus losing the metaphorical, poetic effect of the sense of 'maturation' and the 'analogy suggested between the inevitability of natural cycles of vegetation and the cycles of life', justly pointed out by Wellek and Warren.[80] The analogy establishes a deep poetic connection between the life of the universe and human life, *comprehending* much more than the particular 'readiness' of man which becomes, as always, more concrete through the connection made. By comparison the expression 'readiness', with its *insufficiently mediated* 'concreteness', is a clumsy paraphrase or turning into *prose*.

The same sort of one-sidedness is to be found in those who are misled by traditional romantic and post-romantic aesthetics into thinking of Pindar – the inventor of those poetic flights that bear his name, which are synonymous with the boldest metaphors and thereby of the control of reason and its categories at their highest pitch – and exalting him as a poet merely of beautiful 'images'. Rostagni calls his art 'purely imaginative, free from rational bonds, close to impressionism', no less. Such an assessment of Pindarism is as distorted, though for opposite reasons, as that of Voltaire who was hostile to Pindar on classicist grounds, in the name of a flat 'reasonableness' in poetry.

Nor can the name of Hegel be forgotten in this phenomenology of aesthetic error. His complex attitude towards metaphor is extremely significant and instructive, for because Hegel cannot free himself from the one-sided romantic conception of metaphor and replace it by another which takes account of the importance of the *relational*, and thus rational-intellectual, aspect of metaphor, he is forced by his own rigid and abstract rationalism to undervalue metaphor itself. He allows that metaphor 'is an entirely compressed and abbreviated comparison, in that it does not oppose image and meaning to one another but *presents the image alone* [nur das Bild vorführt]; the literal sense of the image, however, it extinguishes [tilgt] and it makes the actually intended meaning recognizable at once in the image through the context in which the image occurs, although this meaning is not expressly stated'. But he then concludes: 'But since the sense so figurated [der so verbildichte Sinn] is clear [erhellt] only from the con-

---

80. René Wellek and Austin Warren, *Theory of Literature*, London 1963, p. 202.

text, the meaning expressed in metaphor cannot claim the value of an independent artistic representation but only of an *incidental* one [nur beiläufigen Kunstdarstellung], so that metaphor therefore can arise . . . only as a mere *external adornment* of a work of art which is itself independent.'[81] Thus metaphor 'is always an interruption [Unterbrechung] of the course of ideas and a constant dispersal of them, because it arouses and brings together images which do not immediately belong [gehören] to the matter in hand [die Sache] and its meaning'. Hegel indeed tendentiously celebrates the plastic sense of the Ancients which saved them from too frequent a use of metaphor. Let us note here that if Hegel had actually realized his intention of taking account (against Schelling) of the positive nature of intellect, neither the rational–*intellectual* character of metaphor nor its consequences, including a possible reassessment of the classical position, would have escaped him.

We have seen then that poetry, even in metaphor, which is usually said to be proper to poetry, is rationality (in the concrete sense understood above) and truth and knowledge. In no way therefore is it 'prior' to all distinctions between real and unreal, as claimed by aesthetics of the mysticizing breed. Try *not really thinking* the 'water' or the 'gold' of Pindar's first Olympian ode, try *not taking seriously* these everyday terms of our experience *in their usual lexical meaning* and just being content with their purely expressive or imaginative aspect *without* any *precise signification*, and then honestly say how much of that poetic emotion which Pindar meant to communicate to us through his *transferences of meaning* from 'water' to 'gold' to 'sun' and finally to the 'contests' of 'Olympia' is aroused in you or anybody else. The answer will be, none whatsoever. This is perhaps the moment to recall Aristotle's observation that simile, unlike metaphor, 'does not say that this *is* that, so that the mind does not even examine this' (*Rhetoric* 1410b 18–19): an observation of capital importance, but one which to make sense presupposes the recognition in metaphor of a paradoxical *identity* of the *diverse* and thus a harsh intellectuality as in the exemplary case of Pindarism. Now, having reached this point, it remains for us in conclusion to examine the general concept of literary and poetic *abstraction* and the whole problematic which derives from

81. Hegel, op. cit., I, pp. 403–4, and below, pp. 407–8.

it: from the problem of the typical in literature to that of literary symbol and allegory.

10. The Literary Symbol

From the foregoing, and in particular from the nature of poetry as concrete intellectuality, as logical-intuitive complex, and in this sense as discourse, we can, if we are not mistaken, justifiably derive the *typicality* (and hence *tendentiousness*) of poetic values in general. For there is an *artistic* typicality as well as *scientific typicality*. It can be defined as an ensemble of common and specific features or an historical and social essentiality. It should be superfluous to add that, precisely because of its concrete intellectuality, this typicality has nothing to do with any sort of statistical average. In any case, if the typical is the essence of a given historical phenomenon, it cannot be identified simply with the most wide-spread, the most frequent (or quantifiable) or the most ordinary. In other words, typicality, precisely because it is not an average, must be apprehended as something sensuous or concrete or characteristic. It is therefore expressible or valid through a combination of common and specific, rather than simply common and generic, features. It is in short a *characteristic* typicality.

We have already drawn attention when speaking of the 'materialist' aesthetics of George Lukács to the inner contradiction of those who hold that the criterion of art as a 'sensible intuition' without any 'conceptual' or intellectual elements, can be reconciled with that of 'typicality' or artistic intellectuality. We have at this point to ensure that there is not the slightest misunderstanding. Engels, for example, raised in a materialist way the question of tendentiousness (*die Tendenz*) in poetry and pointed primarily to Aeschylus, Aristophanes, Dante and Cervantes as 'highly partisan poets'. He never tires (quite rightly) of warning that 'it is always bad if an author adores his own hero' and that 'the author does not have to serve the reader on a platter with the future historical resolution of the social conflicts which he describes'. But then he pushes his caveat against the prosaic to the point of unbalancing and distorting his just insistence that 'the purpose must become manifest from the situation and the action themselves', by adding the absurd restrictive clause which reads: 'without [the purpose] being expressly pointed out' and concluding, very oddly for an historical materialist, that 'the more the opinions [Ansichten] of the author remain *hidden*, the *better* for the work of art'.[82] It is a conclusion that can only be explained by residues in Engels himself of the romantic fear of thought in poetry (Goethe: poetry 'expresses a particular without thinking of or drawing attention to the universal'). Recall, however, the organically *artistic* character of the 'views' of poets, from Aeschylus to Mayakovsky and Brecht. Then consider the threat that Engels' anti-rational restrictions represent for a poetic of social realism of the kind so warmly approved by Engels himself. What happens in that event to the poetic force of the 'satire' and 'irony' to which Engels himself drew attention in Balzac, to take an extreme and very characteristic example? Indeed the case of Schiller's *Kabale und Liebe*, praised by Engels as the first political *Tendenzdrama* in Germany, becomes extremely awkward and counterproductive for him if it is judged today by his restrictive standards. For paradoxically, it is precisely because it is not sufficiently *thought*, in other words historically *motivated*, that the lack of social realism and the artistic failure of Schiller's bourgeois drama are apparent to us today. Auerbach observed that 'this is not realism, it is melodrama' (a negative characterization of an aesthetic order, it might be worth noting) and, following up a comment by Korff, suggested that the reason was that 'the one motif which is probably of cardinal importance *for the comprehension of the social structure* – the inner lack of freedom of the subjects of the principality, who, in their stuffy, narrow, and misguided attitude of piety toward the burden laid upon them, acknowledge it as an eternal right – this motif does not come out *clearly* enough' (our emphases).[83] Consequently the fact that what should have been a critical, tendentious, bourgeois view of that lack of freedom under the *ancien régime* in the event remained hidden in Schiller's writing led not to the artistic success but to the failure of this (bourgeois!) tragedy.

But once we have done away with these romantic residues and understood the concept of poetic typicality with materialist rigour, it is not difficult to see how such typicality will include not only literal poetic meanings but also, given the concrete intellectual nature

---

82. Engels, letters to Minna Kautsky of 26th November 1885 and to Margaret Harkness of April 1888, in op. cit., pp. 368 and 380.
83. Auerbach, *Mimesis*, ed. cit., p. 442.

of metaphor, metaphorical or hyperbolic meanings. For these too compose an ensemble of common and specific features or historical and social essentiality. Thus broadly we find typicality of the *letter* in:

> From a loom inside rose a singing voice,
> of goddess or woman (Homer);
> this sickness sent by a god, (Sophocles);
> Poor help to raise an old man fallen in youth (idem);
> A bull thou seem'st that leadeth on before (Euripides);
> Three hundred chains
> Lustful Pirithous keep. (Horace);

metaphorical typicality in:

> But when he had donned the yoke of necessity (Aeschylus);
> invidious misfortunes (Pindar);
> The shadow of a dream
> Is man (idem);
> But no man knoweth how her [hope's] gift may turn,
> Till 'neath his feet the treacherous ashes burn (Sophocles);
> which appeared in its leanness to be
> charged with all cravings (Dante);
> this cramping earthly life (Goethe);
> One mind for thousand hands suffices (idem);
> Stetson!
> You who were with me in the ships at Mylae! (Eliot);

and *hyperbolic* typicality in:

> look never beyond the sun
> by day for any star shining brighter
> . . .
> nor any contest than Olympia greater to sing (Pindar);
> So that,
> the very first cry of
> 'Comrade!' –
> shall spin into one this very earth (Mayakovsky);

and so on.[84] We have here a little pattern-book, as it were, of 'lyric',

84. Perhaps it would not be superfluous to recall what Aristotle has to say about hyperbole in the *Rhetoric*, 1413a, 19 ff.: 'Approved hyperboles are also meta-

'epic' and 'tragic' poetic formulae, which are simultaneously and indivisibly historical and social essentialities, and vice versa. It is noticeable that, however much they seem isolated and fragmentary when they are just quoted like this (while in reality they are living and vital cells of real poetic organisms, ranging from the *Odyssey* to Goethe's *Faust* and Mayakovsky's *Of This Love*), each of them still preserves so much truth and typicality as to reflect at a glance some aspect of the life and culture of the society in question: the archaic period or fifth century B.C. in Greece, the Latin world of Horace, the Middle Ages, Goethe's bourgeois epoch (post-French Revolution), Europe after the First World War, or the first socialist state.

It goes without saying that the literary symbol (which is synonymous with characteristic typicality, whether literal or metaphorical) always needs to be distinguished from allegory. Allegory is a poor copy and counterfeit of symbol, an artistic non-value. Everyone agrees on the need for the distinction between them, but there is no agreement about the only thing which can give it a precise and rigorous sense: the respective concepts of symbol and allegory. Though it has its limits, the account given by Goethe is still the most fruitful; at least it has not so far been bettered. Symbolism, in Goethe's words, 'converts the phenomenon into an idea and the idea into an image in such a way that in the image the idea always remains *infinitely effective* [*wirksam*] and, though it be expressed in all languages yet remains inexpressible'. Allegory, on the other hand, 'converts the phenomenon into a concept and the concept into an image in such a way that the *concept* is always *restricted to the image* [*im Bilde begrenzt*] and *preserved* complete in it and expressible with reference to it.' In other words, Goethe says, 'it makes a considerable difference whether the poet seeks the particular as an illustration of the universal or contemplates [*schaut*] the universal *in* the particular. From the former arises allegory, in which the particular is valid only as an example [*Beispiel, Exempel*] of the universal. The latter procedure is proper to the nature of poetry. It expresses a particular without thinking of or drawing attention to the universal. The writer who catches this particular in a living way

phors. For instance, one may say of a man whose eye is all black and blue, "you would have thought he was a basket of mulberries," because the black eye is something purple, but the great quantity constitutes the hyperbole.'

receives at the same time the universal without being aware of it – at least not until later.'[85]

What is true in this exposition is that in symbolism the universal, the 'idea', remains inexhaustible (infinitely active), persists as itself, while in allegory the universal, the 'concept', is limited or restricted to the image, to an image, and in this image is exhausted and in effect destroyed. What is not true on the other hand is that all this means that in symbolism the universal, being inexhaustible or truly *universal*, is thereby 'inexpressible' or mystically ineffable. Nor is it true that one 'is aware' of it only 'later', i.e. too late, while in allegory it is expressible and therefore manifests itself not as 'idea' but as 'intellect' in the one negative sense in which this term is used by the romantics. All this is the oppressive legacy of romanticism in Goethe himself. The profound truth partially perceived by Goethe is that in symbol there is thought, there is that unity which is the universal itself, and there is 'at the same time' the 'living' particular. But the limit to his insight was his failure to see that, if in symbol there is unity and therefore particularity, living particularity, then by virtue of the dialectic of heterogeneities symbol is not mysticism but discourse, intellect – in other words concrete reason, reason become intellect. This is lacking in allegory. Because it is not 'idea' or thought, allegory cannot be image or particular either, other than as an immediate example of an equally immediate concept (abstractly given or pre-supposed, or 'conventional' and artificial, as we generally say). That is why allegory is 'cold'. It lacks a living image or *particularity*, precisely because it lacks *unity* or universality or idea or reason – and vice versa; because in short it is not discourse or concrete intellect. In this respect, compare Goethe with Hegel, who limits himself to the observation that in allegory 'the relation between the sense [*Sinn*] and the external shape [*Gestalt*] is not so immediate and necessary' as in metaphor.[86] The greater richness of Goethe's formulation of the problem is immediately apparent.

In conclusion, the following points should be borne in mind:

(1) The criterion discussed above, whereby symbol can be distinguished from allegory, is not only valid if we assume a given relation *in itself*

85. Goethe, *Maximen und Reflexionen*, nos. 749–51, in *Werke*, Glückstadt 1953, Vol. XII, pp. 470–1.
86. Hegel, op. cit., I, p. 403.

between the two senses, *Sinn* and *Gestalt* in Hegel's terminology, or 'letter' and 'figure' in that of De Sanctis,[87] and then enquire whether or not the relation between them is 'immediate and necessary' (Hegel) or 'essential and precise' (De Sanctis), 'so that the reader can pass easily [or not pass] from one to the other' (De Sanctis). It is even more valid if we examine to what extent that relation-of-senses may *potentiate a context* in respect of the simple 'literal sense, agreeing in its parts and sufficient to itself' (De Sanctis). By proceeding thus, we may hope to avoid the mistake made by De Sanctis when, speaking of Dante's 'wood' (figure) of human life (figured), he claimed that 'human life, by being figured, is presented as devoid of every particular for which and in which it is life; it appears as general and motionless as a concept'. Now, we have already seen how Dante symbolizes mankind as a whole – and therewith the meaning of the context is potentiated from the outset – precisely because he is lost in the wood of error of this life and not in some straightforward material wood. Furthermore, even leaving aside contextual values, it is difficult to maintain that in this relation-of-senses, that which is figured, human life, is presented as devoid of every particular once we acknowledge that its sinfulness (no less) is presented, and precisely with those attributes ('dark' and unbridled, 'savage') which attach to it in the normal parlance of religious and moral thought, at any rate that of the Fathers and the Middle Ages. Thus here 'the literal sense . . . has being', as Castelvetro would say (i.e. the dissimilars, sinful life and wood, have sufficient similarity), and 'the allegory . . . may be . . . taken as good'. In other words it is a matter here of symbol (=metaphor) and not allegory (in the bad sense).[88]

(2) If we say that literary symbol is synonymous with characteristic typicality, and that this can be either *literal* or *metaphorical*, it follows: (a) that it is arbitrary and mistaken simply to identify symbol with metaphorical meaning, as has been the tendency at least since Romanticism, for the purpose of exalting the 'imaginative' and 'mysterious' (=mystical) richness of metaphor, romantically conceived, over against the clarity of 'unpoetic' intellect; as though Horace's 'Three hundred chains lustful Pirithous keep' were less symbolic – in other

---

87. De Sanctis, *Lezioni e Saggi su Dante*, a cura di Sergio Romagnoli, Turin 1955, pp. 578 and 619 ff.

88. Castelvetro: cf. *La Divina Commedia*, a cura di N. Sapegno, cit., I, p. 10.

words, less expressive of a universal meaning, of a whole society – than Pindar's 'invidious misfortunes . . .'!

(b) that this tendency, being contradicted by the facts and therefore shown to be erroneous, confirms by its very error the opposite thesis of the concrete intellectuality of metaphorical as well as literal meanings and hence the symbolic and typifying capacity of both meanings;

(c) that this intellectual symbolism (there is no other kind) constitutes that sort of abstraction which is literary abstraction: not generic or inferior (invalid) abstraction, but rather concrete *determinate* abstraction, in that the typicality with which it is identified is *characteristic* typicality; in short, abstraction that is valid epistemologically and aesthetically.

(3) It remains for us to see finally how our analysis of literary abstraction, which has so far been conducted from a general rather than a special point of view, may be advanced by an examination of its *semantic component*. This will show us what *specifically* makes a literary or poetic rather than scientific abstraction, at the same time as clarifying further the basic problematic of the literary symbol.

2

The Semantic Key to Poetry

11. Language and Speech

At the very outset of our inquiry, we were obliged to take account of the semantic – verbal or linguistic – aspect of poetic 'images'. The fact that in practice no poetic image exists without lexical and grammatical common denominators, and that the latter are *also* vehicles of concepts, was, it will be recalled, the starting-point for our case against traditional aesthetic mysticism, or the belief that poetry, being 'pure intuition' or 'pure image', possesses a 'cosmic' or universal quality of a mystical and enigmatic kind.

This argument demands some further elaboration, and naturally enough it is to linguistics and the philosophy of language that we shall turn rather than to aesthetics. In particular, we need to spell out the *limits* – as well of course as the positive achievements – of the *romantic* philosophy of language which still lies at the root of modern aesthetic mysticism. To begin with the positive. Philosophers and linguists have long been agreed in postulating that *thought and language are identical*. Marx, starting from the premiss that 'for philosophers one of the most difficult tasks is to descend from the world of thought to the actual world', concludes that 'language is the immediate [concrete] actuality of thought'.[1] Saussure believes that thought, taken in itself, is 'a nebula' in which nothing is distinct before the appearance of

---

1. Karl Marx and Friedrich Engels, *The German Ideology*, London 1965, pp. 503–4. The passage continues: 'Just as philosophers have given thought an independent existence, so they had to make language into an independent realm. This is the secret of philosophical language, in which thoughts in the form of words have their own content. The problem of descending from the world of thoughts to the actual world is turned into the problem of descending from language to life.'

language.[2] Croce admits that 'an image that is not expressed, that is not in some way uttered, . . . even if it is only murmured to onself, is an image that does not exist'.[3] For Wittgenstein, to postulate the possibility of the linguistic sign is to assume the determinancy of the signified, or sense of how things are (even if not what they are).[4] This fundamental postulate of all modern philosophy is a romantic discovery. The *Sturm und Drang* had already perceived that it is only those 'characteristic signs of consciousness', words, which makes things 'distinguishable' and '(re)cognizable' in the 'ocean of sensations' (Herder).[5] But it is in Wilhelm von Humboldt[6] that we find that profound romantic characterization of language according to which: (1) language, being 'eternal mediator' between 'Spirit' and nature, 'is modified according to every gradation and nuance of the former'; it is not therefore an *ergon*, a fixed product or thing or substance, but 'something that must constantly be produced', an *energeia* or 'activity'; (2) 'speech, which makes the concept a member [*Individuum*] of the world of thought, adds to it meaningfully something of its own, and while it gives determinacy to the idea, the idea is within certain limits its prisoner'; thus 'from the mutual dependence of thought and speech it is clear that languages are not so much means of presenting [*darzustellen*] already known truths [*schon erkannte*] as means of discovering truths hitherto unknown.'

The negative side of this philosophy, which is what particularly concerns us, may be summed up in the following principles, also drawn from Humboldt. Firstly, that 'language in the true sense of the word consists in the [spiritual–creative] act of its actual self-production', that is, in *speech*. Thus language, 'in the real and essential sense', is reduced to the 'totality of utterances'. One might compare Croce: 'What is speech if not a continual and perpetual transformation? What is our lord and master Linguistic Usage if not the whole

2. Ferdinand de Saussure, *Course in General Linguistics*, translated by Wade Baskin, Introduction by Jonathan Culler, Glasgow 1974, p. 112.

3. Benedetto Croce, 'Aesthetica in nuce', in *Ultimi saggi*, Bari 1963, p. 16.

4. Cf. Ludwig Wittgenstein, *Tractatus Logico-Philosophicus*, 3.23, 3.221, tr. D. F. Pears and B. F. McGuinness, London 1963, p. 23.

5. Johann Gottfried von Herder, 'Abhandlung über den Ursprung der Sprache', in *Sämtliche Werke*, V, Hildesheim 1967, pp. 34–5.

6. Wilhelm von Humboldt, 'Über das vergleichende Sprachstudium', in *Werke* IV, Berlin 1907, pp. 23, 27, 30; and 'Einleitung zum Kawiwerk', ibid. VII, pp. 45–6, 169 ff.

mass of words which have actually been spoken or written? Fashioning a linguistic usage to serve as a touchstone is merely to create something imaginary.... On any given occasion, one is dealing not with something monolithic but with any number of expressions, all of which are individual and always different from those which had been fixed previously' (see also Vossler).[7] The second principle, namely that 'to break it [the speech-act] down into [lexical] terms and [grammatical] rules is simply a dead and pointless exercise of scientific analysis', follows as a consequence from the first. Again compare Croce: 'extra-aesthetic study is a study no longer of language but of things, that is, practical facts'.

In other words, the grave defect of romantic and idealist linguistics – directly denounced by modern linguistics from Saussure onwards, yet stubbornly ignored by traditional aesthetics from Croce to Hartmann and Richards – is its one-sided and (in the bad sense) abstract reduction of the complex but fundamental fact of natural language to only one of its elements: speech (*la parole*), the subjective speech-act. By ignoring the reality of the language-system, *la langue*, as an historical and social institution or a superstructural phenomenon, it takes no account of the unitary, objective, *system* of verbal signs without which, as preexistent *norm*, no mutual comprehension between speakers would be possible and their very existence as such would make no real sense.[8] In reality, however, both *langue* (system) and manifold *parole* are real, and both mutually condition each other. This has some relevant consequences for aesthetics, first and foremost.

In order to engage with these consequences we should remind ourselves, by way of premiss, of some of the fundamental discoveries of modern general linguistics.

7. Croce, *Problemi di Estetica*, Bari 1966, pp. 155–6. Cf. C. K. Ogden and I. A. Richards: 'such an elaborate construction as *La langue* ... as a guiding principle for a young science it is fantastic', in *The Meaning of Meaning*, London 1923, p. 6. See below, note 16, for further observations of a critical nature on Ogden and Richards's indifference to the Saussurian distinction between linguistic sign and ordinary symbol. On Croce and Vossler in relation to this question, see G. Nencioni, *Idealismo e Realismo nella Scienza del linguaggio*, Florence 1946.

8. Croce's attempt to dismiss real, objective linguistic usage as 'something imaginary', while extolling as the only reality the abstract subjectivity of the speaker *in vacuo*, is a curious and very significant instance of idealist dogmatism, at its boldest and blindest.

12. Some Lessons of Linguistics

We shall start with two propositions from the linguistic writings of Edward Sapir and Louis Hjelmslev. These will enable us to test and examine in greater depth Humboldt's brilliant and fruitful, but somewhat hazy, intuition of a mutual dependence existing between idea or *thought* and speech (*parole*), from which he went on to assert that at the same time as the idea receives determination from speech it is within certain limits 'held prisoner' by it (*gefangen gehalten*). They will enable us to probe that insight by converting Humboldt's *mutual dependence of thought and speech* into the *mutual conditioning of langue* (or system or norm) *and parole.*

Sapir has observed: 'In such a Latin word as *cor*, "heart", for instance, not only is a concrete concept conveyed, but there cling to the form [linguistic form or morpheme of the noun], which is actually shorter than its own radical element (*cord-*), the three distinct, yet intertwined formal concepts [i.e. grammatical categories] of singularity [number], gender classification (neuter), and case (subjective-objective)... The significant thing about such a word as *cor* is that the three conceptual [i.e. grammatical categorial] limitations are not merely expressed as the word links into place in a *sentence*; they are tied up, for good and all, within the *very vitals* of the *word* [– "concrete concept" or *thought*] and *cannot be eliminated by any possibility of usage*' (for example, if used poetically–expressively by a Latin writer).[9] Thus, if it is the case, as Louis Hjelmslev has noted, that 'grammatical function' is not to be confused with 'use' (*emploi*) – for 'use does not concern form ... It comes within the compass of signification', it is also the case – as Hjelmslev himself has concluded – that, if an 'adverb' for example is used as an 'interjection', this 'in no way changes' the 'grammatical' function of that element, and that while a given 'semanteme' may well be used as a '*hyperbole*' or a '*metaphor*', its *grammatical* function '*does not change*' as a result.[10]

9. Edward Sapir, *Language*, London 1921, p. 30.

10. Louis Hjelmslev, *Principes de Grammaire Générale*, Copenhagen 1928, pp. 126–7; see also his *Prolegomena to a Theory of Language*, translated by Francis J. Whitfield, revised edition, Madison, Milwaukee and London 1969. Cf. B. Siertsema, *A Study of Glossematics*, The Hague 1965, p. 87. Viggo Brøndal observes in his *Les Parties du Discours*, Copenhagen 1948: 'The norm, the system of signs, is therefore the first

This incidentally confirms the appropriateness of our reference elsewhere to Aristotle's technico-grammatical definition of the *Iliad* as an example of a 'phrase' [*logos*] which achieves unity by the combination of several 'phrases': an instructive definition, particularly from the epistemological and aesthetic point of view, once we recall that for Aristotle the 'phrase' is a 'composite sound with a meaning' made up in large measure of parts which 'mean something by themselves', that is 'nouns and verbs'.[11] Thus, to take an example from the *Iliad*, our ability to perceive an effect of *truth* and poetic credibility in Book I, ll. 200–3 will depend on our having a proper understanding, according to the use of *la langue*, of a particular verb-tense – the aorist *pháanthen*, as used in the line: 'and terribly did [his] eyes flash [*pháanthen*].' Since this is an indefinite tense, one that does not imply continuity or repetition and therefore refers to an instantaneous action, we are bound to conclude that the 'fire' belongs to the eyes of Achilles suddenly offended by the apparition of Athena in favour of his enemies ('Why now art thou come again, daughter of Zeus, who beareth the aegis? Was it that thou mightest see the insolence of Agamemnon...?' and not, as was traditionally thought, to the eyes of Athena who comes to recommend calm and is anyway impassive by definition (see Paul Mazon).[12]

We can now start to see that *the mutual dependence of thought and speech takes shape in concrete terms in the mutual dependence of parole and langue.* Even poetic utterance, as we have seen, which expresses a poetic thought, cannot but be essentially *langue*, and thus grammatical 'form'; and not even the most brilliant or creative metaphor or other poetic symbol

object of all linguistics. It is only by studying the separate signs, hence the words independently of the phrase, and their place in the system that one will understand language in its totality. This fundamental distinction completely escaped Ogden and Richards in *The Meaning of Meaning*.'

11. Aristotle, *Poetics* XX, ed. cit., p. 79 [and cf. translator's note at the foot of p. 78 on use of the term 'phrase' for *logos*: ' "Statement" and "proposition" also cover part of its meaning'].

12. Homer, *The Iliad*, ed. cit. [Murray, like all the translators and commentators consulted, attributes the 'fire' to Athena's eyes rather than those of Achilles – *Tr. note*]. Paul Mazon, in his translation published in *Belles Lettres*, Paris 1956, argues, against the tradition, that the former interpretation is the only one permitted by linguistic usage: cf. my *Poetica del Cinquecento*, Bari 1954, p. 43; and see the fundamental study by Antonino Pagliaro on 'Il Capitolo Linguistico della "Poetica" di Aristotele', in *Nuovi Saggi di Critica Semantica*, Messina–Florence 1956.

can help but be a semanteme, an element of signification, belonging to the pre-existent system of signs that is the linguistic system; and therefore it cannot but possess a grammatical 'value', without which it would be non-expression (=incommunicability) and would not exist as poetic value (thought). But let us now try to form a general picture of what the linguistic sign is and of what the normative sign-system of *la langue* or natural language consists – in other words, that system of lexical and grammatical common denominators of poetic 'images' whose real presence is the prime refutation of traditional aesthetic mysticism and its assertion, in linguistics as well as aesthetics, of an absolute *subjective* 'creativity' and Heraclitean mutation (see Croce above) and hence 'ineffability' of 'speech' conceived abstractly and *in vacuo*.

Natural human language, according to Saussure, has an individual side, 'speech' (*parole*), and a social side, 'language' (*la langue*). Neither is conceivable without the other. *La langue* 'is not a function of the speaker' but 'a product that is passively assimilated by the individual'; it 'never requires premeditation'. *Parole*, on the other hand, is 'an individual act'; it is 'wilful and intellectual'. Within the act it is necessary to distinguish, firstly, 'the combinations by which the speaker uses the language code for expressing his own thought' and, secondly, 'the psychophysical mechanism that allows him to exteriorize those combinations', (ed. cit., p. 14) – although 'the vocal organs are as external to language as are the electrical devices used in transmitting the Morse code to the code itself' (p. 18). *La langue* and *parole* are closely connected, 'each depending on the other'. *La langue* is necessary 'if speaking is to be intelligible and produce all its effects', but speaking (*parole*) is necessary for 'the establishment' of language (*la langue*), and historically the actuality of speaking always comes first (p. 18).[13]

Language (*la langue*) is a 'system of signs that express ideas' (p.16). Some people regard language essentially as a 'naming-process', that is a list of terms corresponding to as many things. This pre-scientific conception is open to criticism at several points. It assumes 'that ready-made ideas exist before words'. It also suggests 'that the linking of a name and a thing is a very simple operation – an assumption that is anything but true'. But 'this rather naive approach' can bring us

13. On the social side of language, see Chapter Three, for a discussion of Stalin's theses on linguistics.

nearer to the truth by showing us that 'the linguistic unit is a double entity, one formed by the associating of two terms' (p. 65). The 'speaking-circuit' (p. 11) shows that 'both terms involved in the linguistic sign are psychological' or mental 'and are united in the brain'. Therefore we can say that 'the linguistic sign unites, not a thing and a name, but a concept and a sound-image'. (pp. 65–6) 'I call the combination of a concept and a sound-image a *sign*, but in current usage the term generally designates only a sound-image. . . . One tends to forget that *arbor* is called a sign only because it carries the concept 'tree', with the result that the idea of the sensory [sound] part implies the idea of the whole . . . I propose to retain the word *sign* to designate the whole and to replace *concept* and *sound-image* respectively by *signified* and *signifier*'. For these last two terms have the advantage of indicating the opposition that 'separates them from each other and from the whole of which they are parts' (p. 67). Now, 'the bond between the signifier and the signified is arbitrary. Since I mean by sign the whole that results from the associating of the signifier with the signified, I can simply say: *the linguistic sign is arbitrary.* [Thus,] the idea of "sister" (*soeur*) is not linked by any inner relationship to the succession of sounds *s-ö-r* which serves as its signifier in French; that it could be represented equally by just any other sequence is proved by differences among languages and by the very existence of different languages: the signified "ox" has as its signifier *b-ö-f* on one side of the border and *o-k-s* (*Ochs*) on the other.' (pp. 67–8). The principle of 'the arbitrary nature of the sign' is 'first principle' of linguistics as a science; its importance is 'primordial', its consequences 'numberless'. It should not cause us any surprise: 'in fact, every means of expression used in society is based, in principle, on collective behaviour or – what amounts to the same thing – on convention'. Thus, the term 'arbitrary' should not make us think that the choice of the signifier is left entirely to the speaker, for 'the individual does not have the power to change a sign in any way once it has become established in the linguistic community'; it means only that the signifier 'is unmotivated, i.e. arbitrary in that it actually has no natural connection with the signified'. One might add that 'signs that are wholly arbitrary realize better than the others the ideal of the semiological process'; which is why 'language, the most complex and universal of all systems of expression, is also the most characteristic' and why linguistics can become 'the master-pattern for all branches of semiology'. The term 'symbol' in its common meaning has been used to designate the linguistic sign, 'or more specifically, what is here called the "signifier" '. But 'our first principle weighs against the use of this term. One characteristic of the symbol is that it is never wholly arbitrary; it is not empty, for there is the rudiment of a natural bond between the signifier and the signified. The symbol of justice, a pair of scales, could not be replaced by just any other symbol, such as a chariot.' (pp. 68–9).

Two possible objections arise, which are easily overcome. (1) '*Onomatopoeia* might be used to prove that the choice of the signifier is not always arbitrary. But onomatopoeic formations are never organic elements of a linguistic system. Besides, their number is much smaller than is generally supposed. Words like French *fouet* "whip" or *glas* "knell" may strike certain ears with suggestive sonority, but to see that they have not always had this property we need only examine their Latin forms (*fouet* is derived from *fāgus* "beech-tree", *glas* from *classicum* "sound of a trumpet"). The quality of their present sounds, or rather the quality that is attributed to them, is a fortuitous result of phonetic evolution. As for authentic onomatopoeic words (e.g. *glug-glug, tick-tock*, etc.), not only are they limited in number, but also they are chosen somewhat arbitrarily, for they are only an approximate and more or less conventional imitation of certain sounds (cf. English *bow-wow* and French *ouaoua*). In addition, once these words have been introduced into the language, they are to a certain extent subjected to the same evolution – phonetic, morphological, etc. – that other words undergo (cf. *pigeon*, ultimately from Vulgar Latin *pīpiō*, derived in turn from an onomatopoeic formation): obvious proof that they lose something of their original character in order to assume that of the linguistic sign in general, which is unmotivated.' (2) *Interjections*, which are closely related to onomatopoeia, 'can be attacked on the same grounds . . . One is tempted to see in them spontaneous expressions of reality dictated, so to speak, by natural forces. But for most interjections we can show that there is no fixed bond between their signified and their signifier. We need only compare two languages on this point to see how much such expressions differ from one language to the next (e.g. the English equivalent of French *aïe!* is *ouch!*). We know, moreover, that many interjections were once words with specific meanings (cf. French *diable!* "darn"! *mordieu!* "golly!" from *mort Dieu* "God's death", etc.)' (pp. 69–70). The signs that make up languages are not abstractions but 'real objects', 'concrete entities'. Two principles dominate the whole issue. (1) 'The linguistic entity exists only through the associating of the signifier with the signified': if one of these elements is ignored, the entity vanishes, just as 'if we divided the spoken chain into syllables, for the syllable has no value except in phonology. A succession of sounds is linguistic only if it supports an idea': *the same is true of the 'signified' as soon as it is separated from its signifier.* (2) 'The linguistic entity is not accurately defined until it is *delimited*, i.e. separated from everything that surrounds it on the phonic chain'. These 'delimited entities or units stand in opposition to each other in the mechanism of language'. The only definition we can give of the linguistic unit (which 'has no special phonic character') is this: 'it is a slice of sound which to the exclusion of everything that precedes and follows it in the spoken chain is the signifier of a certain concept.' (pp. 102–4).

The linguistic mechanism 'is geared to [synchronic] differences and identities' (p. 108), with the further implications revealed to us by an examination of 'linguistic value'. Let us begin with linguistic value taken from a 'conceptual' viewpoint, i.e. that of the 'signified'. This value is undoubtedly 'one element in signification', but 'it is difficult to see how signification can be dependent upon value and still distinct from it'; nevertheless, 'we must clear up the issue or risk reducing language to a simple naming-process' (cf. above [p. 65]). So let us take 'signification' as it is generally understood and as it has been presented so far: as 'the counterpart of the sound-image'. But 'here is the paradox: on the one hand the concept seems to be the counterpart of the sound-image, and on the other hand the sign itself is in turn the counterpart of the other signs of the language' (p. 114). An example: 'Modern French *mouton* can have the same signification as English *sheep* but not the same [linguistic] value, and this for several reasons, particularly because in speaking of a piece of meat ready to be served on the table, English uses *mutton* and not *sheep*. The difference in value between *sheep* and *mouton* is due to the fact that *sheep* has beside it a second term while the French word does not' (pp. 115–16). The fact is that 'the value of a word is not fixed so long as one simply states that it can be "exchanged" for a given concept, i.e. that it has this or that signification: one must also compare it with similar values, with other words that stand in opposition to it. Its content is really fixed only by the concurrence of everything that exists outside it. Being part of a system, it is endowed not only with a signification but also and especially with a value, and this is something quite different' (p. 115). Everything said about words 'applies to any term of language, e.g. to grammatical entities. The value of a French plural does not coincide with that of a Sanskrit plural even though their signification is usually identical; Sanskrit has three numbers instead of two'. If words in general 'stood for pre-existing concepts, they would all have exact equivalents in meaning from one language to the next; but this is not true. French uses *louer* (*une maison*) "let (a house)" indifferently to mean both "pay for" and "receive payment for", whereas German uses two words, *mieten* and *vermieten*; there is obviously no exact correspondence of values'. In all these examples, therefore, 'instead of pre-existing ideas' we find '*values* emanating from the system' (pp. 116–17).

But if 'the conceptual side of [linguistic] value' is made up solely 'of relations and differences with respect to the other terms of language', the same can and must be said of its 'material side': the sound, the phoneme. 'The important thing in the word is not the sound alone but the phonic differences that make it possible to distinguish this word from all others, for differences carry signification', meaning. Indeed, how could the reverse be possible? 'Since one vocal image is no better suited than the next for what it is commissioned to express [see Saussure's first principle], it is evident . . . that a segment of language can never in the final analysis be based on anything except its non-coincidence with the rest. *Arbitrary* and *differential* are two correlative qualities. The alteration of linguistic signs clearly illustrates this. It is precisely because the terms *a* and *b* as such are radically incapable of reaching the level of consciousness – one is always conscious of only the *a/b* difference – that each term is free to change according to laws that are unrelated to its signifying function. . . . In Greek, *éphēn* is an imperfect and *éstēn* an aorist although both words are formed in the same way; the first belongs to the system of the present indicative of *phēmí* "I say", whereas there is no present **stémi*; now it is precisely the relation *phēmí* : *éphēn* that corresponds to the relation between the present and the imperfect (cf. *déiknūmi* : *edéiknūn*, etc.). Signs function, then, not through their intrinsic value but through their relative position.' Furthermore, 'it is impossible for sound alone, a material element, to belong to language. It is only a secondary thing, substance to be put to use. All our conventional values have the characteristic of not being confused with the tangible element which supports them. . . . This is even more true of the linguistic signifier, which is not phonic but incorporeal – constituted not by its material substance but by the differences that separate its sound-image from all others.' (pp. 117–19).

Thus, whether we take the signified or the signifier, the conclusion is the same: 'language has neither ideas nor sounds that existed before the linguistic system, but only conceptual and phonic differences that have issued from the system.' Furthermore, 'a linguistic system is a series of differences of sound combined with a series of differences of ideas', that is an *arbitrary* but strictly functional combination or correlation of the two series or planes. For example, 'the formation of German plurals of the type *Nacht : Nächte*', in which 'each term present in the grammatical fact (the singular without umlaut or final *e* in opposition to the plural with umlaut and -*e*) consists of the interplay of a number of oppositions within the system', for 'when isolated, neither *Nacht* nor *Nächte* is anything' (pp. 120–2). In short semantic functionality obtains not only on one plane but on different planes, between an entity on one plane and an entity on the opposite plane: hence the *biplanar* character of the linguistic sign according to Hjelmslev or Siertsema.

Of the further development by Hjelmslev of the structuralist linguistics initiated by Saussure, we shall limit ourselves here to mentioning the synoptic table of glossemes or structural elements of language, and the correspondences between the two planes – that of the grammatical 'form' of 'content' (the signified, thought) or *plerematic* plane, and that of the phonetic 'form' of 'expression' or *cenematic* plane. In these correspondences the exponent-morphemes of the plerematic plane are of particular interest, in other words, the morphemes of the noun and the verb (case, number, voice, mood, etc.). Hjelmslev's definition of the division of them into intense and extense is also to be noted: those of the verb which 'are able to characterize a complete utterance', he defined as extense and those of the noun, which are not able to do so, as intense.[14] On the cenematic plane,

4. Cf. Siertsema, op. cit., p. 209, and note 15 below.

prosodemes and modulations correspond to the former as extensive components, and accents to the latter as intensive.[15]

But without lingering further over these developments, we shall conclude by touching briefly on the problematic of a general theory of signs or philosophical semiotics, suggested by structuralist linguistics. Our aim will be to see if we can encompass within it the fundamental issues of an aesthetic semiotics or epistemological theory of artistic languages.[16]

To this end, we should: (1) remember that the linguistic sign as such, as well as being 'incorporeal' (system of differences, relations), biplanar and 'empty' (purely functional), and arbitrary (with respect to the signified and indifferent to it), is accidental in the sense that it is conventional, and therefore *tends* – because of its incorporeal and functional character – as it were not to be seen or considered in itself. 'Language wants to be overlooked'.[17] Yet at the same time, the linguistic sign is an essential instrument to its end, which is thought (given our postulation of the identity of language and thought).

15. For further particulars on Hjelmslev's work, see the Note on Glossematics at the end.

16. Not, however, before taking our leave of Ogden and Richards, who, as has already been said, pay no attention in their famous book to modern linguistics. They finish up with the following abstract dichotomy between the 'referential' or 'symbolic' use of words (intellectual or scientific use in general) and a purely 'emotive', or artistic, poetic use: 'Words . . . are instruments. But *besides* this *referential* use which for all reflective, intellectual use of language should be paramount, words have other functions which may be grouped together as *emotive* ['these "non-symbolic" inferences!'] . . . *poetry*, for many reasons, [is] the supreme form of emotive language . . . As science frees itself from the emotional outlook . . ., so poetry seems about to return to the conditions of its greatness, by abandoning the obsession of knowledge and symbolic truth. It is not necessary to know what things are in order to take up fitting attitudes towards them, and the peculiarity of the greatest attitudes which art can evoke is their extraordinary width. The descriptions and ordering of such attitudes is the business of aesthetics' (p. 271; and see I. A. Richards, *Principles of Literary Criticism*, London 1955, especially chaps, XXIII–XXXV). Thus Richards, who has had so wide an influence in the English-speaking world, ends by adopting a psychological and sentimentalist aesthetic, what we might call an aesthetic emotionalism or behaviourism, which is a sort of empiricist translation of romanticism. What interests us here is that this position is quite consistent with his rejection of scientific linguistics and his fidelity, whether conscious or not, to the romantic theory of language as speech-*energeia*. Richards' best qualities, his aesthetic culture and personal taste, may be found in *Philosophy of Rhetoric*, and in *Practical Criticism*, London 1948 – both of which intimately contradict his theoretical theses; assuredly not, however, in the *Principles*.

17. Siertsema, op. cit.

More precisely, as we shall see, it is *one* of the primary and essential instruments without which thought would not exist. (2) We must also point out, however, that those structural features which are peculiar to the linguistic sign, its incorporeality, biplanarity and arbitrariness, are clearly not shared, as can be seen even at first glance, by other primary or essential signs of thought – technico-graphic, figurative, musical, and so on. By contrast the remaining features of the linguistic sign – those that concern not its specific structure but its generic nature as a sign, its emptiness or pure instrumentality and conventionality, can be extended (the latter perhaps only in part) to the other primary signs of thought.

The next stage will be to examine the epistemological, and particularly the aesthetic-epistemological, corollaries which derive from the principles of scientific linguistics discussed above for the art of literature and its respective semiotics. Their premise will be the postulate, now examined in greater depth, of the identity of language and thought.

13. Text and Context

These aesthetic corollaries, particularly as they regard literary poetics or poetics in the strict sense, may be provisionally enunciated as follows: (a) the specific, distinctive, feature of poetry and literature is a *semantic* or technical one; (b) correspondingly and equally, the distinctive feature of science in general is likewise *semantic* or technical. In saying this, we are of course keeping in mind the rule that we have already tested and confirmed, which *excludes* the normal practice of using one or other *common* or general epistemological characteristic – whether it be reason (ideality) or fantasy (particularity) – as a criterion of distinction between poetry or literature and philosophy and science.

A study of textual 'variants', such as we shall now undertake with an experimental analysis of a few passages from Petrarch and Leopardi, will prepare us for the corroboration and definitive formulation of both these corollaries.

Take, for example, the corrections made by Petrarch in his *canzone*, *Rime* no. CCCXXIII, whereby the lines:

In un boschetto novo, a l'un de' canti,
Vidi un giovane lauro verde e schietto,
E fra i bei rami udiasi dolci canti

(In a new wood, at one corner,
I saw a young laurel green and pure,
And amid its fair branches were heard sweet songs)

finally become:

In un boschetto novo i rami santi
Fiorian d'un lauro giovenetto e schietto,
Ch'un delli arbor parea di paradiso;
E di sua ombra uscian sí dolci canti

(In a new wood were blossoming
The holy branches of a laurel young and pure,
Which seemed one of the trees of paradise;
And from its shade there issued such sweet songs) (ll. 25-8).

Or some of Leopardi's corrections to *L'Infinito* (l. 3, 'celeste confine', celestial confine, to 'ultimo orizzonte', furthest horizon; l. 14, 'Infinità', Infinity, to 'Immensità', Immensity) and *A Silvia* (l. 5, 'lieta e pudica', happy and chaste, to 'lieta e pensosa', happy and thoughtful; l. 12, 'dolce avvenir', sweet future, to 'vago avvenir', fair future[18]; l. 62, 'Un sepolcro deserto e l'ombre ignude', A deserted sepulchre and the bare shadows, also 'A me la tomba inonorata e nuda', To me the bare, unhonoured tomb, changed to 'La fredda morte ed una tomba ignuda', Cold death and a bare tomb).

On the Petrarch, Contini comments: 'He has eliminated the padding phrase "at one corner" (a l'un de' canti), supported only by the worm-eaten and anachronistic artifice of the equivocal rhyme [*canti* in rhyme meaning both "corners" and "songs" in the next line but one]; he has got rid of the "green" which was actually tautological in respect of its substantive'; ' "were blossoming" and "issued" are objective images in comparison with the crude subjective statement of "I saw" and "were heard" '; and 'the "shade" in the manner of a

---

18. Leopardi draws on the double sense of *vago* (in poetic usage) as 'fair', 'beautiful' and 'vague', 'indeterminate' [*Tr. note*].

Chinese or impressionist painter for the "branches" is another example of normal ... poetic ... "deformation" ',[19] thanks to which, according to Romanò, the poet is always progressing 'in the direction of objectivization and myth' as in the final version: 'Which seemed one of the trees of paradise'.[20] In the case of Leopardi, as De Robertis points out, 'furthest horizon' has a 'more complete' sense, being more precise and verisimilar, than 'celestial confine' which anyway is too 'affected and precious', while 'Immensity' gives 'a greater idea of space', and thus of something real, than does 'Infinity'; similar points could be made for 'happy and thoughtful' and 'bare tomb' in place of 'happy and chaste', 'bare shadows', etc.[21]

Now, on the basis of these corrections and the observations of the critics, we can draw the following philosophical or aesthetic-epistemological conclusions. (1) The increasing objectivity and truth of the representation, and therewith the intensification of its poetic quality, is resolved into or coincides with a progression of the *linguistic* modulation of thoughts and feelings, that is to say of *communication* in the current understanding of the term. Now, if it is the case that a

19. Gianfranco Contini, *Saggio d'un Commento alle Correzioni del Petrarca Volgare*, Florence 1943.

20. A. Romanò, *Il Codice degli Abbozzi (Vat. Lat. 3196) di Francesco Petrarca*, Rome 1955.

21. Giacomo Leopardi, *Canti*, con l'interpretazione di G. De Robertis, Florence 1945. On the very relevant problem of authors' variants, see Lanfranco Caretti, *Filologia e Critica*, Milano–Naples 1955, especially pp. 11–25. As regards 'prose', if one examines for example Manzoni's successive drafts of *The Betrothed* (from *Fermo e Lucia*, 1820–23, to *I Promessi Sposi*, 1825–27, to the definitive edition of 1840), one is immediately and most obviously struck by the way the writing progresses from generic, conventional and rhetorical expressions to expressions which are increasingly determinate and concrete, more concise and pertinent, and poetically symbolic or true. This progress is achieved through the *internal* medium of poetic self-correction in the expressive process of a discourse which is semantically autonomous (and only semantically, but that is enough). The process is peculiar to the expressive development of a semantic organism: very different, therefore, from the expressive development represented by scientific or philosophical self-correction, which is all the more efficacious and valid the more it is semantically heteronomous or interdependent with countless other contexts, the more then it negates organic contextuality.

Leaving Italian literature, Flaubert's variants in *Madame Bovary* are likewise very interesting and instructive. These can now be read in full in *Madame Bovary, Nouvelle Version, Textes Établis sur les Manuscrits de Rouen*, edited by Jean Pommier and Gabrielle Leleu, Paris 1949. The texts are as they were 'prior to the corrections and sacrifices which Flaubert went on to make'; their enormous expressive lacunae allow us to infer how unjust is the widely held idea of the 'calligrapher' Flaubert as one who made a religion of polishing and repolishing his works.

'lyrical modification' can only be perceived in language,[22] it must also be the case that the traditional equation: poetry = ineffability = expression (the latter being distinct from and opposed to communication) is false. There are certain stylistic critics who, for the sake of methodological coherence, would be well advised to abandon it once and for all, since it is hardly going to be disputed that nothing is more contrary to the ineffable than language(–thought).

(2) But the progression of a linguistic modulation of thoughts and feelings, as itself a progression towards increasing poetic truth, is such as a process which is internal to the texts in question. That is, it relates to and depends on their growth (their history) and their individuation as semantic organisms or *determinate contexts*. That the reasons for the interest and value of 'stylistic' self-corrections or variants by an author in poetic discourse are not purely rhetorical or formal should already have alerted us to this fact; though we may reasonably suppose that this interest and value differ from those of an author's corrections in philosophical or scientific discourse.

Let us now go on to examine a philosophical text, a passage from Bruno's anti-Petrarchist poetic of 'heroic furies': 'You rightly conclude that poetry is not born from rules, except in the most insignificant degree; rather rules derive from poems: and so there are as many kinds and species of true rules as there are kinds and species of true poets'.[23] If we inquire into the nature and manner of the process towards truth which is constituted in its turn by this linguistic modulation of thoughts and feelings, we shall find that for this particular text-as-element-of-a-context to acquire, not the sort of generic or

22. For example, Contini's indication of the elegiac imperfect *credea* ('I used to think') in Petrarch's:

Di mie tenere frondi altro lavoro
Credea mostrarte
(I used to think I might show you
Other labour from my tender leaves)   (sonnet, *Rime* CCCXXII, ll. 9–10)

as a linguistic, grammatical, clue to the lyrical modification undergone by these lines, if we compare them with the previous formulation:

Di mie tenere frondi or qual pianeta
T'invidiò il frutto
(What star envied you the fruit
Of my tender leaves).

23. Giordano Bruno, 'De gli eroici furori' I, in *Opere di G. Bruno e di T. Campanella*, a cura di Augusto Guzzo e di Romanò Amerio, Milan–Naples 1956, p. 573.

vague or unfocussed meaning which is obtained from an immediate deciphering of the lexical terms which compose it, but a precise and articulated meaning which spells out that degree of truth (about the reality of poetry and its relations to rules) which can sustain the argument or philosophical 'thesis' which it communicates or expresses to us, the text-context has to be taken at the very least in a relation of *inter-dependence* with many *other text-contexts* – and not just 'ideas' – which existed before it, and the respective historical experiences expressed in them. These will run from texts of the Platonic tradition on the irrational nature of poetry as *manía,* or divine possession or 'furor', with their devaluation of 'knowledge' or technique (rules) in poetry, to those of Aristotle on the 'rules' of his *Poetics* and also the Italian Aristotelians contemporary with Bruno and the polemics of his time. For the sake of convenience, we can leave out all the subsequent texts that continue right up to the German Romantics or the Italian idealists.

What does all this mean and what conclusions does it lead us to? For a start, in what does the process of truth realized in ll. 25-8 of Petrarch's *canzone, Rime* CCCXXIII differ (one is already aware of a difference) from that realized in Bruno's text? In reply, we can say straightaway that the degree of thought and truth expressed in Petrarch's text is *inseparable from that text*: it is wholly entrusted to it, or to use Humboldt's expression in our own way, 'imprisoned' in it. This much is already clear simply from the comparison with Bruno's philosophical text, the thought-truth of which *presupposes,* precisely in order *to be expressed,* any number of other text-contexts (coming before and after), that is, so to speak, a whole *semantic chain* of which it is a member. Petrarch's text, on the other hand, is so *semantically autonomous* that in its expressive value it presupposes only itself – in other words, at most its own history entrusted to the 'stylistic' variants which led up to its semantic-formal constitution as poetic discourse. The variants which might be discovered in Bruno's text would only be valid as preparatory phases of its *semantic heteronomy* or dependence on innumerable other contexts (omni-contextuality). It is this heter-onomy alone which provides the condition and possibility of the semantic-formal constitution of this text as a philosophical discourse.

To put it more concretely: (1) the philosophical contribution to truth represented by Bruno's passage and by its omitted context, namely that critical and rhetorical rules must not be separated from the living process of poetry and that such rules should be put to the service of poetry case by case and not imposed on it as preconceived precepts – this contribution would be unthinkable and unrealizable, it could not exist, were it not for the *technical* significance, in other words the *univocal semantic* charge, of at least two terms used in the text: 'poetry' and 'rules', within whose meaning are concentrated dialectical references to *at least* the classical and Renaissance texts of the aesthetic quarrel between Aristotelians and Platonists. Bruno's whole argument focusses and turns on these terms, *the special application of which makes them general*: for they are no longer simply the 'poetry' or 'rules' of which we speak in ordinary discourse. It objectifies its 'thesis' precisely through the medium of the *disorganic semantic contextuality* of the two terms (disorganic because it is heteronomous) – in short, through the medium of their character as technical terms.

(2) The poetic contribution to truth represented by Petrarch's lines and their omitted context

> . . . sí dolci canti
> Di vari augelli, e tant' altro diletto,
> Che dal mondo m'avean tutto diviso, etc.

> (. . . such sweet songs
> Of many birds, and much other delight,
> Which had altogether severed me from the world),

namely the way in which nature can be mythicized by a mind in love and inclined to Christian Platonism and other conventions of Petrarch's time, this contribution was made possible and exists by virtue of the internal-contextual – 'stylistic' – semantic charge of the passage. The objectivization of thought that occurs in Petrarch's lines (and in poetic discourse generally) is achieved through the medium of an *organic* contextual semanticity, which is the opposite of the disorganic (heteronomous = omni-contextual) contextual semanticity of the technical language of Bruno. It is in short synonymous with semantic autonomy, that is with poetry.

What this means, to put it another way, is that the search for universality or truth proper to scientific discourse in general (involving in the case of philosophy an inquiry such that it admits of no presupposition that is not questioned and resolved in the universal) is realized by means of those technical and therefore omni-contextual semantic values, which we may even call 'prosaic', that are best suited to the purpose by reason of that interchangeability and heteronomy which they possess and in which scientific reflection – whose genera must be univocal – can and does find expression. On the other hand, that search for universality or truth which is proper to poetic discourse is realized by those semantic 'values' which are called 'stylistic', and which we may designate *organic-contextual*. These are best suited to the purpose by reason of that autonomy which they possess and in which literary reflection and abstraction – whose genera, as we shall see, must be *polysemic* so that they may be 'occasional', 'connotative', 'free' and so on – can and does find expression. Thus, on the basis of our initial examination of the semantic aspect of both scientific and poetic thought, we find confirmation that what really distinguishes science in general from poetry (and art in general) is *not* 'abstractness' of thought in one case and 'concreteness' of imagination in the other: but rather, as we are beginning to see, the *omni-contextuality* or technical character of the language used by thought in the first case and the *organic contextuality* of the language used by thought in the second. This will become clearer as we proceed, but in the meantime we must bring to a close our examination of the phenomenology of technical language.

Let us take another philosophical text. the *Phaedo* or *On immortality*, celebrated by the aesthetes as one of Plato's most 'beautiful' works. Its philosophical authority, however, resides in passages such as the following: 'It is not only the *opposite* [the odd, cold, death] that does not admit its opposite [the even, heat, life]; there is also that [e.g. threeness] which *brings up with itself* an opposite [the odd] into whatever *object* it enters [as, for instance, the particular substance consisting of a group of three things]; and that thing, the very thing that brings it up [the odd] with itself never admits the *quality opposed* [the even] to the one that is *brought up*' (105a).[24] The sense of this passage, namely that the presence of a specific nature, e.g. threeness, in a substance or subject implies the presence in the same of the corresponding generic

24. Translation based on Plato, *Phaedo*, tr. with notes by David Gallop, Oxford 1975 (and cf. his notes on the passage, pp. 208–9 and 236).

nature, the odd, and that the genericity of particular things is mediated by the specificity of the generic – this sense cannot be dissociated, in the way that it is constituted and developed from the point of view of truth, either from the sense of *other contexts* preceding it, from the Eleatics and the Pythagoreans to the Socratics, or from that of other contexts coming after it. An example would be Aristotle in the *Prior Analytics* 52b 7 and the *Topica* 144b 16, in which for example we again come across the verbs *epiphérein* ('to bring up') and *synepiphérein* ('to bring up with itself') used to express that introduction of generic nature by means of the specific which is characteristic of syllogisms in Barbara-Celarent.

It is the semantic locus, the omni-contextuality, of these terms (and others, such as 'opposite', 'threeness', etc.) which points to their technical character, along with their univocal speciality. We are shown how the philosophical search for truth proceeds in practice by means of semantic values whose disorganic contextuality alone is suitable or functional to that *universal questioning* of things which is resolved and satisfied (*ad infinitum*) in an increasingly rigorous *univocal* delimitation of the *most equivocally diverse* genera or meanings of ordinary discourse (which instead uses the same terms for very different genera). The poetic search for truth, on the other hand, which is a no less universal questioning (it too casts doubt on the empirical and the unmediated in all things, and replaces it by mediation), this search proceeds by means of organic–contextual semantic values which alone are suitable or functional to the resolution of its queries. These values, with their rigorously *polysemic* terms (the 'suggestiveness' or 'connotations' of poetry) – what is called 'style' – are substituted for all the *most equivocally diverse* genera of ordinary discourse. Thus poetic inquiry is in accord, in this cathartic function, with philosophical inquiry; it differs from it only in the technique which effects the catharsis and – as will become increasingly clear – in its positive results.

Turning now to the historical sciences, it will be sufficient to note: (1) that the optimum which they pursue, to reach – as has been said of Mommsen's best work – general conclusions which fit perfectly with every detail of the known facts, also implies the use of corresponding univocal semantic values, if historians are to articulate and express the possible that has been realized, what has actually happened, and so distinguish it from the merely possible. And (2) that since 'historical study' consists in 'weighing up the probable and the improbable' (Bloch),[25] it does not differ in its general epistemological structure from the poet's balancing of what is verisimilar and what is not or what is and is not credible. We may recall Bloch's comments on the use made by the historians, no less than by the poet when he writes metaphorically, of a *testing of resemblances*, whereby study of historical evidence goes back and forth between the resemblance which confirms and that which discredits. Our experience of and reflection on what has happened, on facts and on reality (which, however, do not themselves exhaust the truth), produces the necessity for a univocal and omni-contextual terminology. It is this necessity which confers its unity on the study of history, enabling it to be instituted and to define itself as such; and which therefore un-metaphysically ensures the specific difference of historical study from poetry, which is defined by means of polysemic and organic–contextual terms.

But it is of course in the physical sciences that the need for the univocal is most directly perceptible, both because of their limited field (they do not have the universal range of philosophy or history) and because of the immediately visible specialized nature or particular technique of their mathematical, at least in part artificial language. Galileo warns us in *Il Saggiatore* that it would be a mistake for a person to say ' "Everything in the world is either large or small." This proposition is neither true nor false, and neither is the proposition "objects are either near or far". From *indeterminacy* of this sort it will come about that the same objects may be called "quite close" and "very remote"; that the closer may be called "distant" and the farther "close"; that the larger may be called "small" and the smaller "large". Thus one may say "This is a very small *hill*," and "this is a very large *diamond*." A courier calls the trip *from Rome to Naples* very short while a great lady grieves that her house is so far *from the church*. In order to avoid *equivocation* Sarsi needed to [. . .] give an exact determination [. . . ,] saying for example: "I call medium a distance of *one league*; far, that which is *more than one league*; and near, that which is *less*." I fail to see why he did not do this, unless it was that he realized his case would be stronger if he advanced it by cleverly *juggling equivocations* in front of

25. Marc Bloch, op. cit., p. 65.

the simple-minded than by reasoning it soundly for the more intelligent. Well, it truly is a great advantage *to have one's bread buttered on both sides*, and to be able to say: "Because the fixed stars are distant, they are not much magnified, whereas the moon is, because it is close," and then to say, if necessity arises, "Objects in a room, being close, are magnified a great deal, but the moon, because it is distant, is little enlarged" [26].

In other words, since terms and concepts like 'far' and 'near' and their comparatives and superlatives are not capable of univocal and rigorous determination, they must in the name of science be replaced or *reduced* to a concept-term which can be treated mathematically. The term 'how far' must be translated into one millimetre, one centimetre, a hundred kilometres, etc. Or, to take some other examples: 'On the scientific level, we have the quantitative coefficient of elasticity instead of the qualitative term "elastic" of the thing-language; we have the quantitative *term* "temperature" instead of the qualitative ones "hot" and "cold"' (Carnap). For it is well known, finally, that the procedures of measuring and quantification too are only (particular, refined) forms of *classification* of *things*, and that the classes and genera of science, must have only one name, must be *univocal*.[27]

But on the other hand, we know that metaphors too are genera of an 'occasional' kind, or however one likes to term it, as are all poetic symbols, inasmuch as they are types and typicality. Here we are once again presented, unavoidably, with that *other* verbal language, or rather the other aspect of language, namely the language of poetic discourse. Possessing a semantic-formal rigour in no way inferior to, even if different from, scientific language, the terms of the language of poetic discourse are not equivocal, like those of ordinary discourse. Neither are they univocal, like those of scientific discourse in general. Rather they are *polysemic*. If this is the case, we should expect that the equivocal character of those undistinguished empirical expressions of Galileo's courier and great lady might be judged somewhat differently when arraigned before the bar of poetry rather than that of science. And

26. Galileo Galilei, 'The Assayer', in *Discoveries and Opinions of Galileo*, tr. Stillman Drake, New York 1957, pp. 249–50.

27. Rudolf Carnap, 'Logical foundations of the unity of science', in *Foundations of the Unity of Science*, vol. I, Chicago 1938, p. 53.

with some curious consequences, given the difference between the semantic procedures of poetry and those of science – and when I say poetry, I mean poetic thought, for can there be a semantic procedure that does not belong to thought in the true and proper sense?

So it could happen, by way of plausible hypothesis, that the words spoken by the great lady and the courier turn up exactly the same (lexically and grammatically) in the context of a story or novel or comedy, where they are so enriched with meaning as to become profoundly comic or dramatic or in some other way poetically truthful expressions. Or again, but no longer hypothetically, an expression like 'have you eaten?' – or others such as 'what's the time?' or 'let's go' which according to epistemologists precisely do not communicate *physical* knowledge – such as expression may turn up unaltered yet enhanced in one of the poetically true passages of Stendhal's *Chartreuse de Parme*, spoken in fact by Clelia when she is afraid that her beloved Fabrice Del Dongo may be poisoned (Book II, ch. 19). Or, even though Aristotle, long before our modern logicians of science, had denied in the *De Interpretatione* that a prayer could be either 'true' or 'false', an invocation to God, a prayer, may nevertheless express a profound (poetic) truth when spoken by the doctor in *Macbeth*:

God, God forgive us all! (V, 1).

Likewise, even an exclamation like – one example among thousands – the 'Ach!' of pain of Alkmene which ends Kleist's very un-Molièresque *Amphitryon* may express a world of human poetic truth; and so on *ad infinitum*. (We can leave aside the question of the simply historical truth or meaning and the respective non-metric–quantitative univocality there may be in expressions materially identical, in vocabulary and grammar, to those above mentioned.)

Thus the difference between poetry and science in general (including philosophy) emerges most clearly in a comparison with the physical sciences and their language. The difference is simply a *semantic* one, not the traditional difference based on an abstract and hypostatized epistemological dichotomy between reason and feeling (imagination), or universal and particular, or abstract and (intuitive) concrete or whatever. For, to repeat in different terms what has already been said in Chapter One, it seems to us difficult to deny that poetry belongs to the realm of reason as much as science, since both are *unities of a manifold* and therefore both equally reason-and-feeling. So far indeed is this the case that we know that the very 'abstractness' of the physical sciences cannot be dissociated from a basic intuitive sense of the 'qualities' of the world, or from a permanent contact with them, as can be seen in the following requirement of a dialectical–semantic order: that the 'reduction chain [from qualitative terms to univocal–quantitative, abstract, terms: see above] must in any case finally lead to predicates of the thing-language [sublanguage which is the part common to prescientific and physical language], and moreover to observable thing-predicates because otherwise there would be no way of determining whether or not the physical term in question can be *applied* in special cases, on the basis of given observation statements'.[28] In the same way, and conversely, we have seen that the 'concreteness' of poetry cannot be dissociated from its typicality, in other words its (determinate) abstractness. The generic nature of language, as combination of *parole* and *langue*, is already in itself sufficient indication of this fact, provided we do not forget that language, being above all a system which regulates meanings and therefore an intellectual instrument of communication, is not and cannot be, in Amado Alonso's phrase, 'impressionist'.[29]

14. *Equivocal, Univocal and Polysemic*

In order to arrive at a more precise definition of the nature of poetry, we shall now consider for a moment the specific semantic character which distinguishes poetry, a polysemic discourse or genre, from science, a univocal discourse or genre. What exactly do the terms 'polysemic' and 'univocal' mean, and what implications do they have for us? Ordinary dictionaries define the words 'polysemic' or 'polysemous' [*polisenso, polisèmo*], which in Italian can be either adjective or noun, as 'having various senses' or 'having many meanings'; the

28. Carnap, op. cit., p. 54.
29. Amado Alonso, 'Por qué el lenguaje en sí mismo no puede ser impresionista', in *Estudios Lingüísticos*, Madrid 1954, pp. 331 ff. 'To say "green" is equivalent to saying "it belongs to the class green", so that our first impression is, as it were, blocked [*tapada*] by the category . . . of speech, or *idiomatic thought*, which is categorical . . . Language imposes an *intellectual orthopaedics* on intuition . . .'

Italian noun can also mean a kind of riddle; while definitions of 'univocal' [*univoco*] include: 'Of or belonging to, characteristic of, things of the same name or species', and, of a word, 'Having only one meaning or signification; not equivocal; unambiguous' (*O.E.D.*); some dictionaries also state that 'genera must be univocal'. On the other hand, we find in the glossary which ends what we might call the Bible of the American 'New Critics', Brooks and Warren's *Understanding Poetry* (1952), the following definition of 'denotation': 'The denotation of a word is its specific signification. For instance, the denotation of the word *hound* is "one of a class of carniverous mammals (*Canis familiaris*) of the family *Canidae*, etc." But the word also has a large number of *connotations*, or implied meanings and associations. The connotations of a word may vary considerably from person to person and from context to context. For instance, in the discussion of the poem "The Three Ravens", it is pointed out that the hounds symbolize fidelity. That is, certain connotations of the word *hound* are emphasized in the poem. But the word also has other connotations which, in another context, might appear. For instance, the word *hound* can be used as an insult.' (p. 685).

Now for the sake of greater rigour we shall replace the Anglicisms 'denotation' and 'denotative' which originate from Mill, with *univocal* (cf. Galileo's 'exact determination') and *equivocal* (cf. his 'equivocations') – depending on whether we mean scientific and philosophical discourse or speech or common, ordinary discourse or speech. For the latter, we shall also use the more rigorous term *literal-material* (see below). This replacement is necessary, among other reasons, in order to avoid the contamination and confusion of scientific and ordinary lexical terms which can be seen in Brooks and Warren's use of the phrase 'specific signification'. And we shall replace the Anglicism 'connotation' and 'connotative', likewise derived from Mill, with the term *polysemic*. The *equivocal* is opposed to the polysemic no less, please note, than it is to the *univocal*.

In order to proceed to the clarification of these semantic–epistemological categories of the univocal, the polysemic, and the equivocal, let us go back to their respective semantic loci. We have already had occasion to mention them when we commented that the progression of the linguistic modulation of thoughts and feelings in Petrarch (and Leopardi) was at the same time a progression of poetic truth – or progression of the language towards style, and argued that this was a process *internal* to *determinate semantic organisms*, to be contrasted with the disorganic omni-contextual character of scientific and philosophical truth.

So, by *omni-textual*, or semantic locus of the *equivocal*, we mean the concrete linguistic unit that is the *phrase* (cf. Aristotle's use of the term) or noun-phrase, as a sum of lexico-grammatical 'values', when it constitutes or is part of a linguistic-formal complex, or one that-communicates-thought, which is generic, and therefore random [*casuale*]. That is, a 'text' which acts as the *literal-material* of other texts which are *contexts*, such as those that are organic-contextual or determinate and those that are omni-contextual. Random textuality is therefore omni-textuality. More broadly we can say that the omni-textual is the semantic locus of ordinary, hence equivocal, discourse.

By *organic contextual*, or semantic locus of the *polysemic*, we mean the concrete linguistic unit, the phrase or noun-phrase (as above), which not only is not randomly textual but whose expressive value or lin-guistic–formal (or thought–) interest is conditional on its capacity: either itself to constitute a linguistic–formal or expressive complex which is sufficiently individuated and organic to stand as necessary and necessitating *con-text* for each of its elements, i.e. each element of that phrase; or itself to be an organic part or member of an expressive organism or context whose core lies either in the phrase itself or in other determinable units, phrases or propositions which are *structural* to the context. All polysemic expressive values arise here: that is, every value constituted by a *surplus* of meaning *beyond* (in a dialectical relation-ship with them, as we shall see) those of omni-textual values, which form random aggregates of meanings, ensembles of equivocation, by comparison. This added plurality of meanings, which is indissociable from a determinate context, by which and for which it is produced, constitutes the thought and discourse of *poetry*, and its autonomy. That autonomy is semantic – in other words, scientifically verifiable and non-metaphysical.

Finally, by *omni-contextual*, or semantic locus of the *univocal*, we mean the concrete linguistic unit, the phrase or noun-phrase (as above), which not only, like the organic contextual, is not randomly textual, but whose expressive value, unlike that of the previous category, is not conditional *on any one determinate* context but *on innumerable contexts*, each one interdependent with the others and all of them constituting a sort of open context or context *in fieri*. This unit then is an omni-contextual expressive value. From this arises the omni-laterality or universality of philosophical and scientific thought which, however, is such *only by virtue of its being constitutionally indissociable* from the semantic (i.e. instrumental) character of omni-contextuality and therefore uni-vocality, and *not* in any way because it is 'universality' or 'truth' par excellence. This it could never be, for we already know that *truth* does not consist only of univocal, or philosophical and scientific, genera but also of polysemic genera, those of poetry. Both of these in fact verify and transcend, in semantic-formal and not abstractly formal fashion, the equivocal or random or vulgar genera of the omni-textual field. This semantic-formal transcendence, a dialectic which constitutes scientific and poetic genera or values, is an end whose means or instrument is the semantic, which we must now examine. In doing so we shall discover, among other things, that the identity of thought and language (here: *langue*) is a dialectical identity between end and means.

For the purpose outlined above, we must make the following points first of all. (1) The terms univocal and polysemic are relative or rela-tional terms; they both already imply a relation to something else, that something else being the equivocal as literal-material. The first implies relation to the equivocal in a transcendence of its equivocality (the use of the *same* term for *different* classes of things or different con-cepts), reducing that equivocality to the formal rigour of univocality or technicality (=the *same* term for the same class of things or con-cept). The second performs the same operation, *mutatis mutandis* – yielding *several* terms for the *same* class or concept contained in the literal-material, and therefore *several* terms for *several* classes or con-cepts. This then gives us the genera of science and poetry.

(2) While this double, or bifurcated, transcendence is indeed the transcendence of *matter* (the literal-material) by *form*, poetic or scientific thought, it should be noted that it is so inasmuch as at the same time, and in order really to be able to be formal, it is a *semantic* transcendence and development. It is therefore grounded on the literal-material no less as semantic means (phrase or noun-phrase) than as end – in other words the equivocal, random thought or meaning that is to be tran-scended or developed.

(3) Here, put another way, we have the necessary dialectical *con-comitance* of the literal-material, as semantic-formal ensemble, in the genesis both of the univocal and of the polysemic, which permits that switch from the literal-material which is its univocal or polysemic supersession.

In the case of the polysemic, this dialectical necessity is confirmed by the problematic fact of the paraphrase of poetry, although the indifference of the aestheticists to linguistic matters prevents them from realizing it. In this light, paraphrase, *correctly understood*, can only be that moment of dialectical comparison between those elements in the literal-material (whether language or thought) which necessarily remain unchanged in the poem and those which, having undergone a development, are necessarily altered. This comparison, as we shall see, serves to aid the critic worthy of the name to perceive and evaluate the genesis and process of the poem as a polysemic entity. A lesser confirmation is also to be found in the case of the univocal; for instance, the dialectical compresence of values of what Carnap calls a thing-language (as a sub-language which is common to pre-scientific and scientific language) within the quantitative language of physics, attested by the application and operability of the latter.

Now in order to comprehend clearly the dual modes of semantic-formal transcendence of the literal-material, and in particular its poetic transcendence, we must specify that the literal-material in-cludes: (a) all the lexical–grammatical and related phonetic elements of a language, in other words the form of the literal (as lexical 'form' and grammatical 'form'), or better *instrumental form* (see above, for example, the exponent-morphemes and corresponding exponent-prosodemes in Hjelmslev); (b) all the corresponding *signifieds*, or 'con-tents', of the literal (as lexical 'form' etc.) – in other words the *end-*thought (historical thought in a broad sense, so including experience in general) of the *instrumental* form. All this, taken as a whole, is in fact the technical material for communication and expression from which poetry and science are composed. It therefore precedes and conditions poetry, entering into the semantic dialectic of poetry (as, *mutatis mutandis*, into that of science) to set in motion its double rhythm of conservation and change. Poetry conserves and changes, in its style, the 'form' of the literal; and it conserves and changes *that amount* of the contents of the literal which the poem *develops* in transvaluating its equivocal and random character into the semantic-formal rigour of the connotative or polysemic. It is obvious that the equivocality of the contents of the literal–material is only measurable with precision *by comparison* (critical–aesthetic paraphrase) with the formal rigour of the polysemic, into whose semantic dialectic, in this particular case, that content has entered in order to be transvaluated and purified (catharsis); or alternatively, by comparison with the formal rigour of the univocal or technical, in the applicability of the results of the semantic dialectic of the latter.

Thus we reach the conclusion that the elements which make up that synthesis which is the *poetic symbol* as *polysemic synthesis* (in other words characteristic typicality) are: (1) the instrumental or semantic which is the 'form' of the literal, given the fundamental postulate of identity between thought and language – now revealed as a dialectical identity between end and means; (2) the end-thought of that instrumentality, which is the content of the literal, whose values (thought) are consolidated and conserved but also developed and changed in an ulterior end-thought, whose sufficient means or semantic instrument *is* the form of the literal, as, however, *a multiplicity of nouns (-phrases)* which is *not reduced*, as in the case of the univocal or the technical noun-phrase, *but is limitless.* Thus both *from* and *over and above* the literal-material 'rose' of the dictionaries, countless other 'roses' are produced: the 'white rose' of Dante's 'saintly host' (*Paradiso* XXXI, 1–2), or Burns's 'red, red rose', for example – produced, of course, in the relevant semantic locus, in this case the organic contextual as locus of the polysemic, or the genera of poetic discourse.

We can now see how the literary critic's first task must be to discern whether and at what point and to what extent the semantic values (but does there exist value or thought which is not *sèma*?) of the text under consideration belong to the category of the polysemic or the univocal or even the equivocal (ordinary discourse). This task can only be accomplished by a precise perception of the semantic locus of the text (and this perception is the condition for the exercise of 'taste' or sense of 'style') – that is by seeing whether the text, as a whole or as an element, is something organic-contextual rather than something omni-contextual or even omni-textual. The rest will follow of its own accord: the reconstruction of the genesis of the poem as a polysemic entity *from* and *over and above* the literal-material; the exercise then of an entirely functional philological criticism, in which a critical paraphrase of the context, once the latter has been registered, is precisely the positive dialectical moment which enables the critic gradually to identify the connotations which transcend the denotative or literal-material, and to establish their validity at each point.

Thus, an error is committed both by those whose abstract rationalism prevents them from making a distinction between literal-material and polysemic contents, as is frequently the case with Lukács and Yvor Winters, and by those who, though they perceive this distinction, are prevented by a residual aesthetic mysticism and an associated indifference to matters of language from grasping the dialectical presence of the literal-material in poetry, and hence from even recognizing the critical function of paraphrase, which for them is simply a 'heresy' (Cleanth Brooks).[30] Brooks himself, consequently, is both right and wrong in his criticism of the rationalist Winters' reading of Browning's line:

So *wore* night; the East was gray . . . :

right when he objects that 'so wore night' and 'thus passed night' can be said to share the same rational meaning 'only if we equate "rational meaning" with the meaning of a loose paraphrase'; but wrong to leave it at that, at the immediately negative aspect of the paraphrase, and not to pay attention to the positive, *critical* function of paraphrase in making us measure and evaluate, by *comparison with* the text of which it is a paraphrase, the *switch* which has taken place between the literal-material of ordinary discourse ('passed') and the polysemic (here a metaphor: 'wore') of poetic discourse.[31]

30. Cleanth Brooks, 'The heresy of paraphrase', chapter 11 of *The Well Wrought Urn*, New York 1947, pp. 163-4. The following assertion is typical of the traditional way of considering thought, even scientific thought, in abstraction from language: 'A *scientific* proposition can stand *alone*. If it is true, it is true' (p. 169). Brooks fails to register those particular semantic features of thought, the organic and the disorganic, without which it is impossible to grasp the real life of thought itself in all its richness and variety. Yet he touches on these problems without realizing it a little further on when he adds that: 'The terms of science are abstract symbols which do *not* change under the *pressure of the context*' (p. 171). But he lacks any rigorous, linguistic-aesthetic concept of what "context" might mean, a term which in his usage and that of other "New Critics" has too vague and generic a sense.

31. For Brooks's opponent Yvor Winters, see *The Anatomy of Nonsense*, New York 1943: 'It is the concept of fire which generates the feelings communicated by

Similarly Bremond, a champion of 'pure poetry' (pure of concepts), is wrong when, commenting on Malherbe's line:

Et les fruits passeront la promesse des fleurs

(And the fruits shall surpass the promise of the flowers),

he observes that 'this line has a sense – there will be a good harvest – but one so thin that it is difficult to see how so much poetry can flow from it': for the sense of this line is precisely the connotative or poly-semic sense that 'the fruits shall surpass the promise of the flowers',

the word, though the sound of the word may modify these feelings very subtly [sic] ... The relationship, in the poem, between rational statement and feeling, is thus seen to be that of motive to emotion' (p. 13). Apart from the 'sound' which is somewhat curiously supposed to modify the feelings motivated by concepts, one might at first sight be inclined to concur with Winters's aesthetic rationalism. But this rationalism turns out to be so abstract as to make paraphrase equivalent to poetic meaning, and to tend towards assignment of priority, as Brooks had already objected, to the denotative over the connotative. Winters is on firmer ground when, along with Alonso and linguisticians in general, he argues that 'the rational content cannot be eliminated from words' and concludes that 'consequently the rational content cannot be eliminated from poetry' and 'if there is a necessary relationship between concept and feeling, and concept is unsatisfactory, then feeling must be damaged by way of the relationship' (pp. 12–13).

The clearest demonstration of the limits of Winters's abstract aesthetic rationalism is of course to be found in the literary-critical application of his criteria, as can be seen in his essays *On Modern Poets*, New York 1959. In the study on Hopkins, for instance (and we choose it precisely because Hopkins is not congenial to Winters whose sympathies go rather to Donne or even ... Robert Bridges), we read the following judgement on *The Wreck of the Deutschland* and other poems: 'The paraphrasable content of all these poems is so slight as to be reducible to a sentence or two for each. The structures erected upon these simple bases are so fantastically elaborated that the subjects are all but lost' (p. 180). Because of Winters's horror for the 'fantastic', for example, he completely misses the metaphor 'Who fired France for Mary without spot' in *Duns Scotus's Oxford*, in which he sees nothing but 'empty epithets' and sentimentalism (p. 166). Likewise he quite fails to understand the fine sonnet which begins 'No worst, there is none. Pitched past pitch of grief', or even to mention (except in connection with metre) *Spring and Fall*, perhaps Hopkins's finest poem. When he does hit the mark, as for instance with the lovely sonnet *In Honour of St Alphonse Rodriguez*, his argument, in the manner of Dr Johnson, is not entirely satisfying: 'It is reasoned from beginning to end, and nothing is superfluous; and the simile in the first half of the sestet is not only precisely applicable to the theme but is beautifully managed in itself' (p. 188). On the other hand, his constant polemic against 'unrestrained indulgence in meaningless emotion' (p. 180) is still useful today; likewise his rejection of Hopkins's moralistic, content-fixated poetic (especially against apologist critics like W. H. Gardner).

E

while 'there will be a good harvest' is nothing but the literal-material sense reproduced in function of a paraphrase which here is negative, uncritical and irrelevant.[32]

The concept of semantic dialectic now puts us in a position to explain the *objective* – ultimately *historical* – feeling or pathos of poetry discussed in Chapter One (Section 5 ff.). We may clarify the question by observing:

(1) that, having established the essential linguistic component of poetry, and postulated a dialectical identity between thought and language that is verified by it, we have shown that poetry belongs to thought in general, as a unity – a discursive and not mystical unity – of the manifold.

(2) From this there arises the semantic possibility, the only non-mythical possibility, of historical (scientific) thought circulating in poetry – that is to say of univocal thought circulating in polysemic thought, and vice versa, through the medium of language and more precisely through the medium of the omni-textual or literal-material.

(3) Where this circulation occurs, given the structure of the semantic dialectic examined above, the poetic or polysemic rethinking of meanings which in our particular case are historical both conserves and simultaneously changes those meanings. It conserves them in their literal-material values, which are developed but also incorporated within their univocal values (see above: 'hubris', 'sinfulness', 'Punic wars', 'communism', etc.); and it changes them by adding to them further senses or values in and through the limitless pluralistic formulation of noun-phrases which is proper to the polysemic. Thus it is through the supremely linguistic medium of omnitextual values that

32. Henri Bremond, *La Poésie Pure*, Paris 1926, p. 21. It is interesting to note, incidentally, that when Bremond says: 'if we add merely the weight of a snowflake to the third of these divine anapaests: "Et les fruits passeront *les* promesses des fleurs", the vessel will break', his little experiment leaves us with the well-grounded suspicion that he is so intent on pursuing the mirage of the poetic 'music' of the anapaests, threatened with discord by the substitution of 'les' for 'la', that he has failed to notice that the chosen vessel of the poem will break simply, which is saying everything, because the plural 'les promesses' ('the promises') does not just alter the line, it makes a lamentable hotchpotch of the unity and power of the metaphor of the 'promise of the flowers'. For the whole metaphor is built precisely on the singular of the definite article and thus on the abstract and synthesizing sense of the substantive-concept-vehicle, from which comes the polysemic *connection* which we know metaphor to be.

omni-contextual values – the univocal and historical meanings in question – are transvaluated into organic-contextual and poetic meanings. We further know that omni-textual values condition even the language of the physical sciences, despite the fact that it is made up in large part of the artificial language of mathematical symbolism; they condition it to the extent that, in order to be applied, it must draw on the omni-textuality of a 'thing-language', common to scientific and pre-scientific language.

(4) It follows that the circulation of historical (univocal) thought in poetic thought and vice versa, since it consists in the mediation of the literal-material, or reference back to the latter as their common basic semantic value, in no way prejudices their independence of and distinction from each other. That distinction is semantic, not metaphysical. This independence and distinction is realized in the semantic-formal transcendence of the literal-material peculiar to each, whether polysemic or univocal: from which we have *polysemic typical abstractions*, or poetic genera, and *univocal typical abstractions*, or scientific genera. Both kinds of abstraction are *determinate*, as we know.

So, to sum up, in the same way as Burns's 'red, red rose' is and is not the 'rose' of the botanical treatise – it is in its literal-material value, from which the treatise proceeds in order to depart from it, and is not because it lacks the technical development of its characteristics as the reproductive organ of the plant etc., given that what the poet is interested in in the 'rose' is its desirability, which he transfers to the person of the beloved – so, in the same way, the 'hubris' of Pindar and Eliot's 'Mylae' are and are not those of the history of Greek moral thought or the Punic wars. They share a literal-material aspect, as names and concepts in the Greek and Latin languages; but they lack technical particularization, which is substituted in Pindar by 'invidious misfortunes' and 'fatal insolence', and in Eliot by 'Stetson! you who were with me . . .' That is, it is substituted by meanings which no longer belong *only to the omni-textual order* of meanings of the Greek and Latin languages, which are the basic elements of language shared by both poets and historians; and which do not belong either (except at the cost of confusing and nullifying the poetic synthesis in each case) to the *omni-contextual* order of meanings of the history of Greek moral thought or that of the Punic wars. For the latter know of no 'invidious misfortunes' (or if they do adduce them as sources, they draw on only those elements which can be ordered in the univocal hierarchy of Greek ethical concepts), nor any Stetson at the battle of Mylae.

Substantially the same process occurs when poetry becomes a history of itself in literary criticism. Here the decisive moment is the deployment of *taste*, that is the ability, once the semantic locus of the poem, the organic contextual, has been perceived, to register the passage from language-thought to style-thought – in other words the transition from the random and equivocal sense of the literal-material to the formal rigour of the polysemic. In this, as we know, the critical paraphrase of the contextual is mandatory. For it represents that further – scientific – consciousness of the poetic process which classifies the poem as such by placing its polysemic concepts in a network of univocal concepts. The technical rigour of the latter, though distinguished from it, is not extraneous to the rigour – itself intellectual – of the polysemic; it does not stifle it in any way, for in both cases we are concerned with that unification of the manifold, through language as pure means, which is thought in the concrete. The true, and not dogmatic, concrete universal is the semantic unity of the many, and universal in its semantic particularities. Precisely because the latter are semantic, they are not and cannot be hypostatic 'forms' or watertight compartments of the universal. They are prevented from so being, if for no other reason, by the nature of their instrumental linguistic form: the 'form' of that pure *means* or instrument which is language, the indissociable end of which is true *form*, value, thought, or unity-of-the-manifold (see the conclusions of Section 17). It follows, finally, that the framing of the polysemic in the univocal, the specific task of literary criticism, is possible in so far as the end, thought, bends its means, language, to itself, and uses it as it discourses from concept to concept – from polysemic genus to univocal genus and vice versa: so that the articulation of that thought, proceeding by a series of *switches* (which are not metaphysical, but properly technical, semantic, and linguistic) from the polysemic to the univocal and vice versa, remains unitary, as is in fact attested by the literal-material or semantic base of these switches which express dialectical *developments*.

It is a different matter, of course, in the case of poetry which becomes a source for the history of moral and political faiths and ideologies, or of social behaviour, etc. In that case, the critical paraphrase of the polysemic (the act of taste) has no reason for being and is replaced by the abstraction and identification of contents which can be ordered univocally in preconstituted technical schemas (see above, I, 5, Wilamowitz's technical and historiographical use of a line from Sophocles). Here too, we find confirmed, through contrast, that the task of the literary critic is not, as aestheticist and impressionist criticism claims, to renounce univocal schemas in which the poetic may be framed. Rather it is not to abstract contents or concepts from the organic-contextual, and to be able instead to recognize contents or concepts in their precise organic contextuality by means of those indispensable *semantic indices*, 'quotations'. That is, to recognize them as formal polysemic contents, and then to characterize them specifically in adequate univocal schemas or concepts pertaining to a concrete sociological poetics and stylistics.[33]

33. Some further clarification of what has already been said on the subject of *critical paraphrase*.
(1) Although our analysis of the concept of paraphrase starts inevitably from that well-known phenomenon which the dictionary defines as a more or less 'free', 'circumlocutory' and 'explanatory' rendering of 'any' text, it immediately departs from that definition in showing the particular role and pertinence of paraphrase in the case of the poetic text. (2) This is explained by, and in turn explains and confirms, what we have observed as characteristic of the poetic text, namely its organic contextuality, and hence its semantic autonomy: for in the case of the poetic, polysemic text, paraphrase – the *regression* to current linguistic use, in short to the omni-textual, of words and phrases – constitutes the premise of an internal *progression* of thought and *sèma* or truth, an internal variation and development of meanings, which is disclosed or resolved precisely in a *critical* paraphrase or philological comparison (in the widest sense of 'philological') of the paraphrase with that which is paraphrased. This comparison is the *beginning* and *end* of a whole process (reconstitution of a dialectic) of truth. Which once again confirms for us the fact that poetry, albeit in its own particular semantic ways, is like science the expression of image-concepts which are identical with verbal meanings. (3) This description frees the paraphrase of poetry from the disreputable features (superfluity, indeed harmfulness) attributed to it by traditional post-romantic and decadent taste, which elects to ignore the discursive and dialectical nature of poetic truth revealed by critical paraphrase, and to confer a mythical and dogmatic character on it by endowing it with 'intuitive' immediacy. Our account also avoids the uncritical equation of the paraphrase and the paraphrased poetic text into which abstract aesthetic rationalism falls. It acts on the other hand as a decisive confirmation of what distinguishes poetry from science, namely the absence in the latter of a function of paraphrase as determinant as that of the paraphrase of the poetic text. For the truth of the scientific discourse or context (unlike that of poetry) does not consist in a self-verification [*auto-verifica*], nor therefore in an *internal* dialectical comparison of that discourse with the current use of words and phrases, but rather in a verification

A rapid examination of other modern and contemporary documents of *polysemic rationality* will cast further light on poetic genera or polysemic typical abstractions, and help us to see what distinguishes them from and what links them to scientific genera or univocal typical abstractions (univocal rationality).

Burns again:

> The wan moon sets behind the white wave,
> And time is setting with me, Oh:

Here the effect of poetic melancholy arises from the connotative, polysemic connection between the setting of the moon and the passing of time for me, for us, through the attribution – by transference – of the idea of 'setting' to 'time', leading to the extension and transference of the literal, denotative wanness and whiteness of the (setting) moon and of the wave (at moonset) to human things, which thus also wane and fade away. Notice the exercise of the intellect involved even in this order of association between such vague external and internal impressions. We may be excused a comparison with the much deeper reflection of Horace, in all its simplicity, and one much more moving in its effect:

> Yet swiftly in the sky the moons restore
> Their losses; but when we go down to where
> Are Tullus, Ancus and Aeneas, more
> We shall not be than dust and shadows there[34]).

This presence of the intellect was ignored and denied both by Yeats,

from outside itself, a hetero-verification [*etero-verifica*] as implied by the semantic inter-dependence or heteronomy which is indissociable from the historical or experimental imperative of scientific discourse. It follows that the paraphrase of a scientific text only makes sense *after* the results of its heteronomous semantic constitution, that is in the *application* of its phrase-formulae, in short after its experimental or historical verification (which is semantically a 'hetero-verification'): for instance, in the field of natural sciences, in the thing-sublanguage which mediates the language of science and physics with pre-scientific language, or the language of ordinary use. So we may conclude that, while the function of the paraphrase of a poetic text is to *reconstitute* the truth of that text or poetic truth, the function of the paraphrase of a scientific text is simply complementary – in the formal sense – to scientific truth.

34. Horace, Ode VII 'To Torquatus', in *Collected Works of Horace*, tr. Lord Dunsany and Michael Oakley, London 1961, p. 100.

who thought that poetic relations were 'too subtle for the intellect',[35] and by Brooks and Warren who discount any 'logical' connection here at all.[36] Of course, the connection between the setting of the moon and human time is not a univocal scientific proposition, and in astronomy it makes no sense whatever. Yet it is so rational, it makes so much sense of another kind, that it proves to be as subject to the principle of non-contradiction as any univocal connection (remember Galileo: 'true things, those which are necessary, that is, those which could not be otherwise').[37] This is borne out for us by the congruence of sense of the two poetic propositions in question. For if indeed you change the predicates in the first proposition and replace 'wan' and 'white' with 'gold' in both cases, as Brooks and Warren acutely (but unwisely for their aestheticist thesis) suggest, the poem collapses. It does so, precisely because of the removal of the logical congruence between the elements of the two propositions. For that congruence, indeed *coherence*, is demanded by the metaphor whose vehicle or occasion, the idea of 'setting' – which acts as the mediate term of this poetic discourse – includes the notation of the 'wanness' of the moon and the 'whiteness'of the wave. If you change or replace them, the vehicle is altered, the tenor of the metaphor blurs and dissolves, and the poetic effect of melancholy is no longer produced.

Goethe's *Wanderer's Nightsong II*:
> O'er all the hill-tops
> Is quiet now,
> In all the tree-tops
> Hearest thou
> Hardly a breath;
> The birds are asleep in the trees.
> Wait; soon like these
> Thou too shalt rest.[38]

35. Robert Burns, 'Open the door to me Oh', in *Poems and Songs*, ed. James Kinsley Oxford 1971, p. 541; Yeats's essay 'The symbolism of poetry' (*Essays*, 1924, pp 191–2) quoted (with corrections to Yeats's quoting of Burns) in F. W. Bateson *English Poetry: a Critical Introduction*, London 1966, p. 87.

36. Brooks & Warren, op cit., pp. l–liii.

37. Cf. Giulio Preti, *Storia del Pensiero Scientifico*, Milan 1957.

38. Goethe, 'Wandrers Nachtlied II', in *Werke* I, Zurich 1950, p. 69; translated by Longfellow (cf. below, pp. 159–160 and Note 73).

Here the idea of the peace of nature, obtained with a description as realistic as it is spare, gives rise through natural affinity and contrast to the idea of the peace not only of our body but our soul, a peace which is entire only in death: a general symbolic conclusion which is expressed by the unavoidably metaphorical character of 'thou too shalt rest' (*ruhest du auch*). There is of course a modern, pantheistic sense of the relations between nature and the human 'spirit' behind the verse. No Greek, not even Alcman for example with his famous lines:

> Now sleep the mountain-summits, sleep the glens,
> The peaks, the torrent-beds; all things that creep
> On the dark earth lie resting in their dens[39]

has given us anything similar, nor could they: that immediate introduction of the self, that 'thou', placed in contact-contrast with nature, is thoroughly modern. But above all we have to bear in mind, in this case as in most others, the sense of *another kind* (than the univocal or scientific kind) which constitutes the reasonableness, the rationality, and the coherence of Goethe's text. This polysemic sense, produced by the organic-contextual nature of the text, is very clear in the *semantic switch* of the metaphorical *connection* (verb-metaphor), and its inevitability or necessity – to the eternal surprise of the aestheticist waffling about imaginative *raptus* or pure intuition.

Hölderlin:

> *The middle of life*
> With yellow pears the land
> And full of wild roses
> Hangs down into the lake,
> You lovely swans,
> And drunk with kisses
> You dip your heads
> Into the hallowed, the sober water.
>
> But oh, where shall I find,
> When winter comes, the flowers, and where

39. Alcman, fragment 89, in *Greek Poetry for Everyman*, tr. F. L. Lucas, London 1951, p. 236.

The sunshine
And shade of the earth?
The walls loom
Speechless and cold, in the wind
Weathercocks clatter.[40]

Here the general symbolic sense of a substantially realistic representation is expressed by a noun-metaphor (winter = old age). It is an obvious metaphor, yet it is justified afresh and made necessary purely by the *context*. The idea of winter expands in a natural way from the directly concrete literal representation of the succession of the seasons, from summer to winter, to embrace that of the fading and decay of all things, including man. Or to put it another way, it tacitly becomes a metaphorical connection as well; and it is this alone which gives the representation fullness of meaning by expressing its general sense in a polysemic rather than univocal mode, in short as a poetic symbol.

Rimbaud's *Aube* ('Dawn'):

I embraced the summer dawn.

Nothing was stirring yet on the facades of the palaces. The water was dead. The camps of shadows in the woodland road had not been struck. I walked, awakening vivid warm breaths, and the precious stones looked up, and wings rose without a sound.

The first adventure was, in the path already filled with cool, pale gleams, a flower which told me its name.

I laughed at the blond waterfall, dishevelled between the fir trees: in the silvery peak I recognized the goddess.

Then I lifted the veils, one by one. In the avenue, waving my arms. On the plain, where I declared her to the cock. In the city, she fled among the belfries and domes, and, running like a beggar across the marble quays, I chased after her.

At the top of the road, near a laurel wood, I surrounded her with her heaped-up veils, and I felt, a little, her immense body. Dawn and the child fell down at the bottom of the wood.

When I woke up it was noon[41].

40. Friedrich Hölderlin, *Poems and Fragments*, tr. Michael Hamburger, London 1966, pp. 370–1.
41. Arthur Rimbaud, 'Les Illuminations' XXII, in *Selected Verse*, tr. Oliver Bernard, London 1962, pp. 268–9.

In this poem, the modern parable of the child who is fascinated by nature as a mysterious world of sublime sensual experiences, a world of dreams and adventure, springs from a representation of dawn filled with both precise details and transferred meanings, a *coherent* whole rich in truth: from the first early-morning impressions halfway between real and unreal (those vivid, warm breaths and the pebbles which are made to shine like precious stones by the touch of first light) to the encounter with the noble whiteness of the divine body of dawn, evoked by the silvery tops of the trees, chased away by the advance of daylight, and on to the awakening, after the child-like ecstasy, in the sad reality of noon. Rimbaud's poem is an 'illumination' or immediate vision which only in appearance and for the aestheticists has no rational ties or rational sense. Actually it is a notable document of polysemic discursiveness, and this discursiveness can only be ignored by those who look in it for univocal connections – without finding any – and so imagine all sorts of mysterious or purely fantastic 'suggestions' and so on. Yet in this case, as always in poetry, the presence of language, the literal-material (transcended but present), should make any kind of aesthetic mysticism suspect – were this natural suspicion not thwarted by that indifference to language, a product of the Humboldtian and romantic linguistics of the *parole*, which is a sort of second nature to the aesthete.

The examination of the following sonnet by Mallarmé, celebrated for its hermeticism, will provide us with the final confirmation of what has just been said, and will enable us to close our accounts with the poetic (at its most rigid in Mallarmé's case) of 'not saying but suggesting':

À la nue accablante tu
Basse de basalte et de laves
A même les échos esclaves
Par une trompe sans vertu

Quel sépulcral naufrage (tu
Le sais, écume, mais y baves)
Suprême une entre les épaves
Abolit le mât dévêtu

Ou cela que furibond faute
De quelque perdition haute
Tout l'abîme vain éployé

Dans le si blanc cheveu qui traîne
Avarement aura noyé
Le flanc enfant d'une sirène.

(Kept silent to the overwhelming cloud lowering with basalt and
lavas, even to the slavish echoes, by a trumpet without virtue,
    what sepulchral shipwreck (you know it, foam, but slobber
there) abolishes the stripped mast, a supreme piece of jetsam,
    or this that, furious for want of some lofty destruction, the
whole empty abyss displayed
    in the lingering, most white hair will avariciously have drowned
the flank, child of a siren.)[42]

The first thing to notice is that Mallarmé's wish to suppress logical
continuity by means of inversions and ellipses, whose function is to
render back to words their greatest possible immediacy and sensuousness, their utmost mystical essentiality, and to remove from them the
customary and banal meanings which they usually have in 'reasonable' everyday discourse, is a completely vain one, here as elsewhere
in his work. The reason is not only that, in practice, 'we are left with
nothing by which to decipher this poem except the guidance of
syntax', whose exact rules 'which he knew better than we', he 'never
violated' (E. Noulet), but also that our appreciation of the sonnet's
poetic content depends precisely on our deciphering – in other words
understanding – it. This decipherment or understanding depends in
turn on our ability to identify its syntax and therewith those semantic-
formal linkages or language-thought without which none of its words
– which Mallarmé's poetic misunderstood as platonic and mystical
essences – would possess even sensuous value, that is value as images.
Just to take the 'lowering with basalt and lavas' of the second line: it
is by virtue of its *apposition* to 'cloud' that it acquires a meaning (a para-
phrastic meaning first and foremost: the black weight of low cloud)

42. *Mallarmé*, introduced and edited by Anthony Hartley, London 1965, pp.
101–2.

and therefore can strike us with its sensuous and imaginative qualities, which are sensuous and are images only *together* with their sense or conceptual meaning as a metaphor. Such, again, is the dialectic of heterogeneities.[43]

From this we may draw the following conclusions. (1) If Mallarmé's poetic (the greatest and most representative poetic of symbolism and decadentism) was right to protest against the banal and etiolated discursiveness of ordinary or unpoetic discourse, it was wrong to rest on a principle of anti-discursive mysticism, as the obvious concrete discursiveness and linguistic-stylistic values of his successful poetry in general, and this sonnet in particular, make plain. (2) This discursiveness can only be, in view of what we have said so far, polysemic discursiveness or rationality. (3) It follows that our very enjoyment of the poem in question is conditional on our apprenehsion of it according to the internal stylistic order of its metaphors and connections, which alone can capture its polysemic expressive values in their original wholeness and not confuse or replace them simplistically with paraphrase (see above, the 'black weight'). Paraphrase should serve its usual function of clarifying and assigning a value to the polysemic poetic formula by indicating its equivalents in the literal-material; though these are always approximate, they allow us to perceive *in the comparison* the *gap* of expressive value between them and the higher poetic formula.

At this point we must take issue with Kant. In the *Critique of Judgement,* Section 49, Kant brings his aestheticist criterion of poetry as 'purposiveness without purpose' (Section 10, p. 68) – that is as something not measurable or reducible to a determinate concept or end – to bear on the problem of those 'aesthetical attributes of an object' or 'aesthetical ideas' which include metaphors and similes. That is to say, those 'secondary' and 'kindred' representations which 'arouse *more* thought than can be expressed in a concept *determined by words*', and more exactly 'accompany the logical [attributes] and stimulate the *imagination*, so that it thinks *more* by their aid, although in an *un-*

43. E. Noulet's exegesis, *Dix Poèmes de Stéphane Mallarmé*, Lille-Geneva 1948, from which I have quoted (pp. 130 ff.), is the best, even though the author indulges in the aestheticism which seems almost obligatory for critics of Mallarmé. On the sensory or the musical in poetry in general and for the difficulties which Mallarmé himself felt on the subject, see his instructive confessions discussed below, section 15.

developed way, than could be comprehended in a *concept* and therefore in a *definite form of words*': so that every 'aesthetical idea' is 'a representation [which] adds to a concept much *ineffable thought* [*viel Unnenbares*], the *feeling* [*Gefühl*] of which *quickens* the cognitive faculties, and with language, which is the mere letter, *binds up the spirit* also'.[44] It should be noted here how the poetic spirit is infused into language-as-mere-letter only in the shape of feeling, those kindred representations which are undeveloped and full of ineffable thought, and *not* that of concept. Romanticism, down to its symbolist descendants in Mallarmé and others, will ask for nothing better, proceeding coherently to reduce this 'language' to subjective 'speech'. We should note, in short, the extent to which the discursive or (concrete) intellectual nature of metaphor and simile remains hidden from Kant, and how far he fails to see that simile and metaphor demand *no less conceptual determination* in those of their constitutive representations which are 'kindred' to the 'logical attribute', namely the term of the tenor or comparison, than that present in the logical attribute or vehicle or thing compared. If this is not so, the very process of metaphorical transference breaks down or appears botched and false. For is it not in fact that *not* 'undeveloped', but defined, determinate meaning of the tenor or comparison, *that particular* concept belonging to it *and not any other*, which makes possible the congruence and unity of the tenor or comparison with the vehicle or thing compared, in which metaphor or the grafting of genera or concepts in a new genus or concept consists? One should add that the more the resemblance, the 'kinship', and therefore unity of the dissimilars of tenor and vehicle is clear (being not arbitrary), and thus the more salient is the rational coherence of the relation which is instituted between them, the more successful and more beautiful is the metaphor or simile. Thus the genius of Góngora in his masterly sonnet on the 'deceptive brevity of life' has recourse to the shared (well-defined!) nature of the tenor and the vehicle, two heavenly bodies, in order to achieve an effect of enormous logical–polysemic contrast in the line

'cada sol repetido es un cometa'
(every sun repeated is a comet).

44. Immanual Kant, *Critique of Judgment*, tr. with introduction and notes by J. H. Bernard, London and New York 1892, pp. 199–201.

But if you replace 'comet' with 'flash of lightning', something of a different nature from the sun, the poetic effect immediately dissolves.[45]

Our disagreement with Kant, however, also forces us to ask whether metaphors are the only or principal aesthetic (here: literary or poetic) attributes of an object, as Kant seems to believe, and to review the phenomenon of *literal poetic symbols* with the help of some documentation from modern and contemporary poetry. In other words, we should now extend our documentation of polysemic rationality as constitutive of poetry to other texts. Wordsworth's *She dwelt among the untrodden ways*:

> She dwelt among the untrodden ways
>   Beside the springs of Dove,
> A Maid whom there were none to praise
>   And very few to love:
>
> A violet by a mossy stone
>   Half hidden from the eye!
> – Fair as a star, when only one
>   Is shining in the sky.
>
> She lived unknown, and few could know
>   When Lucy ceased to be;
> But she is in her grave, and, oh,
>   The difference to me!

Here the following points should be made. (1) The whole discourse is articulated in terms which are neither literal-material, despite the apparent, almost prosaic, simplicity of the diction; nor univocal, despite the non-equivocality of the meanings. Yet neither are they polysemic-metaphorical – with the exception of the 'violet' and the 'only star', both of which, however, are subordinate to 'A Maid whom there were none to praise'. Rather these terms are substantially *polysemic-literal*. (2) In fact, the polysemic or poetic value of each of these literal expressions – from 'she dwelt among the untrodden ways' to 'few could know', and 'oh, the difference to me!' – relates to the

45. Luís de Góngora y Argote, 'De la brevedad engañosa de la vida', in *Obras Completas*, Madrid 1943, p. 449.

symbolic conception of the poet's feeling of love for a young woman who loses none of her humanity by her poor and humble social condition, which the poet consciously shares: a conception which, as Edwin Berry Burgum has shown, presupposes and is inseparable from an era of rapid social change, a time of democracy and individualism.[46]
(3) It is this idealized social and historical substance, expressed in polysemic literal terms (containing nothing univocal or technical which might turn the symbolic protagonist into an historical personage, consequently no chronological or sociological setting) which reveals to us how deceptive the almost prosaic simplicity of the diction is, indeed how complex it is in reality. It is this which makes it a poetic discourse in which the literal-material is only a dialectical *precedent* as it is of every discourse, whether it be in a metaphorical polysemic mode or in a univocal mode. It is only by applying the epistemological-technical and aesthetic category of the polysemic, both literal and metaphorical, and the other categories connected with it, that we can surmount the objection, advanced for example by Wimsatt and Brooks against Burgum, that he had simply treated Wordsworth's poem as an historical 'document'.[47]

46. E. B. Burgum, 'The cult of the complex in poetry', in *Science and Society* XV (Winter 1951), pp. 31–48: an important article not only for the remarks on Wordsworth which immediately concern us, but above all for its critique of the Empsonian concept of poetic 'ambiguity': 'Empson . . . employs the word [ambiguity] solely to denote the fact . . . that a poetic statement holds in suspension a great variety and intricacy of interpretations. But this is all that has been traditionally meant by the word "metaphor".' While Empson possesses the merit of having insisted, against Richards, on the cognitive character of poetry, the limit of his position is his lack of any criterion which might explain the poetic quality of word-associations, or 'implications' as he calls them, that is, their greater or lesser necessity from case to case and text to text. What is missing is the criterion of contextual rigour or semantic organicity, with everything it involves. An appeal to the lexical richness of languages and the relevant historical backgrounds certainly does not of itself resolve the problem: it is merely an embarrassing aspect of it. Empson's motto, 'the more [goes on in our minds] the better' (*Seven Types of Ambiguity*, New York 1955, p. XVIII), is confusionist.
47. William K. Wimsatt, Jr. and Cleanth Brooks, *Literary Criticism*, New York 1957, pp. 648–9. On Wordsworth and this poem in particular, see for an assessment that differs from our own: F. W. Bateson, *Wordsworth. A Reinterpretation*, London 1954, pp. 30 ff., of which this one example may be sufficient: 'if the verbal contradictions – to use language so loosely that *untrodden* need not mean "not trodden", that *love* cannot connote *praise*, and that *unknown* obtains a positive sense ('known to a few'), *and yet be completely intelligible* – are disregarded, we are left with a crude and almost vulgar statement of the case for a Rousseauist escapism. God made the country and man made the town.'

Rimbaud's *Ouvriers* ('Workmen'):

O that warm February morning! The untimely South wind came and awakened our absurd paupers' memories, our young destitution.

Henrika was wearing a cotton shirt in brown and white check, which must have been fashionable in the last century, a bonnet with ribbons and a silk scarf. It was far sadder than mourning. We were taking a stroll in the suburbs. The sky was overcast, and that South wind stirred up all the nasty smells of the ravaged gardens and the dried-up meadows.

It can't have wearied my wife as much as it did me. In a sheet of water left by the floods of the previous month near a fairly high path, she drew my attention to some tiny fishes.

The town, with its smoke and its noise of factories, followed us for a long way down the roads. O other world, dwelling-place blessed by the sky, and the shadows! The South wind reminded me of the unhappy incidents of my childhood, my summer despairs, the hideous quantity of strength and knowledge which fate has always kept far from me. No! we shall not spend the summer in this miserly country where we shall never be anything but betrothed orphans. I do not wish this hardened arm to drag, any longer, a *dear image*.[48]

This text is so different stylistically from the previous poem that we must once again explore the question of the polysemic-literal and to clarify further its aesthetic significance. Here, unlike Wordsworth's smooth and simple, literal discourse, we have a literal discourse built up of synthetic formulae of a polemical and allusive, hence symbolic, character. They sometimes come close to metaphor, or rather hyperbole, and we cannot say with confidence that they always avoid it. The text is one of those not infrequent cases which make us realize how uncertain may be the dividing line between the polysemic-metaphorical and the polysemic-literal at given junctures. The synthesizing formulae, which generate the polysemic unity of this description of a working-class couple walking on the outskirts of the

48. Rimbaud, 'Les Illuminations' XIII, in ed. cit., pp. 254-5. For some interpretations of Rimbaud, etc., see W. Fowlie, *Rimbaud's Illuminations*, New York 1953, p. 98.

city, are the following: 'absurd paupers', 'our young destitution', 'It was far sadder than mourning', 'O other world [of the rich], dwelling-place blessed by the sky, and the shadows!', 'the unhappy incidents...', the 'betrothed orphans', '... any longer, a *dear image*' (in other words no longer a woman merely imagined, dreamt of, a happy bride in that other world).[49] The reader is left with the sense at the end that the *betrothed orphans* of this poetic discourse, which at every point presupposes and reflects the industrial society of the time, still lay the blame for their tragedy simply on an anonymous, mythical 'fate' rather than other men, an exploitative class (the bourgeoisie). At any rate one constitutive element of the 'pathos' of this 'illumination', it seems to us, is resignation; not a 'tolerant resignation' as some interpreters have imagined, but rather a resignation filled with violent anguish at the class-exploitation of a worker who is not yet conscious of class injustice, but suffers only from an injustice that is obscure and against whose obscurity he vainly reacts.

To see more clearly the way in which the ideological position of the poet, whatever it may be, constitutes the 'tone' and 'atmosphere' of his poetry as much as its substance, one might compare for example the passage in *Archipelago*, where the romantic humanist Hölderlin likens his age, the onset of the 19th century – albeit to denounce it for its lack of 'sanctuaries' comparable to those of antiquity – to an enormous and joyless 'workshop':

> ... yet always and always
> Vain, like the Furies, unfruitful the wretches' exertions
> remain there.[50]

Let us now, however, pass to the contemporary poetry of Bertolt Brecht.

To Those Born Later:

(I)

> Truly, I live in dark times!
> The guileless word is folly. A smooth forehead
> Suggests insensitivity. The man who laughs
> Has simply not yet had
> The terrible news.

49. Ibid.
50. Hölderlin, ed. cit., pp. 226–7.

What kind of times are they when
A talk about trees is almost a crime
Because it implies silence about so many horrors?
That man there calmly crossing the street
Is already perhaps beyond the reach of his friends
Who are in need?

. . .

I would also like to be wise.

. . .

Also to get along without violence
To return good for evil
Not to fulfil your desires but to forgive them
Is accounted wise.
All this I cannot do:
Truly, I live in dark times.

(II)

I came to the cities in a time of disorder
When hunger reigned there.
I came among men in a time of revolt
And I rebelled with them.
So passed my time
Which had been given to me on earth.

My food I ate between battles
To sleep I lay down among murderers
Love I practised carelessly
And nature I looked at without patience.
So passed my time
Which had been given to me on earth.

. . .

(III)

You who will emerge from the flood
In which we have gone under
Remember
When you speak of our failings

The dark time too
Which you have escaped.

For we went, changing countries oftener than our shoes
Through the wars of the classes, despairing
When there was injustice only, and no rebellion

And yet we know:
Hatred, even of meanness
Contorts the features.
Anger, even against injustice
Makes the voice hoarse. Oh, we
Who wanted to prepare the ground for friendliness
Could not ourselves be friendly.

But you, when the time comes at last
And man is a helper to man
Think of us
With forbearance.[51]

Here the moral and ideological climate which constitutes the poetic
'tone' is, unlike Rimbaud's *Ouvriers*, revolutionary. To be exact, it is
Marxist. The historical specification is imposed by the metaphor 'we
went . . . through the wars of the classes', from which the whole contextual energy which makes the text poetic is released like a flash of
light. It is sufficient to note the theme of the introduction of socialist
solidarity ('And man is a helper to man') as a new 'friendliness' – to
be achieved through a class-struggle or a rejection of 'friendliness' in
a humanitarian or lay-christian sense ('to get along without violence',
etc.), which can only favour class-collaboration. This ideological motif
lends precision, particularly of a literal polysemic kind, to all the other
expressive formulae in the poem – some of which are practically not
even 'dormant' metaphors: from 'Truly, I live in *dark* times!' and the
'*smooth* forehead' which 'suggests insensitivity' and the 'talk about trees'
which 'is almost a crime' to 'Love I practised carelessly'. In other
words, it is this moral testament that the author is a socialist – rather

51. Bertolt Brecht, *Poems*, edited by John Willett and Ralph Manheim, London
1976, pp. 318–20.

than bourgeois – revolutionary, which confers its particular poetic 'accent' or 'tone', its specific 'pathos', on the text as a whole.

Now, before proceeding to our conclusions on poetry and literature, we should examine two important questions: euphony or the so-called 'musicality' of poetry; and the translatability of the poetic text.

15. *Sound and Meaning*

It is clear today that there are very strong arguments of a linguistic and aesthetic order against the contaminatory reduction of poetry to music. Such a contamination has been a dominant tendency in criticism and taste from (to take it no further back) the poetics of Bembo, who wrote: 'there is no more important consideration than that of stress; the stresses give the sounds their harmony and concert, which is as much as to say giving life and soul to bodies',[52] to that of Verlaine:

> Music before everything, and for that prefer the Uneven hazier and more soluble in the air with nothing in it weighty or fixed.[53]

The tendency has persisted right up to the poetics of American New Criticism. For example Brooks and Warren, already cited several times in the course of this study, update the teaching of Pope ('The sound must seem an Echo to the sense')[54] with the pronouncement that: 'The function of the verse as such is highly important . . . in supporting and stressing the meaning'. At the same time they seek to distinguish 'onomatopoeic' effects, which are 'only occasional in poetry', from other 'sound effects' of poetry.[55] Before we go on to set out the arguments against this view – they are in any case contained implicitly in the preceding paragraphs – let us take one or two other significant

---

52. Pietro Bembo, *Prose della Volgar Lingua*, a cura di Mario Marti, Padua 1955, Book II, p. 77 (and see Cesare Segre, 'Edonismo Linguistico nel Cinquecento', in *Giornale Storico della Letteratura Italiana*, CXXX (1953), 390, pp. 145–77, from whom we borrow the formula 'linguistic hedonism' which we use below in a wider, more general, sense.

53. Paul Verlaine, 'Art poétique', tr. in *The Penguin Book of French Verse, 3: The Nineteenth Century*, introduced and edited by Anthony Hartley, London 1967, pp. 224–6.

54. Alexander Pope, *An Essay on Criticism*, 1. 365.

55. Brooks and Warren, op. cit., pp. 135–7.

and more or less well-known examples of the approach that has become traditional in literary criticism or appreciation.

Virgil's famous line,

> Tendebantque manus ripae ulterioris amore
> (and stretched out hands in yearning for the farther shore),[56]

expresses the attitude of the shades of the dead as they crowd round the gloomy ferryman Charon. It is rendered all the more beautiful, according to the conventional view summed up by Empson, who in this question of sound in poetry is also a follower of Pope, by the fact that *ulterioris*, the word which indicates the banishment of the shades from the world beyond, is long, and so shows 'that they have been waiting a long time'; as well as by the repeated vowel-sound *-oris amore*, 'itself the moan of hopeless sorrow'.[57] According to Momigliano, we would appreciate what is the classic passage of Dante in this connection (*Purgatorio* VIII, 1 ff.) much better if we bore in mind the following points: 'Notice the cadence of the entire period ...; the sweetness of the words and the sounds; the delaying of the enjambement (ll. 4–5) ...; and finally the second enjambement (ll. 7–8), where the ringing of the bell dies away in a silence lost in dream'.[58] Even Goethe's *Wanderer's Nightsong*, discussed above, a poem as discursively simple as it is sublime, cannot fully be appreciated, according to Emil Staiger (following a good many others, including

---

56. Virgil, *The Aeneid*, Book VI, 1. 314, tr. H. Rushton Fairclough, Cambridge, Mass. and London 1956.

57. Empson, *Seven Pages of Ambiguity*, ed. cit., p. 14.

58. Dante:

> Era già l'ora che volge il disio
>   ai navicanti e 'ntenerisce il core
>   lo di c' han detto ai dolci amici addio,
> e che lo novo peregrin d'amore
>   punge, s' e' ode squilla di lontano
>   che paia il giorno pianger che si more,
> quand' io incominciai a render vano
>   l'udire ...

(It was now the hour that turns back the longing of seafarers and melts their heart the day they have bidden dear friends farewell and pierces the new traveller with love if he hears in the distance the bell that seems to mourn the dying day, when I began to cease hearing ... [tr. Sinclair, ed. cit.])

Cf. *La Divina Commedia*, commentata da A. Momigliano, Florence 1957, pp. 329–30.

the aestheticist Santayana),[59] if one does not bear in mind, for example, that 'in the long *u* [of 'Ruh', rest] can be heard the hush of
twilight', that the pause after 'Warte nur, balde ... ' (Wait now, soon),
is almost the waiting [*Warten*] itself, and that in the last two long-
drawn-out words [of the final line: 'Ruhest du auch', thou too shalt
rest], everything, even the unquietest of beings, man, finds rest'.[60]
Thereafter, for reasons of 'musical' interest, Staiger has no compunc-
tion in linking the name of Goethe to that of Verlaine as author of
the sentimental *Chanson d'automne*, no less

> Les sanglots longs
> Des violons
> De l'automne

> The long sobs
> Of the violins
> In autumn,

in order to make the point that 'the fleeting rhyme *la* in:

> Decà, delà
> Pareil à la
> Feuille morte

> Here, there,
> Like the
> Dead leaf

removes the last weight from language: so that one could almost say *one hears*
something hopelessly lost' (*op. cit.*, p. 14). With which he appears to
have trumped even the good abbé Bremond, the intrepid defender of
'nonsense' in poetry in the name of musical 'magic', who opined that
if 'Victor Hugo's storks came from Mulhouse and not from le Caystre,
one glorious stanza of the *Mages* would lose its brilliance'.[61] How that

59. Emil Staiger, *Grudbegriffe der Poetik*, Zürich 1951, p. 13. Cf. George Santayana,
The Sense of Beauty, New York 1955, pp. 167–8.

60. Cf. B. Tecchi, in his translation and commentary to Goethe's poems (Bari
1949), where even the assonance of two diphthongs and the contiguous rhyme
Walde and *balde* are summoned to support the conclusion that every sound effect
'helps to give an impression of solitude, peace, and "stillness" '.

61. Bremond, op. cit., p. 20.

compliment would have delighted the poet of *Booz endormi*, for which he did not hesitate to invent the city of 'Jérimadeth' for reasons of euphony!

Similar examples could be drawn from commentaries on Leopardi. De Robertis, for example, in his edition of the *Canti* already cited, assays a couple of samples of a 'musical appreciation of *L'infinito*: "Sempre caro mi fu" (Always dear to me was): *fu*: the stress of the line gives the word an unexpectedly vague idea of distance . . . ; "E le morte stagioni" (And the dead seasons): better than if he had inverted noun and adjective and said "e le stagioni morte". Both sound and sense are more fragile, more remote'. We need not be detained by Tennyson, a conscious seeker of delicate onomatopoeic effects, as in:

> The moan of doves in immemorial elms,
> And murmuring of innumerable bees

– effects which enchanted the Victorian aesthetes. It is scarcely necessary either to recall Poe, the deliberate creator and theorizer of musical atmosphere in 'waves' of metre (think of *The Raven* and *Ulalume*), 'guaranteed permanent', to quote the pitiless judgement of Aldous Huxley, 'like those of the best hairdressers'.[62] But mention of Poe may remind us of the remarks of his tormented musical translator, Mallarmé, who was undoubtedly measuring himself against Poe first and foremost when he wrote regretfully that 'speech fails in expressing objects by corresponding touches of colouring and rhythm, though these exist in the instrument of the voice, amid languages . . .'.[63] We can conclude this 'musical' review of literature with the recent critical comment of Dámaso Alonso on Góngora's line in the *Fábula de Polifemo y Galatea*

> infame turba de nocturnas aves

> (vile swarm of birds of night):

the poet *also* gives us a 'phonetic image of darkness' which is produced by the two *tur* syllables, the fourth and eighth of the line, its use in

62. Aldous Huxley, 'Vulgarity in Literature', in *Music at Night and Other Essays*, London 1949, p. 300.
63. Mallarmé, quoted in Guy Delfel, *L'Esthétique de Stéphane Mallarmé*, Paris 1951, p. 145.

the eighth syllable 'repeating and intensifying the sensation of the fourth.'[64]

The linguistic arguments against this age-old manner of literary judgement (already Dionysus of Halicarnassus had been struck by how the sound of Homer's verses may give an idea of corporal bulk) may be summed up, firstly, in the demonstration by Saussure and the glossematicians of the purely 'functional' character of the phoneme-ceneme as a planar and interplanar 'relation'; and secondly, in Saussure's equally modern demonstration of the arbitrary nature of the link between the signifier or phonetic element and the signified, and the lack of motivation of the linguistic sign as a whole. From the latter it follows that even onomatopoeias are in reality an (entirely marginal) element of the system of conventional signs which constitute a language.[65] Thus, Saussure's observation that the idea of *soeur*, for example, is not connected by any internal relation to the sequence of sounds *s–ö–r* which serve as its signifier, and that this idea could as well be represented by any other sequence of sounds, has the value of one proof among countless others of a discovery which, as we have seen, is 'first principle' of linguistics as a science. We know too that a complete theorization of the subversion of the internal economy of the sign that would be involved in its reduction to an expressive musical value could only be accomplished by a unilateral linguistics of *la parole*, as pre-eminently spiritual or creative–subjective energy, not true *ergon*. From such a romantic and idealist linguistics was born the myth not only of form-as-image but also of form-as-image-sound which was to become the idol of generations of decadentist aesthetics. That myth was to lend authority to every fantasy and caprice of impressionistic criticism, all of which amount in effect to a *sensuous dissipation* of the rational-concrete rigour of poetry as polysemic discourse.

But let us spend a little longer over these aesthetic arguments

64. Dámaso Alonso, *Poesia española*, Madrid 1952, pp. 328 ff. (Not to be confused with Amado Alonso.)

65. By way of contrast, consider the Romantic linguistics of *parole* developed by Humboldt. Believing it legitimate to assert the existence of a 'symbolic character of grammatical sounds', he maintained for example that the phonetic group *st* designates the impression of lastingness and stability, the sound *l* that of fluidity, the sound *v* that of uneven and oscillating movement, and so on. One thus has the *phonetic* expression of certain *feelings*.

against traditional taste. Grounded as they are on scientific linguistics, therefore a rigorous general semiotics, they are of a dual nature. On the one hand, they are based on the linguistic-literary fact in itself, and on the other, on a comparison between the literary fact and the musical fact and their respective semiotics.

Taking the first aspect, the following observations should be made against the more refined supporters of euphony in poetry, and their conviction that it is the phonetic image which brings the overall poetic value of the text to full realization. (1) Their attempts to distinguish in terms of aesthetic values between a simple onomatopoeic effect and other more complex and delicate sound effects are as vain as they are subtle from the linguistic–aesthetic, epistemological point of view (and this is the only one that counts, at least in philosophy). A case in point are the lines already quoted from Tennyson. Brooks and Warren tell us that they contain onomatopoeia proper, that is the sound of a word simply imitating a real sound. Whereas, according to the same critics, in Keats's

> Mid hushed, cool-rooted flowers fragrant-eyed,

we have a 'suggestion of coolness and repose' brought about by the 'hovering accent on the foot *cool-root-*' and by the 'length and sonority of the vowels repeated in the foot' and also by the 'accented word *hushed* just preceding'. This suggestion, naturally enough, is conveyed in the first instance by the 'literal meaning' of the words themselves, which is then supposedly reinforced and underlined by the sound in an integration of phonetic images and images of 'meaning'.[66] But the attempted distinction does not hold, because even in the case of Tennyson's onomatopoeic *moan*, the same critics state that 'if . . . the line were not introduced by the specific meaning of *moan* it is highly improbable that anyone would discover onomatopoeia in the line'. So onomatopoeia and other sound or musical effects are equal in their presumed integrative aesthetic function, and both are equally indicative of epistemological confusion, error and romantic aesthetic projection.

(2) Equally nugatory is the attempt made by Dámaso Alonso[67] to reconcile Saussure's discovery of the arbitrary nature of the linguistic

66. Brooks and Warren, op. cit., pp. 136–7.
67. D. Alonso, op. cit., p. 601.

sign on the one hand ('we believe with Saussure that... there is nothing that links the signifier to the thing signified'), with the thesis that the speaker's sense of motivation behind the signifier should nevertheless be taken into account. This sense, according to Alonso, 'might be an illusion', but even so it is still 'a very real fact of language' which should be borne in mind (wrong: if anything, it is a fact of traditional linguistics and poetics). An eclectic mélange of different poetics and linguistics, Alonso's attempted reconciliation has no chance of success. In particular, it confuses a modern scientific linguistics with a poetics and a rhetoric that are tied to a superseded, pre-scientific linguistics (romantic, in this respect). In fact, in the end Alonso cannot help seriously contradicting himself: withdrawing from scientific linguistics the authority which he had granted it, he accuses it of a 'sad shortsightedness', because it is only able to regard language as 'conventional' (the persistent nostalgia for language as metaphysical *energeia*, and hence *parole-langue* as pure subjective, 'spiritual' 'creation'). In any case, with its apologetic defence of that wholly subjective feeling of the speaker (about the motivation of the signifying *phoneme*), Alonso's position is less advanced even than that of Dr Johnson in the 18th century when he pointed out that: 'There is nothing in the art of versifying so much exposed to the power of imagination as the accommodation of the sound to the sense' and that: 'It is scarcely to be doubted that on many occasions we make the music that we imagine ourselves to hear, that we modulate the poem by our own disposition, and ascribe to the numbers the effects of the sense'.[68] Less advanced too than that of Mallarmé – to take an example of the very opposite type of poetics to the rationalism of Johnson: the Mallarmé we have seen above, with his extreme worry, despite his prodigious mastery of language, about the 'failing', the inadequacy of speech to express objects with the musical touches he desired; whence his very significant conclusion: 'Next to the opaqueness of *ombre*, *ténèbres* gives little sense of darkness; what disappointment at the perversity which confers on *jour* and *nuit* contradictory timbres that are dark and light!'

Turning now to the second aspect of the argument against traditional taste, suffice it to note: (1) that, since the so-called 'melody' of a line of poetry is made up simply of vocal timbres and these,

68. Samuel Johnson, *The Rambler* 92, quoted in Empson, op. cit., p. 15.

because they are not arranged in a scale, are irrational, do not have intervals, it is neither melody nor harmony in any proper sense; for even when there is a clear, perceptible and euphonious phonetic ensemble, this ensemble of timbres is a kind of unison and is not proper harmony. (2) Consequently, even poetic 'rhythm', lacking as it does rational and mathematical rigour, and not being subject to metrical law, is not properly rhythm in the musical sense – indeed, the only distinction which it tolerates is the vague, empirical, one of 'lively' and 'slow'. (3) Since poetry is essentially a verbal, linguistic fact, what is called rhythm in it can in effect only be, as phonic measure, a sort of *auxiliary signifier*. Thus, poetic 'rhythm' is difficult to distinguish from the meaning which it serves. In fact there is a sharp antithesis between the unity of the verbal phrase, which consists in and for the meaning and transcends the sounds, and the unity of the musical phrase, which consists in the sounds. That is why, as has often been noticed, there is something jarring about regularly stressed speech. For it gives as much emphasis to what is not logically important as to what is and forces our attention onto the insignificant.

Behind the 'musicalization' of poetry there lies an unwarranted conversion of mere analogies into identity. We may conclude with the hope that we shall soon be rid of this as of every other kind of extraneous or extra-aesthetic gratification. When this hedonism takes on the paradoxical character of linguistic and rhetorical hedonism, it is perhaps the most serious obstacle to the satisfactory understanding of poetry and literature. Even when it is not bent on converting the means, language, into an end, it creates an upheaval of the internal economy of the linguistic sign so great as to cause a serious aesthetic unbalancing and obfuscation of literary taste. The great literary critics of all periods have been so in their *non*-'musical' analysis of poetry, and it is in this and because of this alone that their heritage survives. Perhaps the most eloquent documents of this obfuscation of taste, which varies from one literary period to another, are translations and their traditional modes and rules.

16. *Translatability*

The following statement by Goethe seems to us most opportune as a way of passing from the question of sound to that of the translatability of poetry: 'I honour rhythm, through which poetry first becomes poetry, as I honour rhyme, but what is truly efficacious [*Wirksame*], deeply and firmly so, what really shapes and stimulates us, is what remains of the poet when he is translated into prose. What is then left is the pure and perfect content, which a dazzling exterior [*ein blendendes Äussere*] can often deceive us into imagining is there when it is not, and conceal from us when it is'.[69] Goethe's 'pure and perfect content' (*der reine vollkommene Gehalt*) may be taken, if the reader will allow, as a kind of anticipation of the *formed content* which for us is poetic *form*: poetic form regarded as thought or concrete discourse or logical-intuitive synthesis in the same way as every other value – limiting ourselves for the moment to the general epistemological aspect of poetry, in abstraction from its semantically specific aspect. His deceptively 'dazzling exterior' on the other hand – what for not only the neo-classical but above all the romantic and decadentist traditions was the essential, 'rhythmical' or 'musical' aspect of form, and at times indeed 'form' itself in all its fullness – this formulation may well assist us to isolate the fallacy of regarding rhythm and sound in general as 'integrative' and coessential elements of poetry. Rhythm and sound are in reality external and instrumental elements; they belong to the order of the signifier and are therefore accidental and liable to change when the poetic text is turned from one semantic system to another, i.e. when it is translated. The criterion of translation therefore can only be that of *fidelity* to the *poetic letter*. Fidelity to the letter, once it is demonstrated that the literal itself is in its expressive and semantic texture a rigorous historical product, becomes *eo ipso* fidelity to the objective, as well as subjective, spirit of the poetic text. The necessary limitations on fidelity are to be found, not in the romantic, idealist and subjectivist principle whereby 'we translate well only when we translate for ourselves, in the same way as it is only for ourselves that we write poetry',[70] but purely and simply in the particular characteristics of the languages from which and into which one is doing the translation: for example, the characteristic use in Greek of anacoluthon which is not found in English, or the dominance of hypotaxis over parataxis in the Romance languages or German as compared with English. But these characteristics are not such as to

69. Goethe, 'Übertragungen . . .', in *Werke* XV, Zurich 1953, p. 1085.
70. Cesare de Lollis, *Saggi sulla Forma Poetica Italiana*, Bari 1929, p. 276.

make it at all or absolutely impossible to translate. For though poetry may seem to be imprisoned by them, it is not and cannot be, given the general principle that *thought* (the universal) remains the *end* and language is always the means (*a* means, to be exact). So that poetry worthy of the name is always translatable – even if the translation of poetry is one of the most difficult and daunting, although meritorious, of undertakings. And since poetry is translatable only in the sense divined by Goethe – and that is, by virtue of that *syntactic*, discursive, 'prosaic' order which alone corresponds to the nature of poetry as discourse, albeit polysemic discourse – what in the end remains as untranslatable or 'ineffable' is not the poem itself (the traditional mysticizing conclusion of romantic aesthetics and linguistics) but its euphony; and this perforce cannot have any exact equivalent precisely because it depends on the phonetic plane, that of the *signifier*, which is arbitrary and accidental, and therefore changes from one semantic system to another. Now this is not to deny the pleasures, which in their own way may be exquisite and enviable, of the translator-musician who is by principle one who translates only 'for himself' and uses the text to be translated as poetic material of his own; nor is it to deny the similar kinds of pleasure of the reader-musician. All we are saying is that these pleasures are not properly of a strictly artistic order, in that they are not of a genuine *literary*-aesthetic order. They remain ambiguous and neutral, somewhere between literary experience and musical experience: para-literary, para-artistic, and perhaps even extra-artistic since they lie outside both literature and music.

But let us now sample a few of the most admired versions of poetry 'i npoetry', whose 'beauty' (according to the romantic and decadentist canon) is attributed to their 'infidelity'. We shall find, on the contrary, that when they are really beautiful, that beauty is attributable to their fidelity to the polysemic character of the original text, *in spite of* their 'success' in finding the 'right' rhythm. Even when the rhythm comes off, there is always still a lot of padding and filling-in of various sorts that needs to be eliminated. We shall find that when they are ugly (often not just in relation to the original), that ugliness is attributable to their 'brilliant', fearless infidelity to the original polysemic discourse.

We shall start with the translation of *Faust* by Nerval which was so dear to Goethe's authorial vanity.[71] It is enough to compare the opening lines of Nerval's version of the 'Dedication' with those of the original, one of Goethe's finest lyrics:

Venez, illusions!... au matin de ma vie,
Que j'aimais à fixer votre inconstant essor!

(Ihr naht euch wider, schwankende Gestalten,
Die früh sich einst dem trüben Blick gezeigt)

Le soir vient, et pourtant c'est une douce envie,
C'est une vanité qui me séduit encor.

(Versuch ich wohl, euch diesmal festzuhalten?
Fühl ich mein Herz noch jenem Wahn geneigt?)

Rapprochez-vous!... c'est bien; tout s'anime et se presse
Au-dessus des brouillards, dans un monde plus grand,
Mon coeur, qui rajeunit, aspire avec ivresse
Le souffle de magie autour de vous errant.

(Ihr drängt euch zu! nun gut, so mögt ihr walten,
Wie ihr aus Dunst und Nebel um mich steigt;
Mein Busen fühlt sich jugendlich erschüttert
Vom Zauberhauch, der euren Zug umwittert).

[Ye wavering phantoms, yet again my leisure
Ye haunt, as erst ye met my troubled gaze.
Still doth mine heart the old illusion treasure?
Now shall I fix the dream that round me plays?
Ye throng upon me! Nay then, have your pleasure,
Ye that around me rise from mist and haze!
My bosom by the magic breath is shaken,
That breathing round your train, old dreams doth waken.]

Des beaux jours écoulés j'aperçois les images,
Et mainte ombre chérie a descendu des cieux;

---

71. Nerval's translation (1828) in Goethe, *Théâtre*, Paris 1942, pp. 953–4. English version, tr. Albert Latham, ed. cit., pp. 9–10.

(Ihr bringt mit euch die Bilder froher Tage,
Und manche liebe Schatten steigen auf;)

[Dreams of glad days ye bring; and well-loved faces,
Dim shades of well-loved faces greet mine eyes.]

Compare the ending:

De mes jours d'autrefois renaissent tous les charmes,
Et ce qui disparut pour moi revit ici.

(Was ich besitze, seh ich wie im Weiten,
Und was verschwand, wird mir zu Wirklichkeiten.)

[All that I have, now far away seems banished,
All real grown, that long ago had vanished.]

This comparison is enough to show how Goethe's lofty and severe
pathos has become in Nerval's 'poetic' version a kind of musical-
comedy sentimentality (in which, apart from anything else, it would
be difficult to recognize the far from banal poet of *El Desdichado*:
'Rends-moi le Pausilippe et la mer d'Italie').[72]

A real miracle of fidelity by comparison, a gamble that paid off, is
Longfellow's 'poetic' version of Goethe's second *Wanderer's Nightsong*,
cited above, even if the gamble is paid for by the padding in the last
line but one ('like these'):

O'er all the hill-tops
Is quiet now,
In all the tree-tops
Hearest thou
Hardly a breath;
The birds are asleep in the trees.
Wait; soon like these
Thou too shalt rest.

Über allen Gipfeln
Ist Ruh,
In allen Wipfeln

72. *The Penguin Book of French Verse*, cit., pp. 96–97.

Spürest du
Kaum einen Hauch;
Die Vögelein schweigen im Walde,
Warte nur, balde
Ruhest du auch.[73]

Again pure chance, another miracle, is Stefan George's 'poetic' version of the second quatrain of Shakespeare's Sonnet 99, where the translator has managed to respect the polysemic character of the original with a sort of 'logical interlinear version' (Hennecke) without sacrificing either rhythm or rhyme and practically without padding:

Die lilie klagt ich an um deine hand,
Die mairan-knopse, die dein haar bestahl –
Und *manche* rose bang am dorne stand,
Die rote scham, und jene weisse qual.

(The lily I condemned for thy hand,
And buds of marjoram had stol'n thy hair:
The roses fearfully on thorns did stand,
One blushing shame, another white despair;)[74]

Schlegel's 'poetic' translation of *Macbeth* (not to mention his *Hamlet*) is often a marvel as well, a typical exception. Karl Kraus, incidentally, draws an instructive comparison in *Die Sprache* between Schlegel's translation and the version by Gundolf, arguing that while the latter, for all its 'poeticness', is 'banal' and hence unfaithful because of its pretentious and clumsy 'completeness', Schlegel's often succeeds because of its 'fidelity of thought'.[75]

Turning now to translations of Italian classics, we shall limit ourselves to a very few cases which are exemplary from the point of view of the prose-method which we have argued should be adopted: a

73. Henry W. Longfellow, *The Poetical Works*, 'Albion' Edition, London and New York, n.d., p. 595. Hans Hennecke's comments on this version in his *Dichtung und Dasein*, Berlin 1950, pp. 7 ff. are aberrant: ignoring the problem of padding, he regrets that Longfellow, because of the limitations of the English language, was unable to render the subtle interplay of rhyme and rhythm or the two feminine rhymes *Walde–balde* of the original, while at the same time waxing lyrical at the 'dazzling light' of the 'vowels depicting hell' in Dryden's line, famous as a moral representation: 'And all the sad variety of hell'.

74. Stefan George, *Werke*, vol. XII, Berlin 1931.

75. Karl Kraus, *Die Sprache*, Munich 1954, pp. 200, 167.

method rigorously in function of the polysemic meaning, and hence of the order and unity of the original thought-image. Most of these translations too are by practising poets, and their mistakes are certainly no less interesting and instructive than their chance successes – chances, however, which are only given to translators who are true poets.

Cino da Pistoia translated by Rilke, sonnet CXXIII[76]:

> Den seligen Berg, den hohn erstieg ich, ach,
> anbetend heiligen Fels mit meinen Küssen
>
> (Io fui 'n su l'alto e 'n sul beato monte,
> ch'i' adorai baciando il santo sasso)
>
> [I was upon the height and on the blessed mount,
> and kissed the holy rock in adoration].

Here it may be noted that if metrical reasons, extraneous to the course of the thought-image of the original, had not induced the translator-poet to invert and alter the sense of Cino's representation of the appearance of the mount (in effect 'Den seligen Berg, den hohn' inverts the original order of the images of the mount which, with the naive naturalness of classical poetry, proceed from the physical to the moral), the translation of these first two lines of the sonnet would have been perfect for precision and tone. This is confirmed indirectly if, leaving out the intervening lines which are spoiled by padding and even errors of meaning, we go on to the end of the poem. Apart from one slip (the proper name of a woman, Selvaggia, translated as 'Wildnis', wilderness), the translation does extraordinary justice to the original:

> Doch da mein Herr das Flehen nicht begriff,
> so brach ich auf nach Wildnissen schreiend
> und zog durch das Gebirg mit Laut von Schmerz.
>
> Ma poi che non m'intese 'l mio Signore,
> mi dipartii, pur chiamando Selvaggia;
> l'alpe passai con voce di dolore.

76. R. M. Rilke, in *Insel Almanach* 1954–5, Leipzig.

F

[But since my Lord [Love] heard me not,
I departed, still crying Selvaggia;
I crossed the mountain with a voice of grief.]

We are forced to the conclusion, in spite of this happy but chance 'poetic' result, or rather indeed because of it, that Rilke could have given us a wholly perfect translation of the sonnet if he had chosen – or been able – to give us a translation in prose. In passing, we might notice how Rilke's substitution, as usual for metrical reasons, of the semi-colon at the end of the penultimate line of the original by an 'und' ('and') at the beginning of the last line alters the rhythm of Cino's thought, by suppressing a logical and emotional pause which in the original signified that sense of rupture and disjointedness in the expression of true grief which the Italian poet successfully sought. Rather better is Rilke's rendering of the close of another of Cino's sonnets (CIX):

Hofhalten wollt ich mitten unter Klagen
und alle töten, die ich immer töte
in meinem wilden Denken an den Tod.

e far mi piacería di pianto corte,
e tutti quelli ammazzar ch'io ammazzo
nel fier pensier là dov'io trovo morte

[and I should wish to found a court of tears,
and kill all those I kill
in my wild thoughts where I find death.]

The 'poetic' versions of *I' vegno il giorno a te infinite volte* and *In un boschetto trova' pasturella* and other poems by Cavalcanti given us by Pound, Vossler and Hasslinger are inferior by comparison. The best are those of the poet Pound, for example:

In wood-way found I once a shepherdess,
More fair than stars are was she to my seeming

In un boschetto trova' pasturella
più che la stella bella al mi' parere.[77]

77. *The Translations of Ezra Pound*, London 1953, p. 117.

To revert to Rilke, his version of Leopardi's *L'Infinito* is on the whole superior – not merely in literary quality – to his previous translations:

Immer lieb war mir dieser einsame
Hügel und *das Gehölz*, das fast ringsum,
ausschliesst vom *fernen Aufruhn der Himmel*
den Blick. Sitzend und schauend bild ich unendliche
Räume jenseits mir und mehr als
menschliches Schweigen und Ruhe vom *Grunde der Ruh.*
Und über ein kleines *geht* mein Herz *ganz ohne
Furcht* damit *um.* Und wenn in dem Buschwerk
aufrauscht der Wind, so überkommt es mich, dass ich
dieses Lautsein vergleiche mit jener endlosen Stillheit.
Und mir fällt das Ewige ein
und daneben die *alten* Jahreszeiten und diese
daseiende Zeit, die lebendige, tönende. Also
sinkt der Gedanke mir weg ins Übermass. *Unter-
gehen in diesem Meer ist inniger Schiffbruch.*

Sempre caro mi fu quest' ermo colle,
E questa siepe, che da tanta parte
Dell' ultimo orizzonte il guardo esclude.
Ma sedendo e mirando, interminati
Spazi di là da quella, e sovrumani
Silenzi, e profondissima quiete
Io nel pensier mi fingo; ove per poco
Il cor non si spaura. E come il vento
Odo stormir tra queste piante, io quello
Infinito silenzio a questa voce
Vo comparando: e mi sovvien l'eterno,
E le morte stagioni, e la presente
E viva, e il suon di lei. Così tra questa
Immensità s'annega il pensier mio:
E il naufragar m'è dolce in questo mare.[78]

By way of contrast let us recall Sainte-Beuve's version composed in French alexandrines, whose poverty is not to be blamed entirely on

78. Rilke, in *Werke*, vol. I, Leipzig 1957, p. 379. An English version is given below, p. 164.

a metre which (as Maurois said) gives no idea of the 'rapid, airy rhythm' of the original:

> J'aimais toujours ce point de colline déserte,
> Avec sa haie au bord, qui clôt la vue ouverte
> Et m'empêche d'atteindre à l'extrême horizon.
> . . .
> Le grand âge éternel m'apparaît, avec lui,
> Tant de mortes saisons, et celle d'aujourd'hui,
> Vague écho. Ma pensée ainsi plonge à la nage,
> Et sur ces mers sans fin j'aime jusqu'au naufrage.

On the other hand, the results obtained by John Heath-Stubbs and also by Kenneth Rexroth are already sufficient to let us suppose that someone could draw on their 'poetic' versions for a really good one in prose. I give Heath-Stubbs' translation with lines from Rexroth's intercalated:

> This lonely hill was always dear to me,
> And this hedgerow, that hides so large a part
> Of the far sky-line from my view.
>   [K.R.: which shuts out most of the final Horizon from view.]
>   Sitting and gazing,
> I fashion in my mind what lie beyond –
> Unearthly silences, and endless space,
> And very deepest quiet; then for a while
> The heart is not afraid. And when I hear
> The wind come blustering among the trees
> I set that voice against this infinite silence:
> And then I call to mind Eternity,
> The ages that are dead, and the living present
> And all the noise of it. And thus it is
> In that immensity my thought is drowned:
> And sweet to me the foundering in that sea.
>   [K.R.: And my thought drowns in immensity:
>   And shipwreck is sweet in such a sea.][79]

79. John Heath-Stubbs, now in Giacomo Leopardi, *Selected Prose and Poetry*, edited by Iris Origo and John Heath-Stubbs, New York, Toronto and London 1967; Kenneth Rexroth, in *A Little Treasury of World Poetry*, edited by H. Creekmore, New

In the case of Dante, the great testing-ground, it so happens that the modern aesthetic awareness of the external or extra-artistic character of the poet's medieval conviction of the 'symbolic' importance of *terza rima*, an insuperable obstacle to every translator, combined with the existence of valid prose-translations of the *Comedy*, have made the task of his translators a good deal easier. So to a certain extent the case of Dante can be seen as stimulant and normative for a critical, anti-aestheticist, modern manner of translation – one that seeks to capture and render what is essential in the poetry, its polysemic nature, in other words a thought-image in a certain mode of language that is the organic-contextual or style. As far as English translations of the *Comedy* are concerned, let just this one typical example suffice to show the different economy of 'poetic' and prose versions. *Inferno* XXVII, 61–63

> S'i' credesse che mia risposta fosse
> a persona che mai tornasse al mondo,
> questa fiamma starìa sanza piu scosse;

Binyon (so highly-praised):

> If I believed that my reply were made
> To one who could revisit earth, this flame
> Would be at rest, and its commotion laid

Sinclair:

> If I thought my answer were to one who
> would return to the world, this flame
> should stay without another movement.[80]

In the case of Ariosto's *Orlando furioso*, simply compare Sir John Harrington's classic English verse-translation with the recent prose-version by Allan Gilbert; the passage is from canto XXXVI, 69. Harrington:

> Four horses fierce, as red as flamming fire,
> Th' Apostle doth into the charret set,

York 1952. [Heath-Stubbs's version includes a mistranslation of the lines: 'ove per poco/Il cor non si spaura', which, rather than 'then for a while/The heart is not afraid', means literally 'at which the heart almost is afraid'. – *Tr. note*.]

80. *Dante's Inferno*, with a translation into English triple rhyme by Lawrence Binyon, London 1933. Sinclair ed. cit.

Which when he framed had to his desire,
Astolfo in the carre by him he set.
Then up they went, and still ascending hyer
Above the firie region they did get
Whose nature so th' Apostle then did turne,
That though they went through fire they did not burne.

Gilbert:

Four horses much redder than flame were fastened to the yoke
by the holy Evangelist, and after he seated himself with Astolfo
and took the reins, he drove them toward the sky. The chariot
circled about, rose through the air, and came quickly into the
middle of the everlasting fire, on which the old man acted mira-
culously so that while they went through it was not burning.[81]

It is obvious that it is even less possible to derogate from the norm
of prose-translation in the case of the Greek and Latin classics than in
that of other great poetry – notwithstanding the particular difficulties
of its application (so imagine the difficulties of any contrary norm) in
the rendition of a thought-language which is so distant from our own.

Modern experience and translation theory bear out our general
statement. Goethe's own straightforward line-by-line translation of
Odyssey X, ll. 81 ff. is very much superior to the corresponding passage
in the celebrated version in German hexameters by Voss, though in
the latter, according to Goethe himself, there remained 'a trace of the
true sense' or thought of the original because it was 'closer to the
text' than the 'completely false' translation by the poet Bodmer. In
fact, comparing Voss's and Goethe's versions, we can see that Goethe's
is much more faithful to the concentrated representation of the
original, more so indeed than the recent translation, also in prose, by
Bérard: '. . . où *l'on voit* le berger appeler le berger', etc.[82] In England,
Arnold was a severe critic, notwithstanding their fame, of the translations of Homer in metre and rhyme by Chapman and Pope (the
latter version in particular not without its peculiar gifts), on the
grounds of their rhetorical-Elizabethan and Augustan deformation of

81. *Orlando Furioso*, translated into English heroical verse by Sir John Harrington
(1591), edited with an introduction by Robert McNulty, Oxford 1972, p. 395;
Orlando Furioso, an English translation by Allan Gilbert, New York 1954.
82. Goethe and *The Odyssey: Schriften zur Literatur*, ed. cit., pp. 603–5.

Homer's thought and style. Compare, for example, the original with Pope's translation of Sarpendon's speech in *Iliad* XII, ll. 322 ff., which in other respects is one of Pope's most brilliant literary achievements:

Could all our care elude the gloomy grave
Which claims no less the fearful than the brave,
For lust of fame I should not vainly dare
In fighting fields, nor urge thy soul to war:
But since, alas! ignoble age must come,
Disease, and Death's inexorable doom;
The life which others pay, let us bestow,
And give to fame what we to nature owe;

or see his rendition of Priam's speech of desperation to Hector. Similarly, Arnold warned Ruskin not to transpose 'modern sentiment' and 'sentimentality' into the ancients, à propos of *Iliad* III, 243–4:

'So said she [Helen]; but they [her brothers Castor and Pollux] ere now were fast holden of the life-giving earth there in Lacedaemon, in their dear native land',

which Ruskin's 'tender pantheism' interpreted as though Homer had called the earth *physizoos*, 'giver of life', in order to temper and reconcile the negation and pain of that death, of death itself.[83]

This modern experience and theory – we might add finally Eliot's merciless critique of the 'poetic' version of Euripides à la Swinburne and William Morris, perpetrated by Gilbert Murray[84] – authorizes us to bring our critical focus to bear on the following extreme and typical negative cases of translation from the Greek and Latin classics:
(a) Antigone, in what is certainly the most poetic of all translations of Sophocles, that of Hölderlin, says 'my Zeus' ('Mein Zeus': l. 450), which is a Christianization of Jove and the evidence of a contamination, wholly at the expense of Sophocles, of ancient and modern, Greek and romantic. Schadewalt, who discovered it (along with a number of other errors of the same kind), calls it a 'creative error',[85]

---

83. Matthew Arnold, 'On translating Homer' in *On the Classical Tradition*, ed. R. H. Super, Ann Arbor 1960, pp. 101–2 (and see Lionel Trilling, *The Portable Matthew Arnold*, New York 1956). Homer, *The Iliad*, ed. cit.
84. Eliot, *Selected Essays*, London 1951, especially pp. 59 ff.
85. Wolfgang Schadewalt, *Sophokles: Tragödien*, Frankfurt-am-Main 1957, p. 90.

which it is, but one which has no place except in a work that is itself strictly creative, in which case it would no longer be an error. An instance is the magnificent profession of romantic faith lent to Panthea in Hölderlin's own tragedy *Empedokles*:

> O eternal mystery! that which we are
> And for which we search we cannot find; and that which
> We find, we are not.

There could not be a better expression of the romantic, spiritualist dialectic of finite and infinite.

(b) Virgil's famous line:

> sunt lachrymae rerum, et mentem mortalia tangunt

(*Aeneid* I, l. 462), is still sometimes misunderstood as 'the tears of nature [or: of things] and the mortal sadness of humanity', instead of the proper translation: 'tears are shed for misfortune and mortal fate moves human minds to pity'. The misunderstanding arises because of a sort of 'secondary grafting' of meanings or a 'palimpsest superimposed on the original text' (as Spitzer has observed against Entwistle):[86] meaning a modern, romanticizing, deformation of the original in the direction of *Weltschmerz*. Compare the habit of translating 'uita', life or vital breath, in the last line of the *Aeneid* by 'âme' (Bellessort), 'spirit' (C. Day Lewis), 'Geist' (Schröder), to name only the most recent, with the one exception that I know of, Mackail, who in his by now classic prose-version of Virgil gets it right: 'life'.[87] Of the well-known misfortunes of Horace, just one example from the recent highly-praised 'poetic' version by Leishman of the *Odes* may suffice: *Diffugere nives*, l. 16: 'linger as shadow and dust' for 'pulvis et umbra sumus'.[88]

There remain just a few observations to make in conclusion. We have already enunciated the criterion of *literal fidelity*, which is at the same time *fidelity to the spirit* of the original text. With this criterion, I might add, we may be in a position to refine and develop Leopardi's well-known dictum that 'a translation is perfect when the author

86. Leo Spitzer, *Critica Stilistica e Storia del Linguaggio*, Bari 1954, pp. 156–8.
87. A. Bellesort, *Enéide*, Paris 1952; Cecil Day Lewis, *The Aeneid of Virgil*, London 1954 (and for curiosity's sake, see R. G. Austin, *Some English Translations of Virgil*, Liverpool 1956); C. Schröder, *Vergils Aeneis*, Berlin and Frankfurt-am-Main 1952; J. W. Mackail, *Virgil's Works*, New York 1950.
88. J. B. Leishman, *Translating Horace*, Oxford 1956.

translated is not, for example, Greek in Italian, or Greek or French in German, but *the same* in Italian or German *as* he is in Greek or French'. Now the limitation of this criterion is of course not any difficulty of a spiritualist or subjectivist, or a romantic or mystical-aesthetic kind. It is rather – apart from the fact that 'if one is not a poet one cannot translate a true poet' as Leopardi remarks and the efforts of George and Rilke confirm – to be found in characteristics peculiar to the languages from which and into which a translation is made. Indeed, Leopardi himself, having defined the criterion of perfection quoted above, immediately added: 'that is what is difficult to accomplish, and it *is not possible in all languages'*.[89] Given at once the criterion and the limit on it, it is worth while spending a little time on this particular difficulty.

For it is connected essentially with the *linguistic value* of the word, bearing in mind Saussure's warning not to confuse the *meaning* of a word with its value in the system. This injunction, as we have seen, applies not only to words, but also to grammatical entities and therefore to syntax. It follows that the normative presence of syntactical categories such as parataxis and hypotaxis can decisively prejudice the satisfactory expressive and aesthetic rendition of poetic representations when they are transferred from one language in which parataxis dominates or prevails to another in which hypotaxis is more at home.

This has been demonstrated in a recent study by Wandruszka of the prose of one of Hemingway's novels (and what is valid in the case of 'prose' will be even more so in that of 'lyric poetry', where the syntax of the polysemic is all the more delicate).[90] So when for example the original paratactic English: 'Then he leaned over the side *and* washed the flying fish' is rendered by the French translator as 'Il se pencha, *afin* de laver les poissons volants dans la mer', there is no denying that 'the simple clarity of the separate movements of body and hands is weakened by the introduction of a *subordinate clause* of purpose'. When the parataxis is complicated by differentiations in the verb such as periphrasis combined with participial construction, as in ' "Yes", the old man said. He *was holding* his glass and *thinking* of many years ago', it

---

89. Leopardi, *Zibaldone* 2134–5, in *Tutte le Opere*, a cura di W. Binni e E. Ghidetti, vol. II, Florence 1969, p. 564, and ibid., vol. I, p. 434.

90. Mario Wandruszka, 'Parataxe in moderner Prosa', in *Syntactica und Stilistica*, Festschrift für E. Gamillscheg, Tübingen 1957, pp. 651 ff.

is equally undeniable that the corresponding version allowed by the German language, which reads: ' "Ja", sagte der alte Mann. Er *hielt* sein Glas in der Hand und *dachte* an lang vergangene Jahre', is 'flat and inexpressive' precisely as a rendering of the representation of 'what happened' – not only in comparison with the original English but also in comparison with the version that it is possible to achieve in Italian. ' "Sì", disse il vecchio. *Stava stringendo* il bocchiere fra le mani e *pensava* a tanti anni fa' – this rendering is highly satisfactory, with its past absolute 'disse' supplemented by what Wandruszka calls the almost palpable verbal periphrasis 'stava stringendo' and by the non-limitative imperfect of duration 'pensava'. Here we have a passage which, to use Leopardi's terms, is *the same* in Italian *as* it is in English.

Finally, these observations do not in principle stand in the way of the translatability of classical or authentic poetry in general, or poetry of the first rank (to which category Hemingway, who is sensuous and largely unreflective in his writing, certainly does not belong, while for example Proust, whose writing is eminently hypotactic, does). They do not present a theoretical obstacle, given the principle formulated above that the end is thought and language, or rather languages, are its means (one kind of means). A great writer dominates them to the point where he is no longer held prisoner by them, and so does not prejudice the transferability of his sovereign poetic, polysemic thought from the linguistic medium adopted by him into other, even very different, media. All this is facilitated in the last resort by the *arbitrary nature* and hence *indifference* of the linguistic sign in respect of the signified.

But it is not only, not even principally, that there is no theoretical obstacle. Practically and experimentally too, the difficulties can be overcome, as we see in the translatability of the *perfect content*, in Goethe's phrase, or *concrete form* not only of Homer or Sophocles or Pindar but also, for example, of Sappho. Her fragment, 'The moon and the Pleiades have set . . .' (if she is indeed its author) loses nothing of its essential poetic quality, however modest, either in an Italian prose translation or in a prose version, let us say, in German:

> Unter ging der Mond und die Plejaden, zur Mitte ist die Nacht, vorüber streicht die Stunde, ich aber liege allein.[91]

91. Nicolai Hartmann, op. cit., p. 176. On the problem of translation, see for the

We can now understand in a more reasonable sense Walter Benjamin's well-known but too simplistic saying that 'the interlinear version of the Scriptures is the prototype or ideal of all translation'.[92]

various points of view B. Terracini, *Conflitti di Lingue e di Cultura*, Venice 1957, pp. 49–121: 'Any citizen of his own language ... can rely without limitation on an evocative power of words which, according to Saussure, is based on mnemonic associations. ... This power of evocation is the linguistic element where the translator finds the greatest resistance ... it is here that we reach the insurmountable limit to perfect translation. ... By way of compensation, the translator can rely fully on what we might call the syntagmatic power of evocation of words, whose root lies in the expressive unity of the whole.' There is a strange oscillation here between the temptations to hedonism of the linguist at grips with the words of the language, and a less abstract, more concretely aesthetic, consideration of words in their syntagmatic relations, in the expressive unity of the whole or semantic organicity. The latter is what counts from the artistic point of view and that of the effective translatability of poetry.

See also the American miscellany, *On Translation*, edited by Reuben A. Brower, Harvard 1959 (with bibliography); William Merwin, in *The Kenyon Review* XVI (1954), pp. 497 ff. ('verse translations presuppose that they may be read in some sense as independent writings'); and Robert Lowell, ibid. XVII (1955), pp. 317 ff. (who ventures this splendid portrait of Dryden as translator of Ovid, which is valid for so many poet-translators of poetry: 'he is a smaller man caught between rapid *self-imitation* and *impressionistic* imitations of his originals').

92. Walter Benjamin, 'The task of the translator', in *Illuminations*, tr. Harry Zohn, London 1973, p. 82. Benjamin's linguistic naivety comes of course from his metaphysic of language, indeed is identical with his 'metaphysic of the name' – to use the formula of Renato Solmi in the favourable but interesting introduction to his excellent translation of the *Schriften* in *Angelus Novus*, Turin 1962. For this metaphysic, words are 'something other than signs', and 'through the name man's spiritual being communicates itself to God, for the "true" language is "pure" language' – a conception which, as Solmi rightly observes, echoes the romantic idea advanced by Hamann of an original presence of truth in language, one to be rediscovered in it. Compare Mallarmé quoted by Benjamin: 'The imperfection of languages consists in their plurality', ed. cit., p. 77, fn. The outcome in practice is the following exaltation of Hölderlin's translations of Sophocles on the basis of precisely those aspects which will lead any reader who respects Sophocles's poetry to condemn them: 'In them the *harmony* of the *languages* is so profound that *sense* is *touched* by language *only* the way an aeolian harp is touched by the wind. Hölderlin's translations are prototypes of their kind; they are to even the most perfect rendering of their texts as a prototype is to a model', p. 81. Once again, the criterion (here, a 'purified concept of language' or 'pure language') can be judged by its application, by its fruits or results. To forestall any misunderstanding, we quote in full Benjamin's metaphysical or simplistic argument for the exemplary character of the interlinear version of the scriptures (an exemplariness which we accept, but for opposite reasons to those of Benjamin, namely out of respect for the *sense* of the literal in general): 'Where a text is identical with truth or dogma, where it is supposed to be "the true language" in all its literalness and without the mediation of meaning, this text is unconditionally translatable. In such cases translations are called for only because of the plurality

of languages. Just as, in the original, language and revelation are one without any tension, so the translation must be one with the original in the form of the inter-linear version, in which literalness and freedom are united. For to some degree all great texts contain their potential translation between the lines; this is true to the highest degree of sacred writings. The interlinear version of the Scriptures is the prototype or ideal of all translations' (p. 82). The explanation is such that the metaphysical fantasy manages to obscure even the trivial truth (that it is easier to translate 'doctrinal' texts than poetic ones). But there we are: such is the fate of romantic mysticism, however sophisticated and brought up to date – a late romanticism, actually.

Laocoon 1960

The chief pried into every corner of the cabin, all parts of
which he viewed with some surprise; but it was not possible
to fix his attention to any one thing a single moment. The
works of art appeared to him in the same light as those of
nature, and were as far removed beyond his comprehension.

Captain Cook's *Voyages of discovery*, 1773.

17. The Semantic Dialectic

We shall bring our discussion of poetry and literature to a close. Our
analyses up to this point give us sufficient grounds for defining poetry
as *polysemic characteristic typicality*. Science in general, or prose, can be
defined as *univocal characteristic typicality*. Like that of poetry, we call the
typicality of science *characteristic* because it too is unity-of-a-manifold
or reason-and-sense. For, as we have seen above, and as the semantic
need for a thing-sublanguage demonstrates, the very 'abstractness' of
the physical sciences cannot be separated from a fundamental sense
of the *qualities* of the world and from repeated contact with them.

We shall see in due course that this definition of poetry will *not* do
as a blanket definition of all the other arts or art in general. But it does
in the meantime provide us with an implicit definition of the poetic
or literary symbol, whether it be literal or metaphorical in sense. The
poetic symbol is a polysemic concrete concept, as opposed to the
scientific symbol in general which is a univocal concrete concept. It
is worth reiterating that it is an illusion, or to be more exact an
epistemological error, to speak of 'universality' or 'truth' as belonging
'par excellence' to the scientific symbol. For our postulate of identity

between thought and speech or signs in general means that the universality and omni-laterality – hence truth – proper to the scientific and philosophical symbol depends on, and is indissociable from, indeed we may say it is synonymous with, its omni-contextuality and univocality – in other words its ineliminable semantic aspect. Therefore, the poetic symbol cannot be considered any less uni-versal or omni-lateral, or any less true, simply because its semantic aspect is not omni-contextuality, but organic contextuality. We have seen in fact that the poetic symbol is no less unity-of-a-manifold, or thought, than is the scientific symbol. Thus universality or omnilaterality, and hence truth, are as much proper to the poetic symbol as they are to the scientific symbol.

Therewith we find further confirmation of the concept of literary or poetic *abstraction*, as synonymous with poetic symbol, along with that of scientific abstraction, as synonymous with scientific symbol. Both these abstractions are *determinate*, for both are characteristic typicality or, which comes to the same thing, concrete concept or discourse. We have seen that the discursive nature of the determinate abstraction, whether literary or scientific, is so real and concrete as to be actually dialectical. For it represents a semantic-formal transcendence of the literal-material in two directions: in that of the polysemic (literary abstraction or poetic symbol), and in that of the univocal (scientific symbolic abstraction).

On this point, it is perhaps worth underlining once again the semantic-dialectical *switch* that occurs between the equivocal, omnitextual thought of the literal-material and the polysemic or univocal. That switch represents the enunciation of values in the form of speech (signs), which are a very different matter from our traditional and simplistic, 'pure' values or thoughts or metaphysical 'forms', absolute and absolutist. Such forms are incapable of any 'transmutation' into each other: they remain locked into hermetic compartments of experience, as the 'spiritual forms' of fantasy or logic have shown us. But speech-values – actual thoughts – circulate within each other naturally, because they have the same literal-material base. At the same time, however, their *specific differences* from one another are secured by virtue of their different semantic models: the polysemic and the univocal. These semantic models are indissociable from their corresponding values or thoughts exactly as means are from their ends, in the dialectic of ends and means which the identity between thought and speech or thought and sign has revealed itself as being.

It is not only in order to clarify the role of speech, or the sign in general, in both poetic (artistic) and scientific thought that we make this point. We are also interested, if we may put it this way, in a radical *emendatio* of idealist habits of mind. The idealists believe that they will be more firmly based in reality if they adhere to ends or values or forms that are 'pure' of all means or instrumentality or technique – in other words, if they adhere to hypostases, which are epistomologically without consistency and defective by definition. So we must try to accustom ourselves to the *epistemological import of the sign in general*. This is the only way we shall be able to explain rigorously, that is scientifically, the mobility and variety of reality-thought at the same time as its unity. Only thus can we distinguish a poetic metaphor from a historical fact or a physical or philosophical principle *without losing hold of what unites them*: reality-thought, the uni-versal.

For it is, as we know, undeniable that if metaphors as poetic genera or concepts are 'unreal', it is not in relation to reality or truth in general or *tout court*, but only in relation to scientific genera or concepts. Metaphors only become illegitimate if they are substituted for scientific concepts, with the result that two different orders of truth and reality are confused. The truth of the metaphor-concept 'adolescence the flower of our years' cannot take the place of the truth of a physiological or pedagogic concept of the age of maturation, and vice versa.

This being the case, it seems to us equally undeniable that the differential features of these two types of genera, the semantic organicity and necessity of the poetic genus, and the semantically disorganic scientific genus that is exempt from all semantic necessitation and fixity, enable us not to confuse the poetically credible with the historically or scientifically credible. While the former is defined and contained within the polysemic or 'stylistic' (not 'subjective'!) rigour which constitutes its semantic autonomy and its truth, the truth of the latter attains expression and definition only in the univocal rigour of its genera or concepts. What in fact constitutes the historically or scientifically credible is the semantic disorganicity and heteronomy of its concepts, those features which alone permit us a constant and repeated testing of them against the objectivity of the facts. But not only do they enable us to make this distinction. Since these differential features are not metaphysical, but semantic-epistemological, they also enable us to hold on to the *common nature* of the two kinds of genera or credibility: the fact that they are both reason or thought, that is, unity-of-a-manifold.

We have seen that semantic disorganicity and heteronomy, with its *open contexts*, is that kind of expressive articulation suited to the mind's vocation to experiment and documentation: those activities which characterize the appropriation of the reality and truth of things by science. The semantic-expressive component of thought which is suited to the appropriation of the reality and truth of things by poetry and art is the organic-contextual, with its autonomous or *closed* contexts. Now our analyses have already made plain that this semantic character must of itself expose the falsehood of the traditional, Aristotelian and idealist, preconception of the mere 'ideality' of poetic truth, as opposed to the 'factuality' of historical or scientific truth. For precisely the semantic dimension that is an indispensable component of poetic thought, lending it a real and scientifically verifiable character, renders poetic truth resistant to all metaphysical distinctions within thought itself – whether we call them hypostatic or abstract or absolutistic. Thought is always unity–multiplicity. At the same time the semantic character of poetic thought also effectively conceals it, directly or indirectly through its literal-material contents to what is called experience of the real or historicity in general. That connection of course is assured by a technique that differs from those of experiment and philosophical (-historical) argument – one that is semantically different as well. But our claim is borne out if we recollect that even the so-called 'free flights of fancy' of Pindar, Petrarch, Ariosto and Cervantes are artistic (have poetic value) insofar as they are credible because of the truth they express, and insofar as they are credible because they are *verifiable* by human experience, perhaps only indirectly or through contrast, but still verifiable. We must remember, in short, that the 'unreality' or 'ideality' of Pindar's hind (and Petrarch's) or Ariosto's hippogryph is not 'unreality' or 'ideality' in absolute terms. Each of these creatures has a well-defined and coherent sense, each of them is constituted by a rationale in the same way as any being in the real world. It is sufficient for this purpose that, however 'fantastic' they may be, they should not be Horace's human-head-on-a-horse's-neck. If they are 'unreal' or 'ideal', it is rather in the comparative sense in which metaphors and poetic symbols are 'unreal' genera only in relation to scientific genera and *their* reality and truth, not in relation to reality and truth in general.

The whole import of the semantic-epistemological or scientific sense of the autonomy of poetry should by now have been clarified. This autonomy is to be understood as technical (semantic, precisely). It is not to be taken as a metaphysical autonomy, or as the autonomy of a hypostasis, the hypostasis of Art. There are two variants of the latter: the Aristotelian abstract rationalist hypostasis of the 'ideal' or the 'universal' (as opposed to a hypostasis of the 'factual' or the 'particular' that supposedly characterizes history); and the Platonic, romantic and idealist hypostasis of the particular as 'enthusiasm' or 'raptus' or 'disinterested' feeling or 'intuition' or 'fantasy' (as opposed to a hypostasis of the universal or of 'logical form' that allegedly characterizes history and philosophy). Our exclusion applies to both.

Eduard Norden has rightly observed of Mommsen's *History of Rome* that, however great its intrinsic merits, as a work of science it 'passes over' (*vergehet*) into countless other histories: the truth of 'the knowledge that is gained therein', both in its 'development' and indeed in its very origins, does not come from the 'separate existence' or autonomy (*Sonder-existenz*) of the work. A poem, on the other hand, or a work of art, does not pass over into others in this sense; it 'lasts' on its own.[1] But Norden shares with romantic and idealist aesthetics the mistaken belief that the autonomy of poetry is the result of some mythicized 'individual *creative* force', some *subjective* or imaginative power. It is not. Rather its origin is the peculiar organic semantic structure of poetry, to which the aseity or semantic autonomy of the poem corresponds. The historical or scientific work, on the other hand, is semantically disorganic and heteronomous, and this both explains and confirms the need for it to pass over, forwards and backwards, into countless others. For it is in this way that its own scientific truth comes into being and takes shape. But Norden, not realizing this, is forced into self-contradiction, because at the same time as making his distinction he cannot help but acknowledge that

1. Eduard Norden, 'Geleitwort' to Theodor Mommsen, *Römische Geschichte*, Vienna–Leipzig 1932, p. 13.

there is a 'living creative force' with all its attributes (fantasy, etc.) not only in the poet, but also in the historian or scientist, in this case Mommsen. So that he nullifies the criterion of distinction between art and history which he had started by accepting.

Kant and the romantics made a fundamental error, which we are now in a position to see. We do not thereby mean to ignore their not inconsiderable merit in posing the problem of what was meant positively, anti-platonically, by the autonomy of art. Nevertheless they committed the error, which has persisted in all their various successors and epigones down to the decadent aestheticists of our own day, of mistaking the *semantic immediacy* of poetic speech for a *synonymous immediacy of intuition* or *pure image*. That is, they took the immediacy which is to be attributed to the semantic un-relatedness and autonomy of poetic speech, in other words its *style* qua special technical epistemological condition of poetry and art in general, for an absolutized or abstract, generic aspect of poetry and art. This view rests on a hypostatic distinction between Art (as 'form', intuition, and so on) and non-Art. In short, they confused two things: on the one hand, a *specific* feature of art, which can be traced and identified critically and scientifically, namely the semantic organicity and autonomy of poetic and artistic thought or discourse; and on the other, a dogmatic, metaphysical notion of the abstract epistemological autonomy of a *generic* element (intuition or image) of that same poetic discourse or thought, which in fact *shares* with scientific discourse both intuition and concept.

The error of Kant, the romantics and the idealists arose then from the very proper modern need to give a positive explanation of the immediacy, or un-relatedness, of poetic or artistic values and hence their autonomy. But they could not meet the need to explain this immediacy, which is perceived ambiguously by ordinary aesthetic consciousness pre-eminently if not exclusively in emotional effects, except by drawing on the modern metaphysics of transcendental subjectivity (heir to neo-Platonic aesthetic motifs) and entrusting to the general epistemological category of feeling, that is immediacy or particularity, the task of finding a solution which it could not possibly provide. Since in fact what was being sought was the solution to the problem of *expressive* immediacy, the answer itself could only be found in a special, technical, epistemological examination of the semantic problematic of cognitive expression – in other words of actual concrete thought. A correct explanation of the epistemological phenomenon of expressive immediacy, as opposed to the myths of metaphysics, shows us that it is not at all the same thing as *cognitive immediacy*. The latter is a contradiction in terms, as Socrates and Plato, not to mention the Kant of the first *Critique*, have taught us.

Of course, there is a world of difference between demonstrating what we have just said and actually getting it into the vulgar aesthetic skull, still reverberating, more or less unconsciously, with the echoes of the romantic and mystical aspirations of modern metaphysical aesthetics. The facts that we owe the *truth* of certain unforgettable London fogs in Dickens (to take an example from narrative 'prose') solely to what Dickens *said*, that his statement is *sufficient to itself* (what statement uttered by a geographer or historian, a scientist in short, is sufficient to itself or true for itself?), that any critical account *explicates* Dickens' statement but does not *verify* it, because the statement contains its own verification in itself, since its verification comes from the *contextual dialectic* of a semantically *organic* discourse which brings the truth of that statement into being – these facts, and countless others of the same kind, are probably condemned to long obscurity yet at the hands of the myth-makers of the mysterious powers of 'pure intuition'.[2]

We need to make two further points in order to clarify finally our concept of the poetic symbol. Firstly, if metaphor (and its two extremes, hyperbole and simile), whether living or dead, is a cognitive value in general, whether poetic or ordinary, and if the sense of the poetic symbol or polysemic characteristic-typical concept can be either literal or metaphorical, it follows that the poetic symbol or concept is specified and delimited by its polysemic semantic aspect or character, and thus by its semantic autonomy. Secondly, therefore, poetic symbols in the fullest sense are those meanings, whether literal or metaphorical, whose semantic autonomy endows them with sufficient force – either directly or in combination with others – to develop and structure entire expressive worlds (literary works). The pattern of poetic symbols or semantically autonomous structural concepts in a text can be perceived at first glance, sometimes just from

2. On Dickens, see our 'Discorso Poetico e Discorso Scientifico', in *Atti del III Congresso Internazionale d'Estetica*, Turin 1956.

the title, as in those classic examples: *The Divine Comedy, The Waste Land, Les Parents Pauvres* (literal poetic symbol!), *Madame Bovary* (ditto), *Great Expectations* (ditto),[3] *War and Peace* (ditto), *Babbitt* (ditto), *Ghosts, Ulysses* (and it goes without saying that even a fragment of Sappho can be an expressive world, albeit in miniature).

But the notion of the literary or poetic work brings us back to another problem: that of its ascription to a superstructure and hence its relations to an infrastructure or socio-economic base. We have in fact been working towards a solution to this problem, perhaps unnoticed by the reader, in our conception of the dialectic of history and poetry as a semantic-formal dialectic and, connected to this, in the methodological theory of critical paraphrase. Both of these we have tried to substantiate in our analyses of literary works, while demonstrating, though not always explicitly, the inadequacy of the responses of present-day bourgeois taste, impressionistic and mysticizing, to the questions raised by them. Thus we have shown that the poetry, for example, of Sophocles' *Antigone* would be inconceivable and impossible without the language of the ethical and religious mythology of the caste-society of the poet's time and, implicitly, its associated primitive-economic organization; we have seen how unthinkable would be the poetry of the *Comedy* without the theological, tropological, language of Catholic culture in the Middle Ages and, by implication, an economic organization that was still partly feudal, partly communal; or that of *Faust* without the language of pantheism and idealism typical of bourgeois humanism in the age of Goethe, and the burgeoning free-enterprise economy associated with it; or that of *Lenin* without the language of the Marxist ideology of the October Revolution and the Soviet society, along with its socialist economy, to which the Revolution gave birth – and so on.

It is in fact becoming reasonably clear that a complex and materialist semantic dialectic, which supersedes the gratuitous metaphors of 'mirroring' and 'reflection', can provide us with an explanation or rational understanding of the way in which the substance of history passes over into poetry – how history actually conditions it in its

3. *Great Expectations* (1860–61) is a further example of literal poetic symbol (of Victorian bourgeois society). Harry Stone rightly comments: 'Pip's errors of vision, a result of his and society's upsidedown morality, are at the core of the fable'; *The Kenyon Review* XXIV (1962), 4, pp. 662–91.

specific nature as poetry. For that process occurs precisely through the medium of the literal-material and its associated omni-textuality, which is the infrastructural moment of the dialectic described above. By this I mean that it is through the medium of language-as-letter – a particular complex of instrumental forms and their respective thought-ends – that the whole ideological and cultural substance of a society comes to form the historical humus of the poetic work. The poem born from that humus will be inscribed in a super-structure and in the socio-economic infra-structure associated with it. Yet the poem comes into being by *developing* the thought-ends of the instrumental form (the 'form' of the letter) through which alone a historical humus is effective, and by *modifying* the instrument itself. Thus the literal-material is transcended, semantically-formally, into the polysemic or poetic value. *Mutatis mutandis*, the same dialectic – in the form of transcendence of the literal-material into the univocal – constitutes science, and inscribes it in a given superstructure.

All of this, incidentally, also confirms the fact that language – as a means which cannot by definition be dissociated from its thought-end – belongs in a general and a permanent way to the superstructure, rather than to any particular or privileged moment of the super-structure, Stalinist linguistics was in this respect at once right and wrong in its verdict on language.[4]

These questions were touched on at the beginning of our inquiry. When analysing *Antigone*, we sought to elucidate the poetic–structural complexes of the play and thereby to demonstrate why the literary character of Antigone and other similar characters could not have co-existed with Roberts and Co. The reasons for that fact are now

---

4. Stalin, in his work on linguistics, was wrong to assert that 'language differs radically from the superstructure'. Not only was he wrong, but he contradicted himself, since he had already previously borrowed the principle from Marx that thought cannot exist in separation from language, to use it against Marr. This principle (discovered by Herder and Humboldt) implies that language too is to be located in the superstructure of a society at the same time as thought, given that the superstructure 'comprehends', as Stalin said, 'the political, juridical, religious, philosophical and artistic *ideas* of a society and their corresponding political, legal, etc. institutions'. Of course Stalin had no difficulty in showing against Marr that 'the Russian language has remained fundamentally the same as it was before the October Revolution', and in refuting the idea that it was ever the privileged product of 'a single class' of society, even a revolutionary class. See J. V. Stalin, *Marxism and Linguistics*, Moscow 1951.

clearer. Each of these poetic organisms refers back – in the name of its structural values or poetic meanings – to conditions which are not only historical, social, and by implication economic, but which are also *congruent* and *coherent* with the content-values of the work. In other words, they refer back to those particular circumstances, and not others; the conditions of ancient Greece, not those of the Middle Ages or our own times.

Marx wrote that Greek art presupposes 'not any mythology whatever, i.e. not an arbitrarily chosen unconsciously artistic reworking of nature, (here meaning everything objective, hence including society)', but Greek mythology – 'Egyptian mythology could never have been the foundation or the womb of Greek art', but 'in any case' there was needed '*a* mythology'. In the same way, Greek art presupposed a particular economy (primitive, pastoral, etc.) and not any other. Thus the undeveloped 'stage of society' [and economy] in which that art grew 'is not in contradiction' with the 'charm' which, as the art of a people from 'historic childhood', it holds over us. Rather, that charm 'is its *result* . . . and is inextricably bound up with the fact that the unripe social [and economic] conditions under which it arose, and could alone arise, can never return'.[5]

This is Marx's reply, by the way, to the commonly-held, though abstract and superficial, view that 'in the case of the arts, it is well known that certain periods of their flowering are out of all proportion to the general development of society, hence also to the material foundation . . .'. Careless bourgeois critics such as Wellek and Warren have attributed this view to Marx himself and assumed it to be significant in the sense that 'this passage appears to give up the Marxist position altogether'.[6] In fact, of course, Marx goes on immediately to say that 'the difficulty consists only in the general [i.e. historical-philosophical] formulation of these contradictions. As soon as they have been specified, they are already clarified' (*ibid.*).

Engels' position, already mentioned, is again relevant at this point. We refer to his perception that the 'median axis' of the cultural-historical curve of a given ideological or superstructural sphere (e.g.

5. Marx, *Grundrisse*, pp. 110–1.
6. René Wellek and Austin Warren, *Theory of Literature*, London 1963, p. 107 and note.

that of art) is all the more 'nearly parallel' to the axis of the historical curve of economic and material development 'the longer the [historical] period considered and the wider the [ideological] field dealt with'. He had already observed elsewhere that once discussion moves from the State and public and private law to ideological forms such as 'philosophy and religion' or art, the 'interconnection' [*Zusammenhang*] between ideas and their material conditions 'becomes more and more complicated, more and more obscured by intermediate links', but it nevertheless 'exists'.[7] It is in short characteristic of ideologies and cultures worthy of the name that their *universalism* should embrace *long periods*. During such periods, on the other hand, the corresponding kinds of economic forms can so to speak develop along their own lines, although in evident parallelism with the cultural or superstructural factors. (It is to suggest this parallelism and the problematic associated with it that we have used such expressions as 'implicit' or 'by implication' to characterize the nature of the relation between the ideology of poetic or literary ideas and the 'existent' economic conditions corresponding to them.)

In other words, only if we acknowledge the *intellectual* nature of poetry (concrete though it is), can we demonstrate its power to 'reflect' a society and hence its ideology. It is a flagrant contradiction to emphasize this power and still believe in art, as many self-styled Marxist philosophers persist in doing, as intuitive knowledge or knowledge 'through images', in abstract antithesis to science, understood as knowledge 'through concepts'.

The conception of poetry we have advanced in these pages leads to a way of appreciating the poem and understanding it historically whose philosophical and epistemological rationale has been shown in the critical paraphrase – as a true dialectical articulation of taste and decisive element in the practice of literary history. To clarify further this methodological criterion of the *dialectical paraphrase* of the poetic text, and to define more precisely the historical–materialist solution which we offer to the problem of literary criticism, we shall begin by comparing some of the traditional and more recent methods of literary history. Starting with positivism, we shall go on to examine idealism, present-day Marxism, and neo-stylistics.

7. Engels, 'Ludwig Feuerbach and the End of German Classical Philosophy', in *Marx–Engels Selected Works*, Moscow 1968, p. 617.

We shall take one example of the positivist method: Taine's comment on a famous line by Racine:

Dans le fond des forêts votre image me suit
(In the depth of the forests your image follows me),

of which he says: 'When Hippolyte speaks of the forests in which he lives, read the *grandes allées* of Versailles'.[8] Taine's overriding concern with the historical content of a poetic text is very obvious here, and on this occasion his interpretation is particularly external and gratuitous. Inevitably, his reading of the line misses the polysemic or poetic value of Racine's 'fond', which, as more attentive critics have noticed, expresses a two-fold depth, both physical and moral. The curious thing is, of course, that if one reads the *Phèdre* from within the text, that is, working through its organic–contextual or concrete stylistic values, its links with Racine's Christian–modern epoch are plentiful and obvious, as we have already had occasion to point out. (Our criticism is not intended to deny Taine's very considerable personal taste, which afforded him, in contradiction to his own method, some interesting insights on 'style' in his essay on *Stendhal*, and also on *Balzac*, riddled though these are with preconceptions of a moralistic and conventional character.)

We shall sub-divide the idealist method into (a) the classical-idealist or Hegelian method, and (b) the romantic-idealist method. The limitations of the former lie in its interpretation of the poetic text in terms of its *philosophical content*, in homage to the principle of 'beautiful' form as the 'appearance' of the 'Idea'. The result is a concentration on eliciting the ethos of the text from its style that pays no attention to the style itself. In other words, the classical-idealist method is not concerned with the development of the form and content of the literal into the formality of the poetic or polysemic. An example is Hegel's philosophical reading of *Antigone*, cited above. The great merit of Hegel's approach, on the other hand, was that by distinguishing between classical and modern poetry it drew attention to the historical nature of poetry and art in general. For Croce, with his a-historical 'universality' of 'pure intuition', this was a defect.

8. Hippolyte Taine, *Nouveaux Essais de Critique et d'Histoire*, Paris n.d., p. 127. See also Martin Turnell, in *Critiques and Essays in Criticism*, ed. R. W. Stallman, cit., pp. 424 ff. (and S. J. Kahn, *Science and Aesthetic Judgement*, London 1953).

The romantic-idealist method has been applied in various ways by Friedrich Schlegel, De Sanctis, Croce, and on to the epigones of post-romantic and decadent taste in general. Schlegel's method was to interpret a text philosophically, though with contradictory reliance on an idea of art as 'ironic fantasy', and hence 'beautiful *confusion*' – an *indistinct* unity of opposites. Thus he had a low estimation of French classical tragedy because 'it is empty formalism, without strength, charm or substance', as opposed to Shakespearean tragedy which is 'philosophical'.[9]

In De Sanctis, the method veers brilliantly between two opposite poles. On the one hand, he tended to devote particular attention to content, approaching it from an historicist and Hegelian point of view. This gives us such Desanctisian notions as the preconceived 'ideal', which is allegedly 'realized' by the work of art and yet always remains 'a beyond which is never attained'; and the idea of 'situation', which it has been noted is broader than the notion of 'figure-form', and aesthetically justifies abstract subject-matter by exalting 'stupendous situations'. On the other hand, De Sanctis tends towards a sensuous formalism, an idea of 'plasticity' based on the concept of art as 'fantasy' or 'vision' or 'figure'. Hence, for example, his pronouncement that the ethical 'concept' of Dante's *Inferno* was 'poetically superfluous, serving only to classify'. Further comment is unnecessary.[10]

In Croce's critical work, the method leads to a formalistic impressionism and aestheticism. The *Comedy* for example is reduced to a mosaic of 'lyrical' atoms. Every structural or conceptual element is regarded as 'extraneous' or extra-aesthetic. To judge poetry, furthermore, is simply 'to call attention to what is admirable at this or that point, admirable because it is admirable, not because it is clever syntax or a smart piece of style'.[11] Croce's 'monographic' approach to the history of art is a coherent methodological result of the criterion of form as 'pure cosmic *intuition*', which in turn is a distant echo of Kant's 'disinterested feeling', Schiller's idea of art as 'play', and

9. For his notion of poetry-as-irony (1797–8), see Friedrich Schlegel, *Kritische Schriften*, hrsgg. von Wolfdietrich Rasch, Munich 1938, pp. 10, 11, 60, 88, 93.

10. De Sanctis: as well as his *Storia della Letteratura Italiana* cit. and *Saggi* cit., see for example the *Lezioni e Saggi su Dante* cit. and *Scritti Critici*, a cura di Gianfranco Contini, Turin 1949 (we have borne in mind Contini's introduction to this volume). See also Giacomo Debenedetti, *Saggi Critici*, new series, Rome 1945.

11. Croce, *La Critica e la Storia delle Arti Figurative*, Bari 1946, p. 28.

Schlegel's notion of the 'freedom' (freedom from all 'interest') of creative 'ironic fantasy'.

Let us turn now to present-day Marxism, starting with the merits of its method. Firstly, it has replaced Hegel's philosophical interpretation of the work of art with a procedure that allows for more concrete interpretation. In the words of Plekhanov: 'As an adherent of the materialist conception of the world, I say that the first task of the critic is to translate the ideas of a work of art from the language of art into the language of sociology, to establish what might be called the sociological equivalent of a given literary phenomenon';[12] or in those of Lukács: artistic concentration 'is the maximum intensification in content of the *social* and human essence of a given situation'.[13] Secondly, it has brought about the modern rediscovery of the aesthetic problem of content and its importance in the internal economy of the work of art, as against the formalism of 'art for art's sake'. Plekhanov declared: 'the predominance of form over content produces works that are vacant and ugly; beauty lies in harmony of form and content'. Lukács writes: 'It is pointless to criticize a bad writer simply on the grounds of his formal defects. The contrast between an empty and superficial representation and the actual reality of human and social life ... will make it clear that formal defects are merely the consequence of a fundamental lack of content. The appeal to life is itself enough to expose the emptiness of insignificant artistic reproduction'. Thirdly, both Plekhanov and Lukács have from time to time applied these criteria successfully, when they have been deployed with circumspection. A case in point is Plekhanov's commentary on the novels of Balzac and their value for our knowledge of French society under the Restoration and Louis Philippe (but see Engels' famous letter, already cited, to Miss Harkness of April 1888 for a precedent, to which we shall return). Another example is Plekhanov on *Madame Bovary*. Lukács' essays on European and Russian

---

12. See G. V. Plekhanov, *Kunst und Literatur*, Berlin 1955, especially pp. 42, 219, 225–226, 229, 317, 485, 875–928, 954.

13. Lukács, *Writer and Critic*, cit.; *Studies in European Realism*, intr. Alfred Kazin, New York 1964; *Goethe and His Age*, tr. Robert Anchor, London 1968; *Deutsche Realisten des 19. Jahrhunderts*, Bern 1951; *The Historical Novel*, tr. H. and S. Mitchell, London 1962; *Beiträge zur Geschichte der Ästhetik*, Berlin 1954. And see G. Della Volpe, *Il Verosimile Filmico*, Roma 1954, pp. 121 ff.

realism, especially on Balzac, Stendhal, Zola and Tolstoy, should also be noted.[14]

But current Marxist method is also defective in certain respects. Its limitations are particularly obvious, firstly, where what Plekhanov calls the critic's 'second task', the 'necessary completion' of the first, is concerned: that is, 'the appreciation of the aesthetic values of the work under consideration'. The method runs into trouble here because the criterion of its appreciation or evaluation is whether the work of art contains, not so much an 'ideal content' or ideas in general, which would be acceptable ('art cannot live without ideas':

14. Interest in Zola (as well as in Balzac and Stendhal as social novelists) has been reawakened by Erich Auerbach's magnificent book *Mimesis*. Auerbach has re-established the truth about Zola as a writer and as a stylist – and 'stylist' is the right word. That truth had been glimpsed by De Sanctis (see *Saggi Critici*, a cura di Luigi Russo, Bari 1953, pp. 226–323), but then lost from sight by Croce (in a study which he devoted jointly to Zola and ... the author of *Tartarin de Tarascon*, Alphonse Daudet: in *Poesia e Non Poesia*, Bari 1964) and even by Lukács (in his centenary essay in *Studies in European Realism*). Auerbach shows not only that Zola represents an enormous advance on the work of writers like the Goncourt brothers, but above all that Zola 'is one of the very few authors of the century who created their work out of the great problems of the age' (p. 512). In this respect, 'only Balzac can be compared with him', but 'Balzac wrote at a time when much of what Zola saw had not yet developed or was not yet discernible' (ibid.). That is to say, he does not simply give us a picture of social and political corruption under the Second Empire, as De Sanctis and Croce thought, neither is he simply 'the "historian of private life" under the Second Empire in France in the same way as Balzac was the historian of private life under the restoration and July monarchy' (Lukács, op. cit., p. 85). Zola's writing is always dry, fast, pitiless, material (sometimes, it is true, weighed down by emphasis, but not much more so than Balzac's): a modern poetic writing. It is the writing of one of the masters of Realism, in spite of the narrowness of his positivistic-scientist poetic, or, if you will, against his own theory. The fact is that in his artistic practice, his best works, while there are indeed *things* there is also *judgement*, and the two are inseparably fused in a critique at once of things and of society.

It is no good, finally, Lukács telling us that 'although his life-work is very extensive', Zola 'has never created a single character who grew to be a type, a by-word, almost a living being, such as for instance the Bovary couple ... in Flaubert' (op. cit., p. 92). The criterion of artistic-proverbial universality, or the proverbially universal, is, to say the least, too trivial and empirical (in the bad sense). What are we to make, for example, of the 'unproverbiality' of Madame la présidente Tourvel, the character who is perhaps the most alive, and certainly the most moving and human, in Laclos's *Liaisons Dangereuses*, as against the Vicomte de Valmont who is certainly not artistically superior (in part because of the great precedent of Richardson's Lovelace) but is definitely proverbial? Anyway, isn't Tom Fool proverbial too?

Plekhanov), but, equally and even more importantly, an ideal content which is 'not false' – in other words, one which is progressive and not reactionary. Plekhanov states: 'Not every idea can be expressed in a work of art' and 'false ideas harm a work of art', while for Lukács 'any false conception of the world "whatever" is unsuitable as the basis of realism'. Yet at the same time what do we find propping up this ponderous devotion to content but the old aesthetic epistemology of Kant and the romantics? Thus, according to Plekhanov, someone who proclaims ideas 'prefers to speak the *language of logic*', while the artist 'prefers to speak the *language of images*'. But to his credit Plekhanov then gets caught in a tangle of problems of some significance – a potentially productive one once freed of his premises. He remarks, à propos of Ibsen's 'sermons', that 'If an author thinks in images and figures, that is if he is an artist, the nebulousness of his preaching will inevitably render his artistic images indeterminate'. We might compare our own observations on the organic relation, assured by the dialectic of heterogeneities, between intellectual clarity or coherence of meaning and vividness of image. For Lukács, however, there is not the shadow of a doubt. 'Art makes us intuit sensibly' the 'dynamic unity' of the universal, particular, and individual (the categories of Hegelian logic ever with us!), while science resolves this unity 'into its abstract elements and seeks to conceptualize the interaction of these elements'.

When these criteria are applied to actual literary history, and their inadequacies are not mitigated by the personal sensitivity of the critic (the usual rule, to which the previous cases are an exception), the limitations of the method become all the clearer. One example is Plekhanov's essentially mistaken interpretation of the poetry of Ibsen in *Ghosts, The Doll's House, The Pillars of the Community*, etc. Ibsen the artist is actually reproached for his (clear) bourgeois moral ideas – 'purity of will', ethical 'individualism' – and for his fundamental 'weakness' in not finding 'any way out of morals into politics' (meaning socially militant politics). *On this basis*, Plekhanov dismisses his dramatic moral speeches as incoherent and nebulous rhetoric and criticises his poetic symbols for their 'abstractness', that is 'a witness to his poverty of *social* thought'. The only merit he can divine in Ibsen is as a satirist of the petty-bourgeoisie. Lukács is in this instance more felicitous, linking Ibsen to the 'preacher' Tolstoy, and remarking that

'Ibsen too . . . precisely through his didactic pathos excelled his contemporaries even from the purely artistic point of view'.[15]

On the other hand, we may note the failure of Lukács to understand *Madame Bovary*, a novel which he accuses of descriptivism for its own sake, in short, formalism. The faults of Lukács's fixation with content are exemplified when he complains that Flaubert tried to remedy the 'immobility', the 'empty and dispirited greyness' of his mediocre heroes 'by purely artistic and technical means' (*sic*). This attempt was 'bound to fail' because 'the mediocrity of the average man derives from the fact that the *social antinomies* which objectively determine his existence do not attain their highest degree of tension in him; on the contrary, they are obfuscated and attain a superficial equilibrium'. Flaubert is here condemned for giving artistic life to a social content which is not, for example, that of Zola and does not happen to square with the social ideas of his sociologist critic. But Lukács forgets how much he still owes Flaubert. What he owes him is all the poetic *truth* possessed by that 'mediocre pair', as Flaubert called them, in whom precisely everything, including first and foremost their consciousness of social antinomies, is shown to be *superficial*. Other misinterpretations by Lukács include his studies on Hölderlin, who is seen purely in his progressive or Enlightenment dimension to the exclusion, no less, of the romantic dimension into which it flowed and where it assumed its distinctive power and shape; or on Goethe, where much is lost of the figure of Mephistopheles, as we have seen, and too much is made of the 'small-holding' of Philemon and Baucis that is destined to be absorbed by Faust's large-scale industrial property; likewise his writings on Kleist.

The heroic Gramsci is one exception to this tradition of Marxist literary history. The critical jottings that he left and his notes on

15. Take, for example, the human and social richness of the discussion between consul Bernick and young Johan Tönnesen, just back from America, about Marta, the poor relation in the family in *The Pillars of the Community* (Act II; tr. Una Ellis-Fermor, London 1968, pp. 71–72). Is it a 'sermon', and a 'nebulous' one at that? Or is it not rather – beyond any doubt – one of the profoundest denunciations in poetic and dramatic form of bourgeois hypocrisy in family relations? The relation between poetry and moral and social reality, history, is immediate and organic in Ibsen, as can be seen in the subtle, and aesthetically functional, distinction-opposition between women's subjugation and humiliation in the family in liberal Europe and the freedom, even then, of their condition in democratic America – and the play was written in 1877!

method are unfortunately brief, and he was never able to give them a firm foundation or work them systematically into an aesthetic epistemology. Even so, two themes come through strongly: the need to avoid stressing either content or form at the expense of the other, and the need to work towards a criticism that would be functional as well as materialist. It is enough to recall such observations on method as the following:

> 'Once the principle has been established that all we are looking for in the work of art is its artistic character, this in no way prevents us from inquiring into what mass of feelings, *what attitude towards life*, circulates within the work itself.... What is not admissible is that a work should be beautiful because of its moral and political content to the exclusion of the form with which the abstract content has fused and become one';
> ' "Content" and "form" have an "historical" as well as an "aesthetic" meaning. "Historical" form signifies a given *language*, as "content" indicates a given *way of thinking* which is not only historical, but "sober", expressive ...';
> 'Only by abstraction ... can normative grammar be regarded as separate from living language'.

(There is a residue of idealism in this too generous concession to Croce: 'The formal principle of the distinction of categories of the spirit and their unity of circulation does allow us, in spite of its abstractness, to grasp effectual reality'.)

It is enough also to recall Gramsci's *structural* analysis of Dante's poetry in the Cavalcante episode (*Inferno* X, ll. 52–114). We quote his conclusions: 'The most important word in the line

> perhaps whom your Guido held in disdain (l. 63)

is not "whom" [Virgil] or "disdain" but simply the past definite "held" (*ebbe*)'. For 'the "aesthetic" and "dramatic" emphasis of the line falls on this word "held", which is the origin of the drama of Cavalcante, as interpreted in the "stage-directions" of Farinata: "catharsis" then follows' for 'the structural passage [the *concept* of the damned's foreseeing of the future and their ignorance of the present,]

is then not only structure, it is also poetry, a *necessary element* in the *drama* which
has taken place' (our emphases).[16]
Let us finally turn to the neo-stylistic method. Its undoubted merits
include the following. Firstly, it is based on modern, scientific, Saussurian linguistics, rather than the linguistics of Humboldt and the
romantics. In this it is different from and in opposition to the work of
critics like Croce and Vossler. Spitzer is quite clear about the gulf
between them when he observes that Vossler gives more consideration
'to "individual language" than "common language", *energeia* rather
than *ergon'* in the belief that 'if he steeps himself in the soul of the great
moulder of language, the poet, he will be in the presence of the
creative act of language'. Secondly, it is well aware of the consequences of these linguistic premisses as they immediately affect
aesthetic method and literary history. Thus, 'only after considerable
refinement of the relevant disciplines' have we reached the point of
'regarding language as also *expression* and art as also *communication'*
(Spitzer); and 'the greater the objective certainty at which a stylistic
explanation may aim, the more we shall have overcome the *impressionism* which up to a short time ago seemed the only alternative to a
positivistic study of literature' (Spitzer); and finally, 'even when we
reach what in the abstract seems to be the same conclusion, it possesses
a completely different degree of certainty if it has been arrived at on
the basis of experimental stylistic evidence [i.e. 'a non-formalist
stylistic survey'] rather than by psychologistic procedures' (Contini).
Thirdly, neo-stylistics has attempted, with Auerbach in particular, to
point to the 'literary conquest of modern reality' in the texts themselves, preferably by analysing their semantic contents or meanings
along with the relevant syntactic and stylistic modules. In this way,
there has been a deepening of the stylistic approach, which has been
brought closer and made more functional to the historical and social
body and substance of the work of art.[17]

16. Gramsci, op. cit., pp. 11, 61, 203; cf. pp. 79–81. On Dante, pp. 37–8, 36 [Gramsci
interprets the pronoun 'cui' as referring to Virgil while others, including Sapegno
and Sinclair, take it to refer to Beatrice; yet other interpretations have been advanced, without any final agreement being reached. – *Tr. note.*]
17. See Spitzer, op. cit., especially pp. 29 ff., and *Marcel Proust*, Turin 1959; Contini,
'La stilistica di G. Devoto', in *Lingua Nostra* XI (1950); 'Introduzione' cit. to De
Sanctis, *Scritti Critici*; 'Il canto XXX dell' Inferno', in *Letture Dantesche*, a. c. di G.
Getto, cit., pp. 585 ff.; Auerbach, op. cit.

Against these merits of neo-stylistics are to be set its limitations, and these may be summed up in its unilateral tendency to force our perception of the literary fact into the Procrustean modules of linguistics and stylistics. In doing so, it affords us insights into poetic values which, unlike those of aestheticism and impressionism, are neither gratuitous nor unproductive. Even so, they remain at some distance from those values. They are not, in short, entirely in function of their respective texts. To give just a few examples: Spitzer's efforts to collate generic linguistic features and poetic 'spiritual' etymons (e.g. the verb 'voir' and Racinian tragedy, or 'complex disjunctions' and the reflective poetry of Proust); or some of Contini's writings on Dante, where the conclusions he reaches in the field of the history of Italian are more concerned with Dante's language than his poetry (e.g. his comments on the speech of Maestro Adamo). Contini tries to justify these conclusions with the 'cardinal theorem' that 'the [poetic] invention is not only functional, it is also possessed of an intense *linguistic* historicity'. Here one can clearly see a dangerous tendency to institute a distinction between form and content and to give abstract emphasis to the linguistic historicity of the poetic invention (or the historicity of its technical 'form') at the expense of the overall historicity of form and content together, from which, as we know, its poetic functionality is inseparable. The danger for both Spitzer and Contini is that of falling, even if in different ways, into historicist or philological formalism.

Auerbach, finally, oscillates between two poles. On the one hand, there is his tendency to misuse stylistic or rhetorical criteria, such as the mixture of high and low styles which he draws on to explain Christian and modern realism. Because these criteria have a fixed technical nature, they always risk being relatively external to *determinate* polysemic contents. On the other hand, he tends not to distinguish between poetic contents and historical or even purely diaristic contents in characterizing what he regards as a literary conquest of reality. So he falls out of the frying-pan of stylistic or rhetorical formalism into the fire of an historicist and moralistic criticism of content (the latter sanctioned by such transcendental and heterogeneous categories as 'existential realism' and the 'progress' of history).

Now, taking these observations as our starting point, we shall try to specify why it is that literary analysis based on the dialectical, and therefore critical, paraphrase of poetic texts is in a position to avoid both formalism and fixation on content. (We are still taking both these negative concepts in their traditional sense, but see below.) To begin with the latter. We can see what 'content'-criticism in general is, and thereby supersede it, if we bear the following points in mind. Firstly, once we can perceive the true nature of the so-called philosophical or sociological or historical equivalent of the poetic text, namely that it is a paraphrase (though an uncritical one) of the poetic thought or so-called 'content' in question, and thereby a reduction of it – a putting 'into simple language', one should say – to the thought or 'content' of the letter, or literal-material, or omni-textual (the common source of both science and poetry); then a comparison will necessarily be instituted between this paraphrase and the poetic thought or 'content' which it paraphrases. Why? Because a comparison of this sort is dictated, unavoidably, by a *quid* which separates, or at any rate distinguishes, the poetic thought from its paraphrase; the awareness of this distinguishing *quid* is precisely the beginning of taste, without it there is no literary criticism worthy of the name.

All the same – and this is the second point – the comparison thus instituted *is not immediate*. It is mediated, indeed is dialectical, in the precise sense that the distinguishing *quid* reveals itself to be a gap or switch – between poetic thought and paraphrase-equivalent – of a kind such that the poetic thought *both does not and yet does coincide* with itself in paraphrased form, or with itself, let us say, transferred *back* to the letter: in the same way as any thought which develops and potentiates another – as is the case here – does not and yet does coincide with the latter. The *way* in which a thought or 'content' develops lies, to be sure, in its 'form', but we should be more precise. For what in actual fact makes up 'form' is the same semantic, linguistic means as the means of thought (end) in general, whether the thought is in the act of developing another or is itself developable. Thus the 'form' of thought or 'content' in the act of developing another, in our case the 'form' of poetic thought, likewise *does not and yet does coincide* with the means or instrumental form of the 'content' to be developed, in other words with the form of the latter (language-as-letter or literal-material). It does not coincide in that, as the form of poetic thought, it is style-language – hence semantic organicity. It does coincide in that in the other form it exists in a paraphrase which presupposes the use of the same phonetic–grammatical constituents

G

and exponents, and the same vocabulary, that is the *same* basic instrumental form or form of the letter. Thus the philosophical or sociological *'equivalent'* of the poetic thought is shown, in the light of this dialectic of language-means and thought-end which structures the relation of every form and every content, to be an *uncritical paraphrase*, in other words the *degradation* of a thought belonging to style-language to the omni-textual. Such an 'equivalent' is a *hybrid thought*, neither poetic nor scientific, neither polysemic nor univocal.

The cardinal epistemological theorem of the indissociability of means (language) and end (thought) is thereby decisively confirmed. The theorem, and the aesthetic corollary which follows from it, now read as follows:

(1) Since the semantic component of thought in general, in this instance the instrumental form of the letter, is an indissociable and therefore dialectical means of its end-thought, it is a component of the form, or aspiration to unity or value, which makes thought thought.

(2) It follows, for a semantic–epistemological or special reason as well as for a general one (cf. Section 2), that the aesthetic meaning traditionally given by Kantian romanticism and the idealists to the terms 'form' (i.e. disinterested feeling, pure image) and 'content' (i.e. ends, concepts) must be revised. For form is shown to be style-thought, while content is shown to be images, i.e. *matter*. Notice, however, that the literal-material coincides with matter only as regards the *imaginative*, *perceptual* aspects of its meanings, or virtual concrete concepts; while its phonetic–grammatical constituents and exponents, or instrumental form, come under the heading of the *form* or *unity* of its meanings.

It will not perhaps be superfluous to point out that we have so far been using the negative term 'content' provisionally, in the traditional sense of 'ideas': we shall therefore place it, like its opposite 'form', between inverted commas. Similarly, for the convenience of our analysis, we have spoken, again provisionally, of fixation on 'content' or 'ideas', in the post-romantic and idealist sense – meaning the abstract and mistaken attachment of 'ideas' or concepts to poetic 'form' without these 'contents' being properly 'immersed' in the form. This does not mean of course that we cannot go on using the notion of fixation on content as a negative term in criticism, but simply that its meaning will have to be revised in accordance with the revised sense of the related terms content and form. So it will now come to mean a *deficiency* of *ideas*, or *form*, in the work in question, an excessive amount, without measure or form, of fantasy-matter, and therefore a semantic tendency towards the equivocal and the banal. By the same token, *formalism* should be understood as meaning a *deficiency* of *fantasy*, or the prevalence of ideas or *conceptualism*, and therefore a semantic tendency towards the univocal.

It hardly needs adding at this stage that the critical method of dialectical paraphrase deals a decisive blow to formalism as well, whether taken in its traditional or its non-traditional sense. We shall touch briefly on the thoroughly traditional aesthetic-formalist method (which, being aestheticist, is fixated on 'content' in our sense) and then on the historicist–formalist method (which is formalist in our sense). Because of its inborn aesthetic mysticism and its indifference towards *la langue*, aesthetic formalism has never grasped the dialectical and therefore critical significance of paraphrase. On the contrary, it sees paraphrase merely as something pejorative, an abasement of the 'lyrical' or poetic to the level of prose, in one word a 'heresy'. So that while it sets out to exalt poetry, it actually lowers it to the level of the – gratuitous – play of fantasy or what-have-you. Croce's term is 'pure intuition', while Cleanth Brooks and other American New Critics talk about 'paradox' and 'irony', thereby meandering – for all their 'structural' analyses – in the now somewhat muddled tracks of Schlegel the theorizer of romantic 'ironic fantasy'.[18]

18. Cleanth Brooks, 'The language of paradox', in *Critiques and Essays in Criticism*, cit., pp. 66 ff. 'The union which the creative imagination itself effects . . . is not logical' (p. 76); 'We must be prepared to accept the paradox of the imagination itself' (p. 78). Strangely enough, the example chosen as typical is Shakespeare's *The Phoenix and the Turtle* (quoted on pp. 76–7), a poem inspired by the neo-Platonic and mystical *concept* of love:

> Reason in it selfe confounded,
> Saw Division grow together,
> To themselves yet either neither,
> Simple were so well compounded.
> . . .
> Love hath Reason, Reason none,
> If what parts, can so remaine. . . .
> . . .

Brooks in effect operates an aestheticist *hypostasis* of the characteristic paradox of metaphor or hyperbole (resemblance between things as 'far apart' as possible,

The historicist–formalist approach is taken by a considerable number of the neo-stylisticians. Although the starting-point of the method is modern, in that it acknowledges *la langue* as a positive aesthetic factor, it ultimately unbalances the relationship between language and poetry, by its abstract emphasis on the historicity of poetic language, its 'institutions' and sources, at the expense of the overall unitary historicity – and concreteness – of the *formed content* of poetry, of the polysemic.

On the other hand, there are two points certainly worth underlining in connection with the semantic dialectic which institutes literary criticism as paraphrase. In the first place, we should note the latitude of a paraphrase which has the literal-material or omni-textual as the base and reservoir of its dialectic – that is, the same technico-historical basis on which poetry or the polysemic is originally built. Secondly and most importantly, we should register the epistemological and real import not only of this basis, but also and more particularly of what critical paraphrase aims to elucidate, namely speech-as-style or the organic-contextual. For to that is entrusted, or better, in that consists, the *value* of the semantic switch – i.e. the development of thought from language-as-letter to language-as-style – in its dual differential relationship: what we might call the internal relation between poetic or polysemic thought and its re-thinking in critical-paraphrastic terms; and the external relation between poetic thought and scientific, univocal thought.

Thus, for example, Pindar's styleme 'invidious misfortunes' is real, as an expressive fact, in two respects. Transcending its paraphrase 'hubris', etc., it is constituted as a peculiarly expressive polysemic meaning. But since its transcendence of the literal 'hubris' recalled by the paraphrase is dialectical, it remains – in and through its transcendence – within the uni-verse of communication (*langue*) which confers effective *validity* or universality on the peculiarly expressive meaning which it is. Finally it is related – through the *common* dialec-

in Aristotle's words, i.e. as dissimilar as possible). The result is an artificial and erroneous reduction of poetry to *metaphor* as romantically understood, that is to say as synonymous with every kind of 'fantastic' unity-of-opposites. The latter of course includes *Witz* or *Humor* or *Ironie* after the manner of Schlegel, as discussed above. Thus the noble metaphysical scheme of Friedrich Schlegel's aesthetic is annulled, or rendered merely latent, while its methodological criteria are still mobilized.

tical base of the literal 'hubris' – to all other possible peculiarly express- ive meanings of the same letter, for instance, the scientific historical, or univocal, meaning of 'hubris', at the same time as it is differentiated from them. That is to say, one meaning delimits and is delimited by the other by virtue of the respective peculiarities of the ways in which the letter in question is dialectically transcended.

In other words, given the postulate of identity between thought and language (*sèma*) and our demonstration and specification of it in the sense of a dialectical identity of end and means, we are bound to acknowledge both the epistemological importance and the real significance of language-speech. The same acknowledgment cannot then be long delayed for those modes of the linguistic (semantic) dialectic which, as we believe we have shown in the case of the poly- semic and the univocal, can be ascertained experimentally. Otherwise, the only alternative left – once we have excluded *a fortiori* any kind of positivism – seems to be that of metaphysics, with all the theoretical vitiation and methodological, practical impotence of its spiritual 'forms': 'artistic' form, 'logical' form, etc. Such is the meaning of the radical difference between a semantic dialectic – which, because it is semantic and has its basis in language-as-letter, is historical – and a dialectic of the Idea (specifically, a *beautiful*, sensuous, 'appearance' of the Idea) as in Hegel, or any other dialectic of Spirit or Being.

An obvious corollary of the historicity which is a feature of that dialectic, and of the associated rational character of the dialectically produced poetic symbol, is that poetic truth too is in its innermost being sociological truth. It is therefore always *realistic*. Or, which amounts to the same thing, it is always *verisimilitude*, whether direct or indirect, by analogy or through contrast. Verisimilitude is none other than the truth of ideas tested *by organic–semantic means* against the body of laws and probabilities – or *rationality* – which is the reality of experi- ence and history. The criterion of verisimilitude has always been used, and always will be used, more or less consciously, by every literary critic. Thus, it is destined to survive the romantic revolution too. It is a criterion, whose inevitability is the simplest and surest proof of the rationality and historicity of poetry.

Two consequences follow from this: the feasibility of an aesthetic of literary realism, and hence – in virtue of the philosophical criterion – the validity of a poetic of socialist realism. For only when it has been demonstrated that there is *no* poetry *without ideas in general* will it be conceded that the dominant ideas of our time, those of socialism, also have the right to make poetry. It is a right for which we have the duty to struggle, and one way of doing so is by formulating a rigorous, normative concept of decadent poetry as distinct from contemporary democratic or revolutionary poetry. Our criterion, in other words, is one which enables us not to mistake the degree of artistic excellence in a poem of our times, in other words the semantic organicity of its ideas, while still identifying the degree of *contemporary historical import* or social reflection attained by it. Thus, as we have seen, Eliot's poetry tells us a good deal more, precisely as poetry, than does that of Valéry or Rilke. Which means, among other things, that we can no longer judge poetic value simply on the basis of one, abstract, aspect of form: the superficially semantic aspect of style, understood in a rhetorical sense. It must be judged on the basis of the validity of the *form*, as defined above, as it really functions in the poem: that is, according to the *complexity* or otherwise of the *ideas* which acquire *semantic organicity* and, by implication, the resultant *clarity* or otherwise of their imaginative *content*.

We would hope that it would thus be possible to do justice to all poetry, yet at the same time establish scales of values – though not, we hope, extrinsic ones. Let us take the example of the *decadent* poetry of T. S. Eliot. Eliot, though he is inspired by the Christian ideas of Dante, does not reproduce them, but rather rethinks them in a modern way, reflecting in their light the crisis of our times. (The mystical ideas of Rilke are a somewhat different case, for they are considerably less rich in historical resonance and therefore much less poetic; put another way, they give rise to a more schematic and therefore less complex and significant poetry.) Eliot *does not reproduce* traditional semantic modules either: and thus he achieves semantic organicity and originality in the expression of his ideas. Naturally, for a socialist in our times Eliot is not Mayakovsky. Yet the fact remains, if we may limit ourselves to this one point, that he helps us to understand the greatest communist poet through contrast with him (and is everything not contrast and dialectic in poetry too, if poetry is thought?), much better than do other poets who do not have the rich and profound coherence of that anguished reactionary. He makes us understand much better the *historical* necessity of the ideas which are the form of Mayakovsky's poetry: for example, the idea of socialist optimism – ideas which are forces in themselves, ideas-of-action, to a much greater extent than Eliot's own poetic ideas. For Eliot's ideas echo, even if they do not literally reproduce, other ideas whose historical springtide, so to speak, lies far back in time, and therefore, though they are poetic, they are also decadent.

All these are problems of a poetic of socialist realism based (the only way we can see that it could be based) on the philosophical foundation of an aesthetic of realism *tout court*. But see Appendix I for Engels' clarifications on the poetry of Balzac, and in particular those of Lenin on Tolstoy.

It should now be clear, finally, that a semantic dialectic – in as much as it is a necessarily historical dialectic – cannot be the speculative dialectic of an idealistic *a priori* unity of opposites. Rather, it will be a real dialectic (=tauto–heterological identity), or dialectic of determinate abstractions, both polysemic and univocal: in short a systematic circle of heterogeneities, reason and matter. In this it follows the formula of a materialist, non-Kantian, critique of the *a priori*, which infers the positivity and indispensability of matter as co-element of thought for knowledge (and action) in general, not from an inexistent void but from the sterile and vicious plenitude of all *a priori* reasoning which does not take account of matter as extra-rational.[19]

We can now, if we are not mistaken, proceed to a clarification of the *method* of our philosophical theory of literature, or the demonstrative analysis conducted up to this point. That method is one of epistemological *analysis* of the literary phenomenon in its specific components: characteristic typical abstraction, and then the semantically organic aspect of that abstraction, speech-as-style. At the same time, it is a method of *synthesis,* for it re-connects these elements in the category of *end-thought* and *means-sèma,* in other words in the concept of thought as unity of a manifold (or matter) and in this case language–speech as the indissociable, dialectical means of thought as end. But it should be noted that the method is also one of *experimental* analysis. Thus every theoretical or hypothetical statement concerning the specific elements of the literary phenomenon in general has been closely

---

19. On this point, see our *Logica come Scienza Positiva*, Messina 1956, chap. IV, where the concept of scientific abstraction should, however, be extended to take account of its epistemological-semantic univocality.

linked to a great variety of literary *exempla* or particular poetic instances, in which it has taken concrete form and by which it was verified. It is therefore also a method of *historical* synthesis.

The choice of such a method is dictated by the very nature of the theoretical theses or hypotheses which were our starting-point. For these acquire their sense first and foremost in and for the contemporary, post-romantic problematic of aesthetics in which the researcher is necessarily involved and committed. He is therefore bound to form a retrospective critical judgement – or more exactly, an historical–dialectical and therefore critical–synthetic judgement – of the philosophy and aesthetics that have preceded him. For he must test previous contributions by way of method to see how far they *are or are not at one* with the solutions advanced hypothetically to the questions that exercise contemporary aesthetics. The variety and complexity of the tools to be used in the demonstrative inquiry that will then ensue, ranging from those of epistemology and linguistics to those of literary exegesis or social history, further dictates the scientific–dialectical method of an historical–materialist theory of poetry and art in general.

Those who cannot stop fretting about a 'first and last principle' or absolute will obviously find no relief either in the experimental criterion of poetry as semantically organic concrete ideas or in the concept therein implied of a semantic dialectic. To start with the latter, it is quite natural that those who still accept the Hegelian concept of the dialectic of opposites – as a *circular* movement of negation and conservation of an original, meta-historical unity of opposites or Idea – will be unable to acquiesce in a dialectic of expressive facts (for example 'hubris' and 'invidious misfortunes') which is a real unity of the diverse because it is the unity of an actual manifold – the discrete. Thus to say that neither of the elements of the relation can be reduced absolutely to the other, and furthermore that neither absolutely excludes the other, is not the usual dialectician's game with words, for in effect they do circulate only *relatively* within each other, in the *diversified unity of an historical movement* – historical movement being the only non-mythical movement with which we are acquainted. That movement, it should be noted, is not circular, but rather one of both progression and regression from one element to the other. Therein lies the real, not invented, normative value of this historical–dialectical relation. To identify it we cannot use pure deduction nor an *a priori* or absolutizing synthetic procedure proper to metaphysics. We must instead use a scientific procedure, combining both analysis and synthesis – in other words, we must proceed by both *deduction and induction*.

Our imaginary metaphysician will also no doubt have got the impression that an experimental criterion of poetry gives him little more than the bare fact that the *Divine Comedy* and *Ulysses* exist, and he will probably charge us with constantly begging the question. No-one who aspires to a purely deductive demonstration (deduction from an absolute 'universal' principle) will accept that a deductive–inductive circular procedure such as that we have tried to adopt here demonstrates anything. In particular, the metaphysician will demand a more 'profound', that is a more 'universal', aesthetic criterion. If it is not a Crocean eternal 'guise' or 'form' of the Spirit, it may well be along the lines of Hegel and Lukács, the 'sensible intuition' of the 'movement [of universal, particular, and individual] in its living unity' and so forth.

But then we shall have to invite him once again to show what answers, if any, these 'universal' categories provide to the not inconsiderable number of real and particular problems that are raised again and again by works that are called poetic: poetic both for what they are in themselves and in relation to others that are called not poetic, and again in relation to others which are deemed equally artistic but not poetic. Since these categories explain everything in general and nothing in particular, he will have to think again, and consider with perhaps a little less impatience criteria such as those that we have here tried to put forward. For they are criteria of a scientific, general–historical or historical–dialectical, truth – a truth more sure, if less reassuring, than the metaphysical, eternal–dialectical truths of 'speculation', be it old or new.

18. *Other Sign Systems*

Can the special epistemological criterion of *organic semantic contextuality* be extended to non-literary (non-verbal) works such as painting, sculpture, architecture, music and film, to assess their artistic values? We believe so, though it is extremely difficult to demonstrate.

There are two principal reasons for this. First of all, an unfamiliar effort is needed to trace *thought* not just in what seems its most natural sign, the verbal sign or speech, but equally in quite different sorts of signs, such as the figurative sign in general or the musical sign. This calls for a rigorous conception of the 'other arts' as also being sign-systems or *languages* through which thought is manifested, in other words exists concretely as thought. Having made the effort, however, a second difficulty arises. For we must also understand that, just as in the case of speech or the linguistic sign, here too thought, the end, precisely in order to be expressed and become actual, is forced to *adjust* to the specific nature and respective *limits* of the sign, its means. For it is the organicity (semantic organicity, precisely) of the sign which hypothetically sets the norm of artistic and expressive perfection of the thought itself. In other words the postulate of dialectical identity between thought and language, thought and *sèma*, has to be conceived as broadly and as generally as possible: from which we shall conclude that there exists no thought worthy of the name which is not speech, or line or colour, or spatial volume, or interval and note, and so on.

Our starting-point will be the weakness of the discussions of painting or music in thinkers like Kant and Hegel, when, as is frequently the case, they lose sight of the technical elements (what Hegel calls the 'sensuous material') of the two arts – in short, the elements of pictorial or musical language proper.

The figurative arts, according to Kant, or 'those by which expression is found for [aesthetic] Ideas in *sensible intuition* (not by representations of mere Imagination that are aroused by words [=poetry]), are either arts of *sensible truth* [i.e. the plastic arts, subdivided into sculpture and architecture] or of *sensible illusion* [=painting]. . . . Both express Ideas by figures in space; the former makes figures cognisable by two senses, sight and touch (although not by the latter as far as beauty is concerned); the latter only by one, the first of these [sight]'.[20] But 'among the figurative arts I would give the palm to painting; partly because as the art of delineation it lies at the root of all the other figurative arts, and partly because it can penetrate much further into the region

20. Kant, *Critique of Judgment* cit., Section 51, pp. 208–9 (Kant's emphases). [The term 'figurative arts' has been substituted for Bernard's 'formative arts' throughout. – *Tr. note*.]

of Ideas, and can extend the field of intuition in conformity with them further than the others can' (Section 53, p. 220).

As regards music, Kant thinks of it as the artistic 'play' of the 'sensations of hearing', structured by the 'mathematical element' which is the indispensable condition for the 'proportion' of the acoustic 'vibrations' (§ 51, pp. 212–3). Thus in music 'the form of the composition of these sensations (harmony and melody) only serves *instead of the form of a language* [einer Sprache], by means of their proportionate accordance, to express the aesthetical Idea of a connected whole of an *unspeakable* [unnennbaren] wealth of thought, *corresponding* to a certain *theme* which produces the dominating affection in the piece. This can be brought mathematically under certain rules, because it rests in the case of tones on the relation between the number of vibrations of the air in the same time, so far as these tones are combined simultaneously or successively' (Section 53, p. 218 [D.V.'s emphases]). But on the other hand, 'although it [music] speaks by means of mere sensations without concepts, and so does not, like poetry, leave anything over for reflection, it yet moves the mind in a greater variety of ways and more intensely, although only transitorily'; it is, however, 'rather enjoyment than cultivation (the further [nebenbei] play of thought that is excited by its means is merely the effect of an, as it were, mechanical association); and in the judgment of Reason, it has less worth than any other of the beautiful arts' (Section 53, p. 217).

Hegel observes that in painting 'a *surface* becomes the medium of its representations'.[21] Thus, 'the first thing of importance in this connection [of the 'sensuous material used by painting'] is linear perspective'. (p. 837). But it has to be borne in mind that 'this reduction of the three dimensions to a level surface is implicit in the principle of interiorization [Innerlichwerdens] which can be asserted, as inwardness [Innerlichkeit], in space only by reason of the fact that it restricts and does not permit the subsistence of the totality of the external dimensions' (p. 805). For 'the essential principle of painting' is 'subjectivity of mind' (p. 799), living subjectivity, and 'the chief determinant of the *subject-matter* of painting is . . . subjectivity aware of itself' (p. 802). Note also that 'with painting . . . we enter[ed] the sphere of the *romantic*' (p. 888), and therefore 'the centre of painting' is placed 'in romantic and Christian art' (p. 799).

21. Hegel, *Aesthetic* III, iii. 1. ff., ed. cit., vol. II, p. 805 (Hegel's emphasis).

Coming on to music, Hegel writes that 'the note is not a merely vague rustling and sounding but can only have any musical worth on the strength of its *definiteness* [*Bestimmtheit*] and consequent purity. Therefore . . . it is in direct connection with *other* notes. Indeed it is this *relation* alone which imparts to it its own proper and actual definiteness and, along with that, its difference from other notes whether in opposition to them or in harmony with them. Owing to their relative independence this relation remains something *external* to the notes . . . On account of this externality of the relation, the specific character of the notes and their assembly rests on quantity [*in dem quantum*], on numerical proportions which of course have their basis in the [*physical*] nature of sound itself, but are used by music in a way first discovered by art and most variously modified. From this point of view, what constitutes the basis of music is not life in itself, as an organic unity, but equality, inequality, in short the mathematical form [or intellectual form: *Verstandesform*] dominant in the quantitative sphere' (pp. 910–11).

Thus, 'what dominates in music is at once the soul and profoundest feeling and the most rigorous mathematical laws so that it unites in itself two extremes which easily become independent of one another' (p. 894). But Hegel also states that 'inwardness as such is . . . the form in which music can conceive its subject-matter' (p. 902) and goes on: 'The inner life in its abstraction from the world has as its first differentiation the one that music is connected with, namely feeling. . . . Therefore feeling remains the shrouding [*das Umkleidende*] of the content, and it is to this sphere that music has laid claim' (pp. 902–3). Hence 'the note is an expression [*Äusserung*] and something external [*Äusserlichkeit*], but an expression which, precisely because it is something external, is made to vanish again forthwith . . . the impression . . . is at once made within; the notes re-echo only in the depths of the soul', etc. (p. 892).

Just these few extracts are sufficient to prove our point. As soon as Kant and Hegel begin to wander from their analysis of the technical elements of expression of the two arts in question and abandon themselves to metaphysical distinctions and dogmatic sophistry, their discussion becomes ever more gratuitous and erroneous. In Kant, we find ourselves with that hierarchy of the arts, of an abstract rationalist inspiration, which promotes painting over the other figurative arts and demotes music, some of whose real elements Kant analyses with insight, to the lowest rank – dubbing it 'enjoyment' rather than 'cultivation'. Hegel muddles together in his metaphysical categories of 'subjectivity of mind', 'inwardness-as-such', two artistic phenomena which his (acute) technical analyses had tried to distinguish from one another. The result is that one of them – music, of course – is divested of its own properties and simply identified with inwardness-as-such, decreed the 'form' of musical 'content'. Thus the note, as 'something external', 'vanishes again' into 'the depths of the soul' as soon as it has appeared. In other words, in order for the note to be given a metaphysical value, all the real and specific grounds of its existence are cancelled and devalued.

Nevertheless, there are other comments – in Kant – which are of positive interest for the problem of method. I am thinking of the indications he gives in Section 51 of the principle he has followed, or not followed, in making a division within the fine arts: 'we cannot', he says, 'choose a more convenient [*bequemeres*] principle, at least tentatively, than the analogy of art with the mode of expression of which men avail themselves in speech, in order to communicate to one another as perfectly as possible not merely their concepts but also their sensations'. He goes on to specify that this is an attempt 'to combine the fine arts under one principle, viz. that of the *expression* of aesthetical *Ideas* (according to the analogy of *speech*)' but that the reader should not regard this as a 'definitive analysis' of them.[22] We may also compare the two extremely suggestive points made by Kant on music which we have already quoted: firstly that harmony and melody in music have the same function as 'form' (of the composition of the sensations of hearing) as does the form of language elsewhere, in poetry ('instead of the form of language'); and secondly, that this musical form serves to express 'a wealth of thought' which is 'unspeakable', or non-verbal, because it only corresponds to 'a certain theme' (p. 218).

Encouraged by Kant's obscure and largely ignored attempt to bring the fine arts under the rubric of language, we shall now try to explore the fecundity of the semantic criterion – in other words its applicability to all the arts. True, the encouragement lies more in the force

22. Cf. Kant, ed. cit., pp. 207, 210 note.

of truth which is always contained in an experimental principle, however vague, than in the dubious development of it in the present case. But in examining the general applicability of the semantic criterion, we shall see that it is not just an 'analogous' or generic, external criterion of the artistic phenomena of the figurative arts, music, and film. It is specific to them as well, and stands therefore as their inner principle or norm.

19. Painting – Sculpture – Architecture

In what sense can one speak of a language of painting? Let us start from the hypothesis that such a language exists and that it consists, putting it schematically, in signs composed of surface or two-dimensional line and colour. We shall suppose further that these sign-abstractions (abstractions because neither line nor colour exists in two dimensions in nature) are the means whose end is the idea – or unity of a manifold – of painting: in the same way as phonetic, lexical and grammatical elements are the expressive means of which the end is the idea or thought of poetry. Let us suppose further that these pictorial signs are not, as regards their structure, incorporeal or conventional or indifferent as linguistic or verbal signs are; but rather that, though they may be used differently for different pictorial ends, a vertical or horizontal line or a certain colour always remains a vertical or horizontal line or that particular colour. On the other hand we know that, though the structural features of linguistic signs – incorporeality, biplanarity and arbitrariness – remain unchanged, the signs themselves change from one language-system to another, and indeed within the historical span of a single system. Thus, though pictorial signs, as we have envisaged them, *for themselves* are *empty* (of value or thought) in the same way as verbal and other signs, yet they have a different *function* in respect of the ends or values of painting. They are not conventional, incorporeal or indifferent, but possess in their particular quality a certain stability and concreteness and mandatory positivity. The same can be said, *mutatis mutandis*, for other figurative signs and those of music and film.

In order to advance our discussion beyond these preliminary points, we shall now quote and comment on a fundamental passage from the writings of Konrad Fiedler, the critic from whom it may be said that 'visibilism', the most important, if not the only important poetic of the figurative arts, has developed.

'A modern philologist', says Fiedler, 'has claimed that ". . . without speech it is impossible to realize for a moment the simplest images, such as black and white". This expresses very clearly at once a truth and an error, both of which are stated fairly commonly. It is easy to understand that the ordinary use of sight, for the purposes of practical living and theoretical knowledge, cannot lead to the realization of visual images. But the idea that language has a function here is an illusion. It is not appreciated that, in spite of language and in spite of all the spiritual dominion that consciousness achieves over reality as it develops in language, the material of reality which develops through the action of the visual sense remains in the same state, as though neither language nor conceptualization nor cognitive awareness existed. Clearly, if it is to be possible to realize the existence of a *visual objectivity* in products of a conscious activity, then this can only occur precisely through an activity which is as it were an immediate continuation of the sensuous process to which the very existence of *visibility* itself is due. Now, an activity of this kind is in fact to be found among the many manifestations of life of which human nature is capable. We perceive gestures in ourselves and others which seek to represent a visible thing to the eye; we can also see that when someone draws or paints or models he is more or less perfectly producing something that is destined exclusively to be perceived through the sense of sight. . . .'.[23]

Now, if we are to make the most of this revolutionary assertion of visual values for a new aesthetics, we must first translate it into the problematic of an epistemology of the sign, or a philosophical semiotics. If we do not, it will either fall irrelevantly on the stony ground of the psychology of, more or less, the Beautiful, or else wither into figurative formalisms of the type exemplified, at their best, by Wölfflin. The latter's *kunstgeschichtliche Grundbegriffe* are in fact yoked pairs of categories which try to embrace the history of art in all its aspects from the 'linear (draughtsmanly, plastic) and painterly' and the 'planimetric' and 'recessional' to those of 'multiple unity and simple

23. Konrad Fiedler, 'Ursprung der künstlerischen Thätigkeit', in *Schriften über Kunst*, Leipzig 1896, pp. 267–8.

unity' and 'absolute and relative clearness'.[24] In other words, they embrace too much, and therefore too little.

The exclusion of these alternatives, however, strengthens our original hypothesis: since any other choice would only lead us straight back into the worst sort of dogmatism, whether positivist or metaphysical–ontological, we must proceed with it. So, accepting for the moment the reduction of *visibility* itself to a sign, and therefore a means of expression of end-thought, let us begin by verifying those features which are structural to it, or differential, as well as those which it has in common with other signs.

Take any technical drawing, an economic graph for instance, with its straight lines and its curve. How does its horizontal line differ from the horizontal line of the moulding running all along the back wall and under the back windows and along the two *side* walls in Giotto's *Christ before Caiaphas*? An eminent art critic, John White, tells us that Giotto's 'mathematically straight' line is 'potentially a major *spatial* accent' and 'is used to emphasize the *surface* qualities of the design'. Thus, 'it gives *formal being* to the dramatic unity and tension of the scene' (our emphases; see also the *Wedding Feast at Cana*).[25] By contrast the straight line in the graph, to continue with our comparison, *indicates* let us say a certain *amount* of goods, whose prices are traced in the vertical column, while the curve indicates the movement of the particular economic phenomenon as a whole.

We have then to conclude that Giotto's visual sign helps to produce, or to express, ideas or values (of dramatic unity in space, etc.) by virtue of the structural and differential features it possesses as a visual sign, in this case a straight line. But when the same sign appears in the graph, it helps to produce or express values or ideas not by virtue of itself, in other words its *visualness*, but by virtue of *something else*, the verbal–univocal signs of quantitative, arithmetical values. These are represented by the straight line in its capacity as an auxiliary symbol, a symbol of convenience, which means that it can always be replaced by another (a polar or circular diagram, for example).

To put it another way. In the case of Giotto and the pictorial-artistic sign, the visible feature expresses values by virtue of its *structural*

24. Heinrich Wölfflin, *Principles of Art History*, London 1932, pp. 18, 73, 155, 196.
25. John White, *The Birth and Rebirth of Pictorial Space*, London 1957, p. 64. Cf. Emilio Cecchi, *Giotto*, Milan 1955.

semantic capacities, whereby it is potentially part of an *organic* and therefore *autonomous* semantic context. But in the case of the visual sign as economic or scientific symbol, the visible feature resembles the former only in the abstract. In the concrete, that is, in the epistemological concreteness of its semantic use, it is seen to be a visual sign which does not actually possess the structural capacities of a visual sign. So while as a sign it is indeed part of semantic contexts, those contexts are disorganic and heteronomous, being inter-dependent with countless others, be they technico-visual or verbal-univocal or both (economic theories, in this instance).

This is the only possible basis, first of all, on which to submit the modern idea of 'stylistic unity' as criterion of the artistry or otherwise of a painting to rigorous formulation. Statements about the pictorial opus will then be precise and pertinent because they are semantic: for a painting, like any work of art, is an *expressive fact*, an object to be perceived by deciphering it according to the linguistic code in which it is expressed. The danger of the criterion of 'stylistic unity' is otherwise that it gives rise to contaminatory descriptions of 'formal' or expressive-pictorial data and 'content' or illustrative data, converting either kind, as likely as not, into a more or less elegant *bellettrisme*.

The same principle also provides the only possible basis on which to find a more than approximate solution to the problem of the relation between illustration and decoration. We need to find a solution, that is, which will avoid both the tendency to undervalue the illustrative (as in the formalist poetics of Wölfflin and Berenson) and the tendency to undervalue the decorative (seen at its best in Panofsky's poetic of iconologism[26]). These tendencies would be replaced by the normative criterion of the illustrative (ideas, values) as *ex-pressed* from the decorative inherent in the organic structural features of the visual sign (two-dimensional line and colour), leading ultimately to an unbreakable tension between ends-ideality and means-visibility. Thus those who in practice tend to turn means into ends fall into the error, the negative solution, of decorativism, which ultimately generates such extremes of 'in-formal and anti-academic art as tachisme (at present the furthest limit of abstract art), whose visual material is as uncommunicative as it is stimulating. Those on the other hand who

26. Erwin Panofsky, *Meaning in the Visual Arts*, New York 1957.

tend to turn ends into means fall into the error of mere illustration, which may even embrace the most *pompier* and carnivalesque illusionism (what White calls the 'carnival of the *trompe-l'oeil*'[27]). The twin fate of these trends demonstrates the need here too of a concrete dialectic of end-idea and means-sign, or an *irreversible* order. The same may be said, *mutatis mutandis*, for sculpture and architecture.

These structural features of the pictorial–visual sign point implicitly to the particular kind of *perception* proper to the figurative arts, which lies at the root of their 'sensuousness'. As in the case of music also, the sensuousness of the figurative arts is a characteristic which differentiates them from literary art. But having demonstrated its structural features, we must try to show what it is that the pictorial sign shares with other signs and which confers upon it the status of one of the primary signs of thought. What it has in common is the fact that, because in itself it is empty of values, it is pure means in respect of value or idea as end. It is purely instrumental, perenially mutable in its use, and therefore essentially historical.

Even a very schematic and incomplete look at the history of pictorial means, focussing on the evolution of colour and its effect on line, will provide the relevant confirmation. It is sufficient to recollect how the Renaissance conception of the expressive function of line or design or 'form' has changed between the beginnings of Impressionism and our own day in harmony with the various developments from local colour to tonal colour and finally pure colour. Thus the triumph of linear perspective and three-dimensional illusionism, which lasted at least up to Courbet, gave way to the dominance of (pure) colour over line in Van Gogh and then, with Matisse and Braque, to colour as the quintessence of two-dimensionality (the semantic category par excellence of painting), being seen quite simply as colour *on the surface of the canvas*. We need not even mention Picasso's rigorous use of line in an anti-perspectivist function, etc.[28]

In other words, we have only to remember that a curve, for example,

27. White, op. cit., p. 108.

28. Cf. Hans Jantzen, 'Über Prinzipen der Farbengebung in der Malerei', in *Über den gotischen Kirchenraum, und andere Aufsätze*, Berlin 1951; Wolfgang Schöne, *Über das Licht in der Malerei*, Berlin 1954 (see especially pp. 197 ff. and 242–56); André Malraux, *Psychologie de l'Art*: 'Le Musée Imaginaire', Paris 1947 ('the velvet feel of Chardin's peaches is over; in Braque it is no longer the peach that is velvet, it is the painting'); Frank Elgar and Robert Maillard, *Picasso*, Münich–Zurich 1956.

even though everyone still sees it as a curve, has a great variety of expressive functions, depending on whether it is the curve which creates elementary foreshortening on an ancient vase, or the curve in a Fouquet where there is already the tendency to artificial perspective, or the curve in a Picasso, *Guernica* for example, where all modelling and perspective have disappeared, and so on. To remember this is at the same time to acknowledge, firstly, that if we are not aware of the language of painting and its historical particularity, it is impossible to appreciate any one particular painting properly, however original or brilliant or 'unmistakable' it might be. One cannot, for example, perceive the values of a Cézanne without specifying the semantic means it adopts, and distinguishing them from those of Piero della Francesca no less than from those of Monet.

It follows, secondly, that there are no grounds to the objection that might be put to us, that we have reduced art, in this case painting, to 'technical evolution'. The objection does not stand because the dialectical character of the relation between semantic means and end-idea is such that there is nothing more different and clearly distinguishable from the end, i.e. idea or value or universal, than the semantic means or technique used to express it; while at the same time nothing is more strictly indissociable from it, for the latter is the *indispensable condition* of the former (to follow right through the terms used by Kant in connection with the mathematical-acoustic technique of music).

So it also follows that no attempt to produce a sociology of art, or to locate art in a superstructure, can hope to succeed unless it takes account of this dialectical character of the relation between art and technique. A case in point is the sociology of Frederick Antal, the most serious effort in this direction. Antal tries to individuate and distinguish a *Madonna and child* by Masaccio from a *Madonna and child* by Gentile da Fabriano on the grounds that, with 'due consideration given to the *content* of the paintings' and their relevant social background, 'it is soon apparent that *stylistic* divergences between various works of art are due not only to individual differences between the different artists but also to the fact that these works were intended for different sections of the public or satisfied different artistic needs'. These criteria lead to the usual result, though here it is better hidden than usual by the taste and intelligence of the author: a mechanical juxtaposition of 'content' (abstractly conceived) and style or form, in short, social history and art. A typical example is Antal's comparison of the 'lack of corporeal clarity in the figures and their delicate colouring' in the 'aristocratic-Gothic' and 'religious' Gentile, with the sharp and realistic figures of the 'classicistic and upper-middle-class manner of Masaccio'.[29]

Sculpture. Sculpture is the expression of values or ideas by means of a figurative language of non-metaphorical volumes and surfaces leading into depth. It is a language of free three-dimensional visual forms. In this respect, it differs from architectural language which consists in mathematically or geometrically conditioned three-dimensional visual forms. Sculpture is a language of three-dimensional forms expressive of visual *objects equally visible on all sides.* In this consists the rational character and power of the free sculptural sign; and the sculptural sign is, precisely, different from the mathematical-visual sign of architecture, as it is from the pictorial sign which expresses two-dimensional visual forms.

Benvenuto Cellini had an idea of this character and power of the sculptural sign when he wrote that the work of a bad sculptor is ten times more criticizable 'when you walk round it' than it seemed to deserve 'at first sight'. The reason for this, as Cellini explains in his own way, is that: 'Painting is one part of the eight principal views from which sculpture must be seen. . . . But these views are not eight, they are forty and more, for every time he [the artist] turns his figure, a muscle shows too much or too little, so that enormous variations can be seen.' Therefore, he goes on, 'the artist must lift some of that fair grace of the first view of his figure and spread it around the whole, so as to harmonize that first view with all the rest'.[30]

In support of Cellini's point, one might compare the Archaic bronze of a horse in the Metropolitan Museum in New York with the Hellenistic bronze representing a race-horse in the National Museum

29. Frederick Antal, *Florentine Painting and its Social Background*, London 1948, pp. 7 and 312–3. Cf. Pierre Francastel, *Peinture et Société*, Lyon 1951.

30. Benvenuto Cellini, *Due Trattati . . . Uno dell' Oreficeria l'Altro della Scultura*: con appendice di Lettere sulla pittura, scultura e architettura, Milan 1811; letter to B. Varchi of 28th Jan. 1546, pp. 212–3, 237. It is not of course our intention to prejudge bas-relief, etc., but only to indicate a hierarchy of expressive values, based – and this is unlikely to be contested – on how fully the structural features of sculptural language have been used, i.e. the relative complexity or wealth of the problems to which solutions have been found.

in Athens. The tongue of the race-horse – just to make this one point – is hanging in movement from the open mouth and forms a body in itself (cf. Cellini: a muscle shows too much or too little). As a result, it blocks the harmonization of this one view with all the other views of the horse and so prevents us from perceiving any unity of plastic style. It stands in the way of that *essential* sense of the figure in question (horse), the concept-symbol or value to be expressed which in this case has remained unexpressed. By contrast, the plastic unity of the horse represented in the Archaic piece *does* express it. Similarly, one can take, say, a death-mask, however 'impressive', or casts of human bodies, even as natural as those of the people of Pompeii carbonized by the lava, and, comparing them with genuine sculptures representing the same subject, see at once the cardinal difference between the expressed and the unexpressed.

It is true also of sculpture, therefore, that to decide the artistic status or otherwise of a piece one has to see whether there exists an organic semantic context and hence a symbol or thought or value which is semantically autonomous. It goes without saying that the highest possible degree of potentiation of the structural capacities of the relevant sign (volume, etc.) is as much a feature of the sculptural (figurative) semantic organism as it is of others. It is hardly necessary to add, then, that this semantic means too is purely functional and therefore historical. Because of this, to take just one example, we move between 'closed forms' of sculpture, where the solid, bodily space of the figure is set off from and against the natural, incorporeal and empty space which surrounds it (the stone carvings of Egyptian, Romanesque, and Mexican pre-Columbian art, or Brancusi today); and 'open forms' which expand outwards into natural space where their centre of gravity is located (Baroque sculpture and some of Henry Moore's work).[31]

Architecture. Ideas or values are expressed in architecture by means of a system of geometric, three-dimensional, visual signs. That is to say, architecture uses a language made up of measurements appropriate to the creation of visible order through the repetition of similar masses, the effect of which is to modify the physical environment for the purposes of human need. (It is perhaps not too bold to include architecture among the 'representational' arts, even if only just,

31. Cf. Erich Neumann, *The Archetypal World of Henry Moore*, New York 1959.

leaving music alone as 'not representing' anything.) One must be absolutely clear on the primacy of the *quantitative* character of this visual sign, the fact that this is a language of visible *dimensions*, or visual *proportions*. Otherwise very proper comments on 'the supremacy of architecture in spatial values' or 'interior and exterior' as 'dimensions proper to the spatiality of architecture' enabling us to 'realize a spatiality through form which is immune to natural space', all remain unfocussed.

Here too the aesthetic criterion of organic semantic contextuality must be applied. Once again, it is the criterion of the highest possible degree of potentiation of a sign (the architectural sign) which, like the other figurative signs and the musical sign, is not conventional in the very precise sense in which the linguistic sign is conventional. We must, however, reiterate our distinction between organic semantic context, or semantically autonomous and therefore artistic thought, and disorganic semantic context, or semantically heteronomous and non-artistic thought. Here the distinction is between the architectonic *opus* and the merely 'tectonic' *opus* (from the Greek *tektonikos*, able in construction), or engineering.

Finally, we would draw attention to the great variety and wealth of organic contexts produced by the historical functionality of this proportional–visual sign. They range from the relationsihps between the annulets of the capital, the abacus and the bands of the architrave of the Propylea at the Acropolis, the criterion of these relationships being given by low numbers (ratios such as 7:12 and 6:25); to the inter-relation of the rooms and their relationship with the portico in Palladio's Villa Godi, according to commensurable proportions of height to width and length (series of the total plan: the progression 16, 24, 36); to the inter-relation of interiors and exteriors 'established according to an analytical system of incommensurable proportions (proportional scale based on the series Φ) in Le Corbusier's Ville Savoie; and so on.[32]

32. See P. H. Scholfield's fundamental work *The Theory of Proportion in Architecture*, Cambridge 1958. Note his comments on the ratios 7:12 and 6:25 for the Parthenon: 'The first of the ratios between the actual measurements does approximate closely to 7:12, but the second falls short by an error of about 1%. This error may be regarded as trivial, for it would not be apparent to the eye. It is, however, a fact that... an "incommensurable" interpretation of the ratios is quite as possible as Penrose's own "commensurable" interpretation' (p. 93); and

20. Music

We have long known that the most profoundly problematical or, as Adorno puts it, 'enigmatic' aspect of music is what he calls its 'detachment from the visually and conceptually defined objective world': the world that is expressed in words ('thinking language' par excellence, according to Adorno), line and colour.[33] But there is a serious philosophical objection against taking this as a reason for not trying to approach the problem of music in strictly, or rather rigorously, semiotic terms. For not to do so would mean in effect to deny any *expressive* character to music, and thereby to deny its humanity and rationality. At best, we would be settling for a (perhaps very refined) hedonism, the enjoyment of that play of pure 'sonorous forms in movement' counterposed by the Kantian Hanslick, in part beneficially, to the everlasting vulgar conception of music as the production of thoughts and feelings which can be defined in *words*.[34] The same counterposition recurs today in Stravinsky's poetic.[35]

on Le Corbusier's Modulor: '[It is] not only an instrument of architectural proportion, a means of ensuring the repetition of similar shapes. It is also a system of preferred dimensions intended for standardizing the sizes of mass-produced building components' (p. 122). See also: Rudolf Wittkower, *Architectural Principles in the Age of Humanism*, London 1952, especially pp. 110 ff.; Le Corbusier, *Towards a New Architecture*, tr. F. Etchells, London 1946 ('Architecture is nothing but ordered arrangement, noble prisms, seen in light. There exists one thing which can ravish us, and this is measure or scale. To achieve scale! To map out in rhythmical quantities . . . to balance, *to resolve the equation*. For, if this expression may be a paradox in talking of painting, it fits well with architecture . . . which works by quantities': pp. 150–1).

33. Theodor W. Adorno, 'Über das gegenwärtige Verhältnis von Philosophie und Musik' and 'Musik, Sprache und ihr Verhältnis im gegenwärtigen Komponieren', both in *Archivio di Filosofia* (Rome), 1953 and 1956; 'Klassik, Romantik, Neue Musik', in *Neue deutschen Heften*, March 1959; and *Philosophy of Modern Music*, tr. A. G. Mitchell and W. V. Bloomster, New York 1973.

34. Eduard Hanslick, *Vom musikalischen Schönen* (1854), Leipzig 1922, pp. 1 ff., 62 ff., 78–9 note.

35. Cf. Igor Stravinsky, 'Answers to 34 questions', in *Encounter*, July 1957, pp. 3–7. For example: 'The musical idea: when do you recognize it as an idea?' – 'I recognize musical ideas when they start to exert a certain kind of auditive sense.' – 'Do you think you will ever abandon the tonal identification?' – 'Possibly. We can still create a sense of return to exactly the same place without tonality. . . . Form cannot exist without identity of some sort.' – 'Is there such a thing as a problem of communication?' – 'I use the language of music, and my statement in my grammar will be clear to the musician who has followed music up to where I and my contemporaries have brought it.' – 'How do you understand Webern's

I say 'at best', because the alternative to Hanslick's criticist formalism might well be, is indeed, the supremely dogmatic conception of an ontology of sounds or a metaphysical entification of music. Leaving aside the ancients and their 'music of the spheres', such a view has been propounded by a whole host of doctrinaires of various persuasions, old and new, and still finds support today. Its patron saint is Schopenhauer, whose fancies that music revealed the 'essential nature' of the 'feelings' and the 'inmost nature of the world' were received with some indulgence by Schönberg[36]; its spokesmen would include Hindemith who ontologizes and absolutizes certain historical characteristics of tonal music,[37] and the latest theorists of the electronic production of sounds, a music in which they hear the 'languageless voice of Being'.

But let us see in what the language of music might consist, a language which the suggestions of Kant and Hegel may already allow us to term mathematical–acoustic. The first thing we should register, something that is forced on us by the actual history of music, is the phenomenon of interval and note.

We can start with certain premisses. First of all, the interval, as a relation of distance between two sounds, has a natural, physical basis: this was shown by Helmholtz with his discovery in the vibrations of two sounds of the numerical relations between *Grundton* or basic tone and *Obertöne* or harmonic vibrations.[38] Secondly, although Helmholtz

remark: "Don't write music entirely by ear . . ."?' – 'Webern was not satisfied with the . . . passive act of hearing: he requires the *hearer, whether composer or listener,* to make cognisant relations of what he hears: "you must know why". He obliges the hearer to become a listener, summons him to active relations with music. . . . The idea that the actual pitch of the note is not so important in an absolute sense has been supplanted, to my mind, by the idea that *pitch matters only because of the interval.* Today the composer does not think of notes in isolation but of notes in their *intervallic* position in the series, in their dynamic, their octave, and their timbre. Apart from the series "notes" are nothing; in it, their recurrence, their pitch, their dynamic, their timbre, and their rhythmic relation determine form' (our emphases).

36. Arthur Schopenhauer, *The World as Will and Idea*, vol I, London 1883, pp. 338, 331. Cf. Arnold Schönberg, *Theory of Harmony*, New York 1940.

37. Paul Hindemith, *Unterweisung im Tonsatz*, Mainz 1940 ('Thus the interval, which is formed through the coupling together of two tones, is to be regarded as the true building-block of music').

38. Hermann Helmholtz, *On the Sensations of Tone as a Physiological Basis for the Theory of Music* (1857), tr. W. A. Ellis, London and New York 1895, and *Die Lehre von den Tonenempfindungen*, Brunswick 1863. Cf. also Edmund Gurney, *The Power of Sound*,

was not concerned with this, the natural interval must be distinguished from the interval established and developed between two notes by the techniques of the various musical systems. At the same time, however, it must be emphasized that the interval is the primary expressive cell of music because, apart from being a relation of *pitch*, which by itself is an abstraction, it is also a relation of *rhythmic accent, duration*, and *timbre*. The point is adequately proved by the existence of notable musical works generated by a single interval of two notes (i.e. a self-sufficient interval, without need of the intervention of a third note, even if it is set in a discourse of many intervals). An example in the tonal field is the beginning of Beethoven's *Piano Sonata, Op. 111*, provided by an interval of two notes only, E flat and F sharp, while an a-tonal example is the first of Webern's *Five Movements* for string quartet (Op. 5). This not to speak of the fact that relations of rhythm are no less important in tonal music than those of pitch (high and low) while in a-tonal and electronic music relations of timbre in their turn are no less important than those of pitch and rhythm.

With these premises behind us, we may now assert the following. (1) Only when the four constitutive elements of a sound stated above have been determined through the relation of that sound to another, in other words only when a sound has been subsumed in an *interval*, can the sound become a musical *note*, thereby constituting *modes* and *scales*, in short becoming part of a grammar of music.

(2) Taken for itself, the interval – whether it be the tritone of Gregorian chant (relation of pitch: 8:11), or the interval of a major third (relation of pitch: 4:5), or one of the twelve intervals in the dodecaphonic series – is *empty* of musical values or ideas. That is, musically it can signify anything whatever depending on what musical system it is employed in or to what compositional use it is put. For instance, the interval of an augmented fourth, or tritone, used to be regarded

London 1880; E. G. Wolff, *Grundlagen einer autonomen Musikästhetik*, Strassburg 1934. Armando Plebe's essay on 'L'Estetica Musicale di Hindemith', in *Rivista di Estetica* (Turin), 1959, pp. 399 ff., includes a penetrating analysis of Wolff's theory of the interval – as the original cell of music – compared with that of Hindemith which derives the series of intervals from that of the harmonics. I also agree with Plebe, with whom I have had some interesting conversations, that the limitation of Wolff's theory is his conception of the interval as *Spannung*, tension. This is an extra-acoustic term which solicits us towards psychologism and prevents an epistemological analysis of the interval as musical *sign* through which musical ideas may be expressed.

as *diabolus in musica* because of its dissonance; since then, and not so recently, the devil has come to be quite at home (Hindemith). The interval of a third is dissonance in pre-tonal systems and creative practice, consonance in tonal ones; likewise the dominant interval of a fifth (relation of pitch: 2:3). Similarly, the diminished seventh chord is valid and functional in enharmonic systems and usage, but considered 'worn out' and therefore false in the *neue Musik*, and so on.

(3) The relation between interval-and-note, with its associated grammar, and the musical *idea* (which may be a simple 'motif' or a simple 'phrase', harmony and melody, Kant says, or even one or the other) is the relation between semantic instrument or means and that end or value or form which is precisely the expressed musical idea. It is the same dialectical, irreversible, relation which holds, *mutatis mutandis*, between instrumental form (linguistic-structural elements, line, colour) and form-end or (poetic, pictorial) value.

(4) On the one hand, in fact, the interval-and-note is numerically and mathematically structured; its structure, that is to say, is peculiarly rational. This is what makes it the indispensable condition (as Kant saw) for the proportion or unity of sounds which underlies all music, for, as Landormy has observed, the musical work, even as a straight-forward 'organization of auditive perceptions', manifests 'the characteristic need of reason, the need for unity'.[39] At the same time, the different ways in which it is subordinated *functionally* show it to be the instrumental condition – an indispensable condition or *sine qua non* – for the satisfaction of that need for unity of a manifold which is shared by the musical work too. Which amounts to saying that interval and note can be seen as the semantic means of producing and expressing the end which here is musical idea or form (whose content to be formed is as usual matter, the sensuous, the manifoldness of images, in this case acoustic images).

(5) (a). We should not then be surprised if the musical idea consists in an *unspeakable Gedankenfülle*, or plenitude of thought: taking the term 'unspeakable' not in the mystical sense in which it might be understood by a romantic aesthetician, but in the sense in which a theme-idea or series-idea is and cannot but be unspeakable. That is to say, ideas whose means of expression is a particular grammar of intervals and *notes*, not a grammar of phonemes and *signifiers* (cenematic and associ-

39. Paul Landormy, *A History of Music* (tr. F. H. Martens), London 1923.

ated plerematic constituents and exponents) which is the grammar of the literary or poetic idea, a *speakable* idea. So that, far from being ineffable and indeterminate, the musical idea, as Mendelssohn says, is 'extremely definite' in its own way and 'untranslatable' by other means, be they words, line or colour.[40]

(b). Nor should it surprise us if the 'sense' or meaning of music is to be identified with this unspeakable *Gedankenfülle*, the musical idea produced or expressed by an *order* of personal auditive images whose instrument is a grammatical system of intervals, scales, etc. Specifically because it is such a plenitude of unspeakable *thought*, music (against the view of Kant) is cultivation, or *culture* and humanity, as much and more than it is enjoyment. Indeed, looking at it the other way, it could not even be enjoyment if as thought it were merely play, a *Gedankenspiel* incidentally excited (Kant) by virtually mechanical associations and consisting of all those verbal reflections and feelings which are '*aroused*' or, as is commonly said, 'expressed' by music, but which we shall call 'translated' by it. (For example, Beethoven's sonatas in D minor and F minor and the Farewell Sonata supposedly 'express' *The Tempest* and a sentimental romance respectively; not to mention the 'Napoleonism' of the Third Symphony, etc.) So it seems justifiable to conclude by agreeing with the most modern musical criticism, that the enigma of the 'sense' of music is solved only by him who '*plays it* right in its totality' (Adorno, Castiglioni, etc.[41]).

So we cannot accept that 'music does *not* constitute a system of signs'. It is clear from the foregoing that the theme-idea or series-idea, in other words what the music *says* (Adorno: *das gesagte*), *can* be separated from the music (contrary to the opinion of Adorno and others). This is possible in as much as music means first and foremost the semantic, expressive, technique of interval and note and the various historical grammars related to it: their instrumental nature makes them easily distinguishable and separable from their end, the musical idea.

If this is so, it must be conceded that the semantic criterion of organic contextuality is also applicable to the work of music. This

40. Mendelssohn, loc. cit.; and cf. T. Meyer Greene, *The Arts and the Art of Criticism*, Princeton 1952, pp. 488–9.

41. Niccolò Castiglioni, *Il Linguaggio Musicale*, Milan 1959: 'We would recommend any listener who has been spoiled by romantic dis-education to abstain from dreaming of stories of farewell while listening to the famous *Farewell Sonata*'.

criterion ascribes the artistic status of the musical idea to its *expressive autonomy*, in other words to its organic semantic unity. Therein lies the stylistic unity of music, which, like that of painting, sculpture, architecture and, as we shall see, film, is the highest possible potentiation of the organic capacities of what is structurally particular, positive and necessitating in the musical sign.

The musical sign too, like the figurative and filmic sign, is very different from the verbal sign, which is biplanar, incorporeal and arbitrary, that is indifferent to its respective meaning ('language wants to be overlooked', as the structuralist Siertsema says). Here is the confirmation, and explanation, the 'sensuous' character of the musical idea (as of the figurative and filmic idea): it too is incompatible with the comparative 'coldness' and incorporeality of the literary idea. It can now be seen that it is these structural differences between signs (in this case the musical and verbal sign) which are the biggest obstacle to our accepting music as language, if not also as thought. The same is true for the persistent, if somewhat lesser, difficulty in accepting, not so much painting and film, but sculpture and architecture as language and thought. The authority dogmatically conferred on verbal language, still thought of as the language of thought (or unity of a manifold) by definition, remains the great stumbling-block.[42]

It follows from what has been said that music-with-words, of any kind, be it more or less popular *lieder* or cantatas or oratorios or opera, is to be classified as an impure or hybrid genre, or if you prefer, a compound genre. If anything counts in these compositions, it is of course the music with its untranslatable language, romantic illusions to the contrary notwithstanding.[43] There have been doctrinaire, though

42. Cf. Zofia Lissa, *Fragen der Musikästhetik*, Berlin 1954, especially pp. 197 ff., where she denies that music belongs to the superstructure, because she admits only verbal language and therefore does not attempt an analysis of the musical sign. Nevertheless, this is a stimulating work, and not just in comparison with other Marxist endeavours such as Sidney Finkelstein's intrepidly entitled *How Music Expresses Ideas*, New York 1952.

43. Cf. Suzanne K. Langer, *Problems of Art*, London 1957: on 'imitative' music: 'There is a fine instance . . . in Brahms's song, "The Smith" . . . . The vocal part alone conveys the exciting metallic clang, without any patent reproduction of the characteristic smithy sounds; and . . . the effect . . . is due to the hard perfect intervals and extreme use of contrary motion. The tones themselves are not metallic; the three-quarter rhythm, often contradicted by a two-fourth melodic rhythm, is not a copy. . . . This is a genuine *transformation* of occupational noise into purely musical elements – not a quality of tones similar to the noise, but

brilliant, attempts to justify opera in musical terms. Opera is defined as a 'vocal organization of characters' on the grounds that while the unity of a symphony is 'thematic' that of opera is supposedly 'vocal', and whereas 'the symphony draws on the simultaneity of its thematic elements' opera supposedly ' "superimposes" the characters on the harmonies', for chest-C and vocalization are not 'interchangeable' in the same way as the leit-motif (Leibowitz).[44]

We think we still have the right, indeed the duty, to reply to these endeavours with the *fin de non-recevoir* pronounced by Stravinsky: 'It is strange that skeptics who readily demand new proofs for everything and who usually take a sly delight in exposing whatever is purely conventional in established forms, never ask that any proof be given of the necessity or even of the simple expediency of any musical phrase that claims to identify itself with an idea, an object, or a character'.[45] The problem for Leibowitz and others is that chest-C and vocalization interest us in so far as they are music and hence by virtue of their *intervallic* nature. For example the interval absorbs and fuses into itself the vowels of vocalization, which means that these vowels are a long way away from the *word* which as such, in its semantic integrity, gives consistency to the characters. Such vowels are in fact only extremely abstracted elements of the word, because they are in reality dissociated and transmuted into *timbres*. The thesis, therefore, that opera is a vocal, musical construction of characters does not hold.

As regards *dance*, an art whose means of expression is the human body and whose visual language is made up of gestures (steps and positions), it is sufficient to point out that seldom in its history has it been 'pure', usually being commingled with at least music and mime. Indeed

---

relational effects that belong inherently to harmonic intervals and melodic progressions' (p. 103). The musical analyses and criteria are the best thing in Langer's writings – she remarks elsewhere, for example, that 'music is an audible symbol of what would otherwise remain formless and incommunicable'. Their limitations become apparent when she tries to extend the concept of 'symbol' to the other arts. It then becomes clear that it is an aestheticist notion, of romantic origin, that betrays the lack of a modern semiotic, to the point of being virtually indistinguishable from Clive Bell's platonizing formula of 'significant form'.

44. René Leibowitz, *Possibilités de l'Opéra*, Liège 1950, especially p. 39.

45. Stravinsky, *Poetics of Music*, tr. A. Knodel and I. Dahl, Cambridge, Mass. 1970, pp. 100–1.

increasingly it has tended to become a musical-choreographic-mimic-gestural art, culminating in the modern ballet, seen at its best in the Russian ballet of Diaghilev, Nijinsky and Massine. In this connection, it is quite significant to recall the misunderstanding of audiences watching, for example, the *Spectre de la rose* (music by Weber). The spectator in fact is quite likely to take the dreaming woman who has the main *dramatic* role for the protagonist when in fact it is the man (the ghost) who is the real protagonist of the *dance*. This illusion, the product of semantic contamination, tells us more than might appear; for if we are not overstating the case, it suggests that destiny of expressive confusion to which compound aesthetic works in general are condemned.[46]

Dance is an art which is more exposed than any other to contamination: one might almost say it is a built-in effect of the structure of its gestural, artificial and vaguely 'representational' language. As such, we may conclude that it presents itself as a minor art, though one which is not without a kind of cathartic power of its own. Unless of course one accords with the half-poetic, half-metaphysical musings of Valéry, for whom dance, as 'the very act of metamorphosis' represents 'nothing . . . but everything', 'love, as well as the sea, and life itself, and thoughts': too much and too little.[47]

Post-scriptum 1961. Fedele d'Amico's dissatisfaction[48] with the concept of interval to which I attempt to reduce musical language is probably due to the fact that he is expecting from me something that I cannot, indeed should not, give him at the level of philosophy. D'Amico, whose intervention here is as always extremely rich and instructive, wants a concept of interval which would give a precise, if not indeed an *exclusive* account of tonal language, but which would not at the same time try to cover dodecaphonic language. He is very dubious about the consistency and self-sufficiency of the latter, and his reasons are by no means either hasty or superficial. But dodecaphonic language does exist, and it has a structure of its own which may best be summed up in what D'Amico himself says: 'Schönberg believes . . .

---

46. The ambiguity is discussed in Arnold Haskell, *Ballet: A Complete Guide to Appreciation*, London 1949.
47. Paul Valéry, *Dance and the Soul*, tr. Dorothy Bussy, London 1951, p. 59.
48. D'Amico, in *Il Contemporaneo*, April–May 1961.

that each interval is definable in itself, without relation to the others or a basic tone', so that 'for him a fifth is a fifth, a second a second, and that is that'.

Now, at the level of a philosophical or general theory of music one cannot but take account of this. One can only do so by adopting a sufficiently *comprehensive* and therefore (within reason) *schematic* criterion by which to describe the interval in every sort of music: tonal, a-tonal, electronic. The necessary consequence is our identification of the interval as the original cell of musical language *tout court*.

As regards my undoubtedly scandalous critique of music with words, I am aware that it needs further elucidation and argument, even though it is in direct descent from the aesthetic principle of the *Laocoon*, with which D'Amico does not disagree: that of the plurality of artistic techniques. I would hope that this elucidation might be achieved with the concept of *opus compositum* (artificial opus) – that sort of work whose structure is compounded of heterogeneous syntaxes, and which is therefore to be enjoyed *as a whole* by an *eclectic* taste based on mere linguistic *analogies*. In this sense the opera and theatre in general are typical. It is of course a major phenomenon of taste (in the broad sense), of culture and social behaviour. But the only aspect of it which interests the art of music is that which can be put down on music-paper ('voices' and 'characters' included).

21. Cinema

It is a fallacy to include the cinema among the visual arts and to classify it as a sub-species of painting. The reasons for this can be seen from the following definitions of what is specific to film.
(1) The two-dimensionality of the film itself is a purely physical characteristic, it is quite external to the cinematic work, and extraneous to the sign and value of film. The two-dimensionality of the canvas, on the other hand, is totally intrinsic to the sign and value of painting. So fundamental is this distinction that the tension between surface and perspective background which characterizes the art and history of painting, as well as artistic effects of space such as Giotto's straight lines discussed above, do not exist, and would make no sense, in filmic visual expression. The intrinsic feature of the frame, which is

the basic sign of film, is that it is a reproduction, a cine-photographic reproduction, of the three-dimensionality of real, natural, things in the world.

(2) From this it follows that the frame is essentially documentary–analytical in character (and in this sense 'concrete'). It is of course completed by the synthesis of *montage*, but montage is still the counter-pointing *of frames* and their sequences. For this reason, film is not to be confused with painting or the magic lantern or animated cartoons.

(3) These essential parts of the grammar of film-language must be borne in mind if we are to understand the definition which can be given of the filmic opus: namely, that it consists of *edited photo-dynamic image-ideas* (verisimilitude in film).

The following corollaries may be drawn:

(a) The original black and white of photography, with its particular light-effects and chiaroscuro producing the characteristic 'defor-mations and stylizations of things' pointed to by Arnheim and others, has still not been bettered as a semantic means with virtually inex-haustible possibilities. For example, even Visconti's *Senso*, remarkable though it is as spectacle, represents a contamination of cinema and painting, i.e. colour, and literature – an ensemble of hybrid effects.[49]

(b) Spoken dialogue and scenario help indirectly to make the effects of 'micro-physiognomy', etc. (worked out by Balázs) more complex, that is, to make them denser and more capable of expression.[50] They therefore function as a continual *control* of filmic values or visual-dynamic (photo-dynamic) image-symbols by parallel verbal 'values' with a view to the *reduction* of the latter to filmic-visual or 'plastic' terms. In other words, in the film even verbal values are *occasions of plastic expression*.[51]

As confirmation of this last point, one has only to recall a small number of authentic films in which density of dialogue is *utilized* and

49. Rudolf Arnheim, *Film as Art*, Berkeley and Los Angeles 1957, and see also by the same author, *Art and Visual Perception*, ibid. 1954. Cf. Siegfried Kracauer, *Theory of Film*, New York 1960, pp. vii–viii.

50. Béla Balázs, *Theory of Film*, London 1952 (on micro-physiognomy, the sound-track, etc.; pp. 65 ff.).

51. Cf. Karel Reisz, *The Technique of Film Editing*, London 1957, p. 45: 'The visual contribution to his gags of Groucho Marx' eyebrows is incalculable, and Harpo never says a word. . . . It is not so much the quantitative balance between sound and picture, as the insistence on a primarily visual emphasis which needs to be kept in mind'.

consummated by the documentary-visual emphasis which is proper to the idea of film: works like John Ford's *Grapes of Wrath* (1940, from the novel of the same name by Steinbeck,[52] William Wyler's *The Little Foxes* (1941, from the play by Lillian Hellman), Rossellini's *Paisà* (1946), Dmytryk's *Crossfire* (1947), *Bicycle Thieves* by De Sica and Zavattini, and on down to recent productions like Kon Ichikawa's *Burmese Harp* and Kubrick's *Paths of Glory*. Conversely, we might mention certain films in which cinematic catharsis is not achieved, starting with all the so-called Shakespearean films made by Laurence Olivier, including *Hamlet* (no more than a brilliant, undeniably enjoyable pastiche of film and literature). In such films, the literary wealth and strength of the original dialogue is *unconsummated* and, so to speak, forces its way through the screen, getting in the way of what the film is seeking to achieve in optical-documentary terms but for which the genre clearly does not possess an expressive force equal to that of Shakespeare or the literary genre. Further films which we might mention in this connection include Michael Curtiz's *The Breaking Point* (from Hemingway's *To Have and Have Not*), Clarence Brown's *Intruder in the Dust* (drawn from Faulkner), and others of the same kind. Films, on the other hand, which on the whole have succeeded in becoming art include *The Savage Eye* (1959) by Ben Maddow, Sidney Meyers and Joseph Strich, a film-report on Los Angeles, and Fellini's *La Dolce Vita* (1960), a sort of documentary fresco of the life of Italian high society. These are films in which the literary element has been to all intents and purposes consummated. The fact is that what counts aesthetically in the cinema, as *mutatis mutandis* in the figurative arts, is what we might call the *renovatio* of verbal and literary idea-images, the most everyday and familiar that we possess, or their renewal into filmic, pictorial or sculptural idea-images.[53]

52. Cf. Karel Reisz, 'Substance into shadow', in *The Cinema* 1952, London 1952: 'Adapting another man's novel does not absolve the adaptor from the necessity of creating an integrated work within his own medium ... in the film medium ... John Ford ... has taken Steinbeck's and Caldwell's material and triumphantly made the *Grapes of Wrath* and *Tobacco Road* his own'. One might add the precedent, surely no less exemplary, of Jean Renoir's *La Bête Humaine* (1938) in which, for example, the driver Jacques's beloved engine 'la Lison' acquires an expressive force in comparison with which Zola's insistence on it in the novel seems a little rhetorical.

53. On documentary itself, note Paul Rotha's remarks in *Documentary Film*, London 1936, p. 66: 'Real and creative thought must be about real things....

H

Let us finish with a classic example in this connection, from Eisenstein's masterpiece *Battleship Potemkin*: the montage of the three lightning shots of the stone lion with those of the salvoes from the battleship in revolt, and its effect. It is not just, as Pudovkin says, that this effect can be 'reproduced in words only with difficulty'[54]: it is impossible to reproduce it or translate it into words or verbal 'values' without entirely losing its filmic-visual artistry. Phrases such as 'revolutionary lion' or 'the very stones rise up and shout' and the like, into which we might and in fact do translate this celebrated visual metaphor, are generic, banal and impoverished by comparison with the montage of those shots of the lion. For the latter possess a far superior power of individuation, attained by the artistic use of plastic expressive force: an optical-expressive force achieved precisely in the modes of montage of photo-dynamic idea-images. By the same token, it would be impossible to turn Dante's lion

> holding its head high and furious with hunger so that the air seemed in dread of it (*Inf.* I, ll. 47–48)

into filmic or pictorial or sculptural idea-images without entirely losing its artistry, which is of a poetic and literary character.

Post-scriptum 1961. An artistic effect of space like the pure horizontal line joining the two side walls of the room in Giotto's *Christ before Caiaphas* (see also the *Wedding Feast at Cana*) could not occur and would make no sense at all, as we have said, in a representation on film of the inside of a room. The reason is that, because the basic sign of film-representation is the frame, and the frame is a reproduction – a cine-photographic reproduction to be exact – of the three-dimensionality of real things in the world outside, film can never convey anything but the *actual angles* produced by the walls of a room and so on. It can never therefore produce an effect of *surface* spatial stylization like that of Giotto or painting in general.

Post-scriptum 1962. Cinema and literature. In order to understand the

Let cinema attempt the dramatization of the living scene and the living theme, springing from the living present instead of from the synthetic fabrication of the studio. Let cinema attempt film interpretations of modern problems and events...'.

54. V. I. Pudovkin, *Film Technique and Film Acting*, London 1958, p. 116.

relation between cinema and literature and other relations of the same kind, the following aesthetic-epistemological criteria should be borne in mind.

(1) The criterion of *semantic difference*. This stipulates that the apperception of the artistic 'contents' or meanings of any work whatever is conditioned by the status of its semantic organicity, and thus implicitly by the type of semantic apparatus or language which conveys these 'contents' and the relevant emotions to us. The artistic expressive values of the 'contents' and feelings vary, therefore, according to the different signs or linguistic means which mediate them. Not only, as has been known at least since Herder, is there no thought without language: neither is there thought without a corresponding *sign in general*, line, colour, interval and note, cinematic frame, and so on. Obviously, this involves a much broader concept of thinking or ideation than our traditional inability to separate thought from the verbal sign and the 'discursiveness' of verbal signs, which identifies thought purely and simply with speech, discourse. It involves, in short, the rigorous and unitary concept of thought as unification of the manifold, whatever may be the semantic means, or modes, which thought – as such unification – may use or is free to use.

(2) The experimental criterion of *semantic reduction*, which follows from the first. This criterion demands that the expressive achievements of (say) a film, accomplished by photo-dynamic image-symbols, be compared and tested against those of dialogue or its verbal achievements, in order to see whether or not the latter have been *reduced as expression* to the former, and hence whether or not banality and inexpressive untruth have been superseded in an appropriate semantic reading of the 'contents' of the film in question. The artistry of a work is therefore filmic when its 'contents' or meanings, having been *reduced* to filmic semantic terms, thereby reveal to us their non-banality or truth and thus convey artistic feeling. Similarly with the other various kinds of art.

(3) Lastly, the criterion of *semantic occasion*. Applied to film, this means that verbal values, for example, have the right to exist in a film only as occasion or pretext for the complication and enrichment of visual (or, by transference, 'plastic') effects of micro-physiognomy, or others. Thus it is the fate of dialogue in the artistic film to be no more than provisional, to be *consummated visually*. Think how the face

of Bette Davis dominates in *The Little Foxes*, even though its dialogue is taken from the notable play by Lillian Hellman.

22 Legacy of Lessing

Two final observations. The structural differences between the various means of expression, means which are semantic by definition, give rise to the artistic genres: literature or poetry, painting, sculpture, architecture, music, and film. The philosophical justification of the different genres lies in the *epistemological* effect or import of their structural differences in means or technique. (This is clearly not the case with the various literary, pictorial or musical sub-genres or species; though they are called 'genres', this misnomer is applied to external differences which, being merely empirical in the bad sense of the word, are aesthetically inessential and unimportant.) Such epistemological import is confirmed experimentally, as we have seen, in the non-convertibility or untranslatability of one genre into another. If such translation occurs, it is at the price of the thoughts thus translated descending into the generic and banal and losing artistic effect. The genres are *united*, that is to say they are all artistic, by virtue of that feature which they have in common: namely, the *specific contextual dialectic* of thought-end and semantic means that is the semantically organic discourse, in which *artistic* thought consists (given the verified general postulate of the identity of thought and language).

The consequence is that one cannot simply locate art in the super-structure in the uniform and undifferentiated way hitherto typical of Marxists. Such an approach fails to see, and assumes that it can ignore, the differences in expressive techniques arising from the structural differences of the signs. In talking in the same breath of 'social' ideas in music and social ideas in literature, without discriminating between them, it improperly reduces musical ideas to the type of expressive module which is proper to literary ideas. Instead what is needed is a clear articulation of the differences in the superstructural collocations of art according to the different genres and their respective semantic techniques.

Thus the historical and social conditioning of a literary work like *Faust* is revealed in the superstructural value constituted by the verbal *bourgeois ideas* of the protagonist. But the historical conditioning of a musical work, for example Beethoven's Third Symphony, the *Eroica*, is revealed in the superstructural value constituted by Beethoven's *musical ideas*, to the extent that their expression is indissociable from the musical *grammar* of *romanticism* (Rameau's grammar of the perfect, or tonal chord) and its fulfilment in a particular poetic of listening: that which prescribes a disturbing, moving, subjectivist-idealist, in short romantic, hearing of music. In other words, historical conditioning in this case is not exhibited superstructurally in Beethoven's 'Napoleonism', which is of the order of verbal ideas, not musical ideas. The same rule obtains throughout the various semantic techniques, depending on whether or not they express idea-representations, in other words pictorial or sculptural or filmic ideas which have verbal ideas as the occasion or pretext of their plastic expression (the architectural idea is really on the border here, further perhaps from the verbal idea and less distant from that of music than any other).

In other words, the inscription of artistic ideas in the superstructure is determined both by the emptiness, that is the historicity and functionality, of the expressive sign in general, and by the specific differences between one sign and another. This amounts to saying that the inscription of artistic ideas is a special instance of that dialectic of means-*sèma* and end-idea which embraces every cultural aspect of the superstructure.

The solution we are suggesting here to the problem of artistic genres is an attempt, if nothing else, at a more modern formulation of the approach to the problem taken by its discoverer, Lessing, when he rebelled in his *Laocoon* (1766) against Horace's famous simile which had likened poetry to painting ('ut pictura poesis'), the first unwitting step towards the unification–confusion of the arts.

The sort of revision we have in mind may be shown if we take an example: Lessing's analysis of Ariosto's literary description of Alcina. He asks whether the author makes us *see* the proportions of her figure: 'A brow . . .

Che lo spazio finia con giusta meta

(Which finished with perfect measure);

a nose . . .

> Che non trova l'invidia, ove l'emende

> (Envy itself can find no way of bettering it);

a hand . . .

> Lunghetta alquanto, e di larghezza angusta

> (Tapering somewhat, and slender):

what kind of *picture* [was für ein Bild] do we gather from these *general* formulas?'[55] But Lessing's aesthetic critique misses the point that, even were it true that Ariosto's literary representation is defective in the way he claims, there is no literary work worthy of the name, including therefore the *Furioso*, which does not have detailed descriptions, or *more detailed* descriptions than this one, which Lessing calls 'general'. But however detailed they may be, they *are no less distant* from pictorial or sculptural (or filmic) representations, because we 'see' them – these literarily more or less detailed things – in a totally metaphorical sense of the verb 'see', not in any *visibilistic* or literal sense. Therefore we must shift our philosophical attention away from the objects represented by poets, painters, etc. – objects which in themselves are philosophically abstract, refer to something else – and towards the respective *means of expression* and their particularities. In so doing, we shall not be able to agree with Lessing that 'what painters can by line and colour best express can only be badly expressed by words' (p. 76). Rather, we shall conclude that when poetry makes use of words, which is its semantic means of expression, it is no less able to express and therefore particularize than is painting through the use of line and colour, sculpture through volume, and so on. Finally, acknowledgment of the *plurality of these means* of expression must at the same time, if it is rigorous, involve acceptance of the equal artistic rights of the variety of literary or poetic or pictorial ideas which are the ends of those means. It signifies, in other words, *the peaceful co-existence of the arts* on equal terms. The danger of descent into the generic and the

---

55. Gotthold Ephraim Lessing, *Laocoon*, or 'The limits of painting and poetry: with incidental illustrations on various points in the history of ancient art', tr. W. A. Steel, London 1930, Chap. XX, p. 77; Ariosto, *Orlando Furioso*, VII, 11–15.

banal only arises, as we have seen, when an attempt is made to turn the achievements of one art into those of another.[56]

But the gratitude we owe to Lessing for having posed the problem of the artistic genres (glancingly touched on by Diderot[57]) can only be measured by those who – in the wake of romanticism – strive not to relapse into that indistinction and confusion of the arts bequeathed us by the metaphysical-idealist concept of art as creative imagination or cosmic intuition *tout court*; not to mention Schiller's, or even worse Schelling's, conciliation-cum-confusion of art and nature, which is not dead even today, strange as it may seem. All these confusions, especially the last, recall to mind the story told by the great traveller James Cook of the Maori chieftain who came to his cabin and was

56. Wellek, *History of Criticism*, cit., Vol. I, pp. 160 ff., analyses Lessing's Chapter XVI in detail, but over-estimates the theoretical importance of the didactic and content-oriented arguments which lead him to the conclusion that the subject of painting should be bodies and that of poetry actions. The argument is based on superficial aspects of the pictorial sign (signs arranged together side by side) and the verbal sign (signs which succeed each other). Even so, it cannot be denied that Lessing's distinction led at the time (as Wellek reminds us) to the condemnation, in the first case, of allegorical painting and, in the second, of descriptive poetry.

With respect to the empirical and superficial division into artistic sub-genres or literary, pictorial, musical, etc. 'genres' so-called, one cannot but recall the first scientific critique of literary genres made by no less than Aristotle, *Poetics*, 1451 b 1 ff. (and cf. 1447 b 14 ff.): 'The difference between a historian and a poet is not that one writes in prose and the other in verse – indeed the writings of Herodotus could be put into verse and yet would still be a kind of history, whether written in metre or not. The real difference is this, that one tells what happened and the other what might happen' (ed. cit., p. 35). We call this the first scientific critique because it is the first rigorously to respect the greater or lesser epistemological import of the two so-called literary genres, *verse* and *prose*. Aristotle's critique has none of that pre-conceived and mystical repugnance for the diverse or manifold of artistic experience that one finds in metaphysical and idealist critiques of the literary or pictorial genres, which indiscriminately bundle the artistic genres together with these pseudo-genres.

57. Diderot wrote: 'Why would a picture which is admirable in a poem become ridiculous on canvas? The head of the god [Neptune] is so majestic in the poem [et alto/prospiciens, summa placidum caput extulit unda – and gazing/on the deep, he raised his head serene above the waves: *Aeneid* I, 11. 126–7] – why looking like nothing but a man with his head cut off, would it make a bad impression on the waves [in a painting]? Why is it that what delights our imagination is displeasing to our eyes?' ('Lettre sur les sourds et les muets', in *Diderot Studies* VII, Génève 1965, p. 82). 'Even Racine did not express himself with the delicacy of a harp. . . . His melody was heavy and monotonous in comparison with that of an instrument' ('Addition à la lettre sur les aveugles', in *Oeuvres*, Paris 1946, p. 896).

'unable to fix his attention on any one thing a single moment'; unable to tell the difference between painted fruit and real fruit, 'the works of art appeared to him in the same light as those of nature'. What the metaphysician and the Maori have in common, the former as a matter of principle and habit of mind, the latter due to lack of education is impatience with analysis, or more simply with distinctions.

Appendices

Engels, Lenin, and the Poetic
of Socialist Realism

We have drawn attention above to a number of critical errors in Plekhanov and Lukács. If we consider the nature of these errors, we are forced to the conclusion that their radical misinterpretations of the poetry of Ibsen and Flaubert are the clearest proof that these two critics have not understood the fundamental lesson of Engels's verdict on the realist writing of the politically reactionary Balzac – a lesson that was to be applied later by Lenin to the case of Tolstoy.

What does Engels say? (Here too he was in agreement with Marx.) 'The realism I allude to, may crop out even in spite of the author's *opinions*. Let me refer to an example. Balzac, whom I consider a far greater master of realism than all the Zolas . . . , in *La Comèdie humaine* gives us a most wonderfully realistic history of French "society", describing, chronicle-fashion, almost year by year from 1816 to 1848 the progressive inroads of the rising bourgeoisie upon the society of nobles, that reconstituted itself after 1815. . . . He describes how the last remnants of this, to him, model society gradually succumbed before the intrusion of the vulgar moneyed upstart, or were corrupted by him; . . . and around this central picture he groups a complete history of French society from which, even in economic details (for instance the re-arrangement of real and personal property after the Revolution) I have learned more than from all the professed historians, economists and statisticians of the period together. Well, Balzac was politically a Legitimist; his great work is *a constant elegy* on the irretrievable decay of good society, *his sympathies are all* with the class doomed to extinction. But for all that his satire is never keener, his irony never bitterer, than when he sets in motion the very men and women with whom he sympathizes most deeply – the nobles. And the only men of whom he always speaks with undisguised admiration, are his bitterest political antagonists, the republican heroes of the Cloître Saint Méry, the men who at that time (1830–36) were indeed the representatives of the popular masses. That Balzac was thus compelled to go against his own class sympathies and political prejudices, that he *saw* the necessity of the downfall of his favourite nobles, and described them as people deserving no better fate; and that he *saw* the real men of the future where, for the time being, they alone were to be found – that I consider one of the greatest triumphs of realism . . .'. For realism, he had already said in the same letter, 'means, in my opinion, not only *truth* of *detail*, but also the faithful reproduction of typical characters in typical circumstances'[1] (our emphases).

And Lenin? Lenin at the beginning of his 1908 article, daringly entitled 'Leo Tolstoy as the mirror of the Russian revolution', acknowledges there is a problem: 'To identify the great artist with the revolution [of 1905] which he has obviously failed to understand, and from which he obviously stands aloof, may at first sight seem strange and artificial.' But he gives an immediate reply: 'If we have before us a *really* great *artist*, he must have *reflected* in his work *at least some of the essential aspects* of the revolution' (our emphases). Then he goes on to give the following reasons for his bold thesis. Firstly, 'Tolstoy's ideas are a mirror of the weakness, the shortcomings of our present revolt, a reflection of the flabbiness of the patriarchal countryside and of the hidebound cowardice of the "enterprising muzhik" '. Thus, 'Tolstoy reflected the pent-up hatred, the ripened striving for a better lot, the desire to get rid of the past – and also, the immature dreaming the political experience, the revolutionary flabbiness'. Secondly, an article written in 1910 explains that 'the history and the outcome of the great Russian revolution [of 1905] have shown that such precisely [as represented by Tolstoy] was the mass that found itself between the class-conscious, socialist proletariat and the out-and-out defenders of the old regime'. In conclusion, 'by studying the literary works of Leo Tolstoy the Russian working class will learn to know its enemies better . . .'[2] (Compare Krupskaya's *Memories of Lenin*, where she says

1. Engels, letter to Margaret Harkness (April 1888), ed. cit., pp. 380–1, 379.
2. Lenin, 'Leo Tolstoy as the mirror of the Russian revolution' and 'Tolstoy

that for him 'the whole of Russian literature' was 'one of the sources of knowledge of reality').

So Engels and Lenin give different answers, yet one and the same answer, to the question on which a realist aesthetic and hence a poetic of socialist realism depend: should a literary work contain *ideas* in general, without prior definition as to the sort of ideas, or should its ideas be *'not false'*, i.e. progressive rather than reactionary? Whether we are looking at a French artist in the 1840's whose opinions were monarchical and legitimist, or a Russian artist in 1905 with mystical-populist ideas, the answer is the same. Both are realist artists.

But the important point to notice is that they are both realist artists *in spite of* the *different* ways in which the truth of their writings comes across. The truth of Balzac's art – what earns him the name of realist – consists in the fact that he 'saw' the 'real men of the future', his bourgeois enemies, against his own ideological sympathies. That of Tolstoy's writing, on the other hand, consists in the fact that he saw men and things in *conformity* with his own ideological sympathies. Yet he was able to teach the revolutionary proletariat 'to know its enemies better', precisely because in this sense he reflected 'at least some of the essential aspects' of the 'revolution' in his literary work and showed that 'such' was the 'mass' of the peasantry, rebellious in spirit but unprepared. In other words, Balzac's artistic realism is a matter of seeing his (progressive) enemies not less but more truly than those on his own side, while Tolstoy's is a matter of seeing his own side and his own (unprogressive) ideas more truly. But both lead equally to truth – artistic truth, which brings with it an inestimable gift, especially to the revolutionary worthy of the name. For it permits (by these artistic, not scientific, means) a *better knowledge of reality*, and of its progressive and its reactionary antecedents: a knowledge which is indispensable to action itself.

The mistake of Plekhanov and Lukács is their failure to grasp this basic aspect of the lesson of Engels and Lenin. Their error is all the more serious when it comes to their substantial misunderstanding of Ibsen and Flaubert, two writers who are certainly no less instructive for the socialist revolutionary than Balzac or Tolstoy.[3] Ibsen, restless

and the proletarian struggle', in *Collected Works*, ed. cit., Vol. 15, pp. 202 ff. and Vol. 16, p. 353 [emphases mainly D.V.'s].

3. Unlike Pasternak, for example, who is not enough of an artist. See Mario

liberal democrat that he was, remains unsurpassed in his representation of the cruel hypocrisy and the lies of the bourgeoisie, thus the
antinomies within the moral code of individualism. Of course these
antinomies cannot be resolved *from within*, but without Ibsen we would
understand very little of a socialist dramatist like Brecht. Or rather, if
there were no Ibsen with the world that he reflects, there would be
no Brecht – he would make no sense. We owe something too to that
political agnostic Flaubert, who brought to light one of the profoundest patterns in bourgeois mores, the vice of romantic escapism
in women who do not work, in a word *bovarisme*.

So the answer to the basic question posed above appears to be this.
Literature should contain *ideas* or ideology, but without prior definition as to the sort of ideas. Or to put it another way – but it amounts
to the same thing – what matters *in literature as well* is truth. Such truth,
as we know, is not in conflict, indeed it coincides with, tendentiousness – and related typicality: the examples abound, from Dante to
Mayakovsky.

What we have said, however paradoxical it may sound, does not
exclude a *poetic* (not an aesthetic) of socialist realism. On the contrary,
it implies it by virtue of the two principles we have argued: firstly,
that no literature exists without ideas in general (and that includes
our ideas today, therefore); and secondly, that all ideas are tendentious, in other words exhibit an inevitable historical *determinacy*. Thus,
in our times, the only possible practical artistic ideal, which alone can
be realized, is *socialist* realism. We do not just claim the freedom to
fight for it, we have the right to do so. The reason is precisely that we
have had to grant equal aesthetic rights to the artistic ideals and
poetics of the past in the name of the sociological and realist truth of
literature in general. There seems no other basis on which to found
a poetic of socialist realism, I mean, to justify it with rigour.

Of course there arise a mass of problems. To name but two: that of
the modes of a poetic or artistic truth which cannot for example
exclude anachronism; or what exactly is meant by 'decadent poetry'.
But it does not look as though we can evade these by treating them as
pseudo-problems, the sophistry of contemplative philosophers. That
path is blocked by the observations of Engels and Lenin, if by nothing

Alicata, *Sul Caso Pasternak*, Rome 1958, and Richard D. Stern, '*Doctor Zhivago* as a
novel', in *The Kenyon Review* XXI (1959), pp. 154 ff.

else. We still await the necessary demonstration that those observations are not just felicitous but local critical comments, which is
the belief of the great majority of Marxists both at home and abroad,
but rather, as we believe, premises from which an objective aesthetic
law in the proper sense of the term can be developed.[4]

Note on Lukács and the Concept of 'Critical Realism'. Let me say at once that
Lukács' methodological concept of 'critical realism' as the forerunner
of socialist realism, with its leading representative in Thomas Mann,
leaves me doubtful, if only because of the negative literary–historical
judgements to which it leads. I refer to his unsatisfactory assessment
of the poetic originality of Proust, Joyce and Kafka, the last great
decadent bourgeois novelists, as compared with the refined but
second-hand bourgeois art of Thomas Mann, an occasionally brilliant
epigone of nineteenth-century realism.

In concrete terms, I am thinking of Proust's *Recherche*, Joyce's
Ulysses, Kafka's *The Trial* and *The Castle* as well as his short stories, and
the quality of the poetic testimony to the crisis of the bourgeoisie
represented by these works. Unlike Mayakovsky or Brecht, who
judge the crisis to overcome it, these writers suffer it, and it is precisely
because they only suffer the crisis of a civilization that they can be
called decadent. But think of the quality of Proust's analysis of the
decline of the French élites in the period around the First World War.
The intellectual method of this analysis, it should be noted, could not

4. On the problems of realism in general and socialist realism in particular,
see Bertolt Brecht, 'Weite und Vielfalt der realistischen Schreibweise', in *Versuche*,
Heft 13, Berlin 1958: 'Nothing prevents the realist Cervantes from seeing knights
tilting at windmills or the realist Swift from seeing horses founding states. It is
not the idea of narrowness but that of breadth that goes with realism. . . . When it
comes to literary forms, one must question reality, not aesthetics, not even the
aesthetics of realism. There are many ways in which truth can be concealed and
many ways in which it can be told . . .': pp. 106–7, our emphases. See also *Volks-
tümlichkeit und Realismus* (1938), in *Sinn und Form*, 1958, Heft IV: Lukács's essays 'throw
light on the concept of realism, though in my opinion they define it rather too
narrowly'; 'Realist means: revealing causal connections in society, unmasking
dominant points of view as the points of view of the dominators, writing from the
point of view of the class which is ready with the widest solutions to the most
pressing difficulties in which human society is enmeshed; underlining the moment of development, concreteness and the possibility of abstraction'; for this
reason we will allow the artist to bring his whole imagination, his humour, all
his powers of invention into play. We will not be holding to over-detailed literary
models . . .'.

be more significantly bourgeois-individualist, conducted as it is through an internal and contemplative memory, which yields a narrative that is a kind of *artistic* autobiography of the author-cum-protagonist. Or take *Ulysses*, which is a summation and judgement of our humanitarian bourgeois civilization in the sense that the justification of that civilization is reduced to the terms of its now lifeless commonplaces. The literary technique of interior monologue is used to orchestrate Joyce's negative, ironic, anti-heroic counterpointing of classical myths and everyday events. Remember, for example, the solitary protagonist Bloom in that den of modern Cyclops, the Dublin pub where perfectly normal, nationalist and racist, 'citizens' gather, and the effect of pathetic absurdity in his affirmation there:

... it's the very opposite of that that is really life.
– What? says Alf.
– Love, says Bloom. I mean the opposite of hatred.

(Think by contrast of the positive atmosphere in which Tolstoy's heroes, active and alive, move with such confidence.[5]) Finally, recollect Kafka's stories and novels, with their hallucinating satirical allegories of existential, religious and metaphysical anxiety. Lukács does make the attempt to analyse Kafka's narrative poetry a little, unlike that of Proust or Joyce, and in doing so he runs the risk of

5. James Joyce, *Ulysses*, London 1969, p. 331. See Richard Ellmann, *James Joyce*, New York 1959 (especially pp. 1 ff., 367 ff.): 'Joyce's court is, like Dante's or Tolstoy's, always in session. The initial and determining act of judgement in his work is the justification of the commonplace.... There is nothing like Joyce's commonplace in Tolstoy, where the characters, however humble, live dramatically and instil wisdom or tragedy in each other', etc. (p. 3). Note also S.L. Goldberg, *The Classical Temper: a Study of James Joyce's Ulysses*, London 1961 (especially pp. 100 ff., 142 ff., 248 ff): 'The result is a comment on the age far more mature, because far more dramatic in this sense, than that of *Bouvard et Pecuchet* or *The Waste Land*..... . The drama of the book derives from Bloom's ambiguous relations to his society, from the interplay between his limited values, his social exile, and his underlying sanity,' etc. (p. 142). Unfortunately, the author of this excellent book misses the historical and sociological origin and import of some of the artistic formulations of *Ulysses*. When he speaks, for example, about Stephen's fear of 'history', a 'nightmare', Stephen says, 'from which I am trying to awake', he does not take account of the fact that this is a moral trait which brings to perfect fulfilment the figure of the bourgeois intellectual, a Platonist thirsting for eternity in his conception of art as 'epiphany' and 'stasis'. Stephen represents the true completion of the poetic survey and judgement of an epoch that is Joyce's novel.

profoundly contradicting himself. For he calls the work 'allegory' in a negative sense and argues that Kafka's 'allegorical transcendence' prevents him 'from investing observed detail with typical significance'. But at the same time he admits that Kafka's 'attitude to detail is selective, not naturalistic', which makes it effectively able to emphasise the essential.[6]

With all this in mind, consider for a moment the meaning, as artistic representations of the modern bourgeois epoch and as compared with a passage from Proust or Joyce or Kafka, of scenes from the bourgeois writer who for Lukács is 'always immanent', Thomas Mann: the death of the Wildean aesthete in Venice, the romantic-decadent artist's confession of his egoism in *Tonio Kröger*, the tragic passing of the great Hanseatic family in *Buddenbrooks*. Now, Mann's achievements are by no means inconsiderable. His artistic realism is certainly superior to the self-satisfied decadence of a Gide, for instance. Even so, these books are only *episodic* visions of a crisis such as that which our era is living through. They are episodic, because they lack any profound problematic core. One might add that the legacy of Kafka is very clear in Camus (in *L'Etranger* and *Le Malentendu*, for example), that of Proust in Virginia Woolf, that of Kafka and Joyce in Beckett (*Waiting for Godot*), and of Joyce again in the farces of Ionesco. But Mann's art, though it too is bourgeois and related to the crisis, has left no heirs of whom we are aware. This too has its significance.

We would reiterate that where you have authentic poetry – but you have to make the effort to perceive it, beyond any preconceived schema of a book's 'contents' – you always have sociological truth. That is, you have realism – polysemic-symbolic representation (which therefore in one way or another *passes judgement*) of an historical and social reality. Such realism can as well be the optimistic and constructive bourgeois realism of Fielding and Balzac (as Lukács believes) as the pessimistic and constructive realism of Swift (here we agree with Brecht, thinking not only of the Houyhnhnms in *Gulliver's Travels*, but of the *Modest Proposal*). Equally, it can be the different versions of a pessimistic and apocalyptic realism we find in Eliot, Proust, Joyce and Kafka, or the modest 'immanent' realism, the *hic et nunc*, of Mann.

6. Lukács, 'The Ideology of Modernism' and 'Franz Kafka or Thomas Mann?' in *The Meaning of Contemporary Realism*, tr. J. and N. Mander, London 1963. Our criticisms notwithstanding, this is one of Lukács's most stimulating works.

I

Finally it can be the new constructive optimism of the socialist realism of Mayakovsky and Brecht (for all their parables and hyperbole).

For if there were no room in poetry for any idea or conception whatever of the world, there would obviously be no room either for the socialist idea. Neither would there be any justification for the current interest of democrats in a socialist–realist poetic. The upshot would be to make poetry, considered philosophically or in general terms, organically resistant to ideas – in conformity with the belief of romantic, post-romantic and decadent bourgeois aesthetics. But we think we have some reason to believe that things are otherwise. We believe too that we are supported in this by the example of a revolutionary like Lenin. Lenin was able to understand the truth that emerges from Tolstoy's artistic depiction – with its negative, mystical and reactionary ideological basis – of the conditions of the Russian peasantry towards 1905; and he saw it as an instructive lesson for revolutionaries themselves. Does it really demand so much greater an effort that we should find it impossible (but it isn't) to understand today, as socialist democrats, the lessons that the great decadent literature of Eliot and Proust and Joyce and Kafka teaches us about the crisis of the present time? It is a negative lesson of course, but what an instructive one! For it is true with the truth of art, which is also sociological truth.

Let us pause for a moment over Kafka. Who can deny the educative force of that sense of moral nightmare aroused in us by the depiction of the life of K and of the others in *The Castle*? That life is sordid in the extreme, almost sub-human, because it is subject to the most basic form of alienation – that religious alienation which is historically and effectively co-substantial and concomitant with every other form of alienation suffered by men in fear of oppressive authorities, in their own way transcendent like the divinity which consecrates them. It is hard to deny the essential and instructive truth in this sort of black humour, which Thomas Mann acutely described as Kafka's 'religious humour'. But still in order to understand it, we must work from within the artistic expression of this humour – in other words its polysemic symbols, starting from the Count's inaccessible 'castle' and its cruel and hypocritical 'administration' of the 'village'. In the inner workings of that administration, for example, the poetic motif used by Goethe and Ibsen, and much earlier by Dante, of intercession and redemption by the eternal feminine, is reversed. The woman is pre-ordained to prostitution and the procurement of 'bureaucratic' favours for her lover, 'from above'. What one must not do is start from external considerations, as Lukács does when he simply refers to 'the world of the Hapsburg Monarchy' *without the mediation* of these poetic symbols and the related sense of nightmare which is central to the book.[7]

Thus, the final alternative formulated by Lukács – the choice between Franz Kafka and Thomas Mann, 'between an aesthetically appealing, but decadent modernism, and a true-to-life [*lebenswahr*] critical realism' – seems to us an artificial one. It is likely to side-track us from an adequate, concrete aesthetic appreciation of the two authors. Neither of them in his art is a forerunner of socialist realist truth. But at the same time, Lukács's characterization of Mann's *art*, decadent-bourgeois though it is, as 'critical realist' is otiose. At any rate it *does not serve* to prove that the *distinctive* character of this art is a 'true-to-life' critical realism. There are two reasons for this. Firstly, in general terms, authentic poetry is always realist (sociological) truth, and therefore is also 'critical' – for since it is truthful, it is not one-sided. Secondly, there is the particular point alluded to above: that the 'immanence' which characterizes Mann's work, in other words its episodic and chronicle cast, is far from being a distinct and superior merit if it is compared to the profoundly allegorical or, if you prefer, symbolic art of Kafka. Rather, it is a clear sign of Mann's limitations and the relatively lesser value as truth of his art, compared with that of Kafka (or equally, to keep to the novel, of Proust and Joyce). Thus we should, if anything, reverse the order of Lukács's 'choice' – if there were any sense, from the point of view of aesthetic method, in talking about choices or alternatives.

7. Cf. Kafka, *The Castle*, tr. Willa and Edwin Muir, London 1957. The 'Count': 'What, you don't know the Count?' 'Why should I?' replied the teacher in a low tone, and added aloud in French: 'Please remember there are innocen children present' (p. 16). The 'Castle' bells: '. . . a bell began to ring merrily up there, a bell which for at least a second made his heart palpitate for its tone was menacing, too, as if it threatened him with the fulfilment of his vague desire' (p. 22).

2

On the Concept of 'Avantgarde'

It is my opinion that the concept (and the term) 'avantgarde', referring to avantgarde *poetics*, is of no help to us Marxists. It is too compromised historically, and can only create confusion and misunderstanding.

What in fact is meant by an avantgarde poetic? All the avantgardes have shared an anti-academic attitude in their programmes or manifestoes. They have been against the traditional 'forms' and techniques of art (figurative, musical or literary) and therefore the 'contents' rhetorically associated with them. This is the historically fruitful and positive side of the avantgardes – the side that has led to original artistic achievement, particularly in the figurative arts, from Manet to Van Gogh to Braque to Picasso.

But the trouble is that as time went by the change of 'contents' related to the change of 'forms' became indifference to and abstraction from *content* in general. The shift away from objectivity and reality has led finally to the desperate formalism of 'informalism' (meaning the negation of all traditional forms), the drips and splashes of painters like Pollock. For the true soul of avantgardism is the worship of form-as-pure-sensuousness. This is what has brought it in the end to the cult of 'matter' practised by the informalists and the *tachistes*. Avantgardism has come then to signify formalism par excellence. The consequence is that it seeks to stake the whole future of art, so to speak, on one (idealist) card: that of creative subjectivity and extreme individualism, in other words fantasy/form or sensuousness.

So I cannot agree with De Micheli (*Il Contemporaneo*, Oct.–Nov. 1959) that the avantgarde, even in its better aspects, is opposed to capitalist civilization. Capitalism is frantically individualistic in all its manifestations; the avantgarde is its legitimate offspring, in its good productions and its bad. The bad was well suggested by Picasso when he protested that he and the others had been reduced to painting only 'monsters'. He was stressing the inhumanity of a formalism which tends to abstract as far as possible from the contents and therefore also the values of human and social life.

In other words, the *antitheses* represented by the avantgarde always remain *internal* to capitalist, individualist culture and civilization. A familiar, if not typical, example is the conflict of life-style between the conforming traditionalist and the Bohemian artist-'anarchist'. What could be more romantically individualist than Gauguin's rebellion and his (exotic) escape? What is more historically *bourgeois* than attitudes like these? Nevertheless, Gauguin's painting remains, as does Van Gogh's. Some of their technical achievements also remain, to be employed in a new figurative poetic of realism, achievements such as the anti-Renaissance sense of pictorial space suggested by the works of Picasso's communist period, Léger, the early Pignon, Guttuso.

But we must conclude that the term and concept of the avantgarde can be of no further use to us Marxists. It means too many things historically and today gives rise to too many ambiguities. Lukács was right to alert us to the close relations between decadentism and avantgarde, and De Micheli has perhaps not taken his point sufficiently to heart. As we struggle for a new poetic, we must replace the concept of avantgarde by that of socialist realism. As its very name makes crystal-clear, the poetic of socialist realism aims to avoid formalism or any other imbalance between form and content. In its restitution to art of its full humanity (which is reason and senses combined), it aims to restore the fullness of art itself. It seeks, finally, to foster that vocation to the classical which is the hallmark of the authentic work of art.

Thus, if we may close our remarks with a reference to literature, we are already aware of the *classical* completeness of some of the democratic and socialist poetry of Mayakovsky and Brecht. Their work is illustrative of the poetic of socialist realism, which rose up against the (bourgeois) literary avantgardes: naturalism and verism, symbolism and expressionism, surrealism and hermeticism.

.

3

The Crucial Question of Architecture Today

As I understand it, the essential and positive thrust of Benevolo and Tafuri's line of reasoning (*Argomenti di Architettura*, 2, 1961) is this. The widest possible definition of the term 'architecture' was given by William Morris. He tells us that it embraces the whole physical environment of human life because architecture seeks to meet human needs by altering that environment. But even if we start just from this very broad definition, we must acknowledge that the ambiguity in Morris's original outlook has not been resolved even today. For there was a contradiction between his insistence on an architecture for all, not just the few, and his rejection of technology; yet not even after the revolutionary and constructive changes brought about by Gropius, Le Corbusier, Aalto and others, has an answer to it been found. We are imprisoned today in an agnostic acceptance of a mechanistic, 'functional' rationality, in a cultural and social automatism, in an ever more uncontrolled process of 'quantification' (implicitly divorcing the architect and the engineer), and so on. The result is that the mass of ordinary people – in this self-styled civilization of mass-democracy – still live in homes that are ugly and inhuman and in cities beset by chaos. Our houses and towns are striking and disturbing symptoms of human alienation.

But what sort of remedies do the writers propose for the state of affairs revealed in this diagnosis? Benevolo concludes that Morris's 'illustrious and traditional notion of "architecture"', the ambiguities of which are still unresolved (with the consequence noted above), 'is changing before our eyes; historical development itself will show how far its scope extends today'. But he himself suspects his argument of circularity. Tafuri reminds us, quite rightly, that the definition of those ethical and social contents which are 'the starting-point' of the modern revolutionary movement in architecture, owes much to the Enlightenment. 'With increasing methodological rigour,' he tells us, 'the most committed contemporary architects are tending to look for "continuity" ' (with this revolutionary movement). But in trying to give 'a very precise content' to this continuity in philosophical terms, he proposes a criterion which in practice is rather generic. He wants an inquiry 'whose aim is to define the human condition of the architect in the web of its relations with the social world towards which his activity is directed. It must therefore start from the present and turn towards the past; then, returning from the past to the present, still taking the present as its starting-point, move on towards the future' (see Husserl and Paci). He concludes with an aestheticizing reference to 'the problems opened up by the painting of Klee': Klee 'discovers the undeniable reality of the *image*, as something that is part of our existence, and affirms it *against* the abstractness of *form*', and so on.

To a greater or lesser extent, we all find ourselves in something of an impasse with regard to these problems. But one possible way out, it seems to me, might be suggested by a very perceptive comment of Benevolo, with which Tafuri agrees, about Morris. The contradiction in his outlook mentioned above shows, according to Benevolo, how 'Morris's sensibility leads him, not to appreciate reality directly, but rather the image of reality as *reflected* in the forms of *culture*'. This critical–historical insight is apposite, if I am not mistaken, both to Morris's poetic of craftmanship, a poetic based on the past, on nostalgia for the Middle Ages, and to the romantic socialism which derived from it. I think we are justified in drawing from it a genuinely topical warning for theorists of art (in general) and architects as well. It is that we too must not lose contact with the reality of our time, its economic, social and cultural reality. We too must be careful not to take refuge in a reflected reality, in the forms of a culture that belongs to the past and now is worn out and decayed: which means, in our case and in this particular instance, bourgeois aesthetic culture with its various metaphysical 'solutions', whether they be romantic, idealist or phenomenological. The alternative is to remain trapped by the aestheticism or over-estimation of the *image* (which in architecture means ornament) at the expense of the *concept* (that is, the useful and the humanly functional), against which the modern revolutionary movement in architecture fought with such success.

Clearly, to liberate ourselves from every residue of romantic and decadentist aesthetics presupposes not only that we be fully aware of the co-presence of both reason and image in every work of art, but also that we acquire a new, 'positive' concept of expressive technique and hence of the various artistic *languages*. In that way we shall be able to maintain a clear distinction, for example, between the architectural figure and the sculptural figure. All of which presupposes in its turn no longer a metaphysical conception of society and culture, but a scientific, in fact historical–materialist, conception, so that the modern ethic of socialist democracy which follows from it may guide us also in our artistic activity. In architecture, which we are concerned with here, it will give us that support which cannot come from a more or less romantic, utopian, socialism à la Morris. There is no hope of finding a way out of the grave difficulties discussed above without a keen awareness, in architecture too, of the new 'contents' which demand ever more appropriate, and in this sense truly new and original, 'forms'.

4

Linguistics and Literary Criticism

1. These remarks are prompted by the *Inchiesta su Strutturalismo e Critica* (Inquiry into Structuralism and Criticism), edited by Cesare Segre, and published in Milan in 1965. My purpose is to try and define how modern, anti-romantic Saussurian linguistics and post-Saussurian structuralism relate to the aims and methods of a literary criticism that seeks to be historical-materialist by the canons of *Critique of Taste*. In other words, I shall be comparing and contrasting these canons with the criteria of the several committed representatives of the most *outré* 'aesthetic structuralism' who replied to the inquiry in question. It will not be out of place to recall that the first utilization of Saussurian linguistics for the purposes of a poetic, and within the framework of a philosophical aesthetics, is to be found precisely in *Critique of Taste*.

The clarity and balance of Roland Barthes' contribution to the inquiry demonstrates, if demonstration were necessary, how far superior he is to his imitators and impersonators. Let us start with the points that find us in agreement. He begins by stating that, though 'there is a lot of confusion in the term "structuralism" ', in his opinion 'it designates any systematic research concerned with matters semantic and inspired by the model of linguistics'. He narrows this down further by adding that 'reference to Saussure leads to a more specific, or, if you prefer, more responsible, structuralism'. The use of Saussurian linguistics is discriminating in that 'it implies the decision not to limit the systems of signification to the signifiers [phonemes] alone, but to include the study of the signifieds themselves'. This is an important decision 'because, if one moves on to connotative systems (literature being a case in point), the signifieds form nothing less than the ideology of the society which uses the system'. It follows that 'the principle [of literary criticism] will be to consider the work of literature (or a group of works, a corpus) as a *system of signification*'. However, 'since this system is "supported" by a pre-existent body of information, namely articulated language (French, for example), we are dealing in literature with one of the kinds of *meta-language*. Along with Hjelmslev, we can call this meta-language *connotation*'. (Our emphases for the most part.)

We can say right away that these comments tally with the general aesthetic-linguistic approach of *Critique of Taste* (from its first 1960 edition onwards), with the following specifications, however.

(1) Reference to Saussurian linguistics and its glossematic-structural developments in Hjelmslev, is inevitable for a sociological, non-romantic criticism and aesthetics. The reason is two-fold. Firstly, Saussurian linguistics takes as its object *la langue* or *glossa*, regarding it as a real, historical and social fact (or we could say, a superstructural phenomenon). It concerns itself, in other words, with the objective, unitary system of verbal signs, the *norm* which pre-exists individual speakers and makes them such. It is the opposite of romantic, Humboldtian, linguistics, which reduced natural language to just one of its elements, *la parole*, the subjective speech-act. Whether it is aware of it or not, traditional aesthetics and literary criticism (from Croce to Nicolai Hartmann or I. A. Richards) is based on this romantic linguistics. Secondly, Saussurian linguistics is the first to give us a complete, rigorous and unitary, concept of the verbal sign. As Hjelmslev himself says, there are two particular features of modern linguistics: 'that of insisting on the [linguistic] form which has hitherto been neglected in favour of substance [whether that be thought or the signified; or the signifier, the material aspect of sound or writing, or the material aspect of phonetic "expression"]; . . . [and] that of seeking to include within linguistic form not only the [phonetic] form of expression, but also the [grammatical] form of content [=the signified or thought]'.[1] Barthes's summary remarks on the 'decision not to limit the systems of signification to the signifiers alone' correspond to those principles.

(2) The linguistic 'form' so rigorously defined as at once grammatical

1. Cf. above, Sections 11-12 and the Note on Glossematics.

and phonetic (or, in glossematic terms, *pleremes* + *cenemes*, elements that 'can be filled' with thought and those that 'cannot'), functions as *instrumental form* – instrumental to the communication and expression of meanings, or thoughts or values; and hence as technical *means* towards *ends* – in other words, thoughts or values or *forms*; in short as 'form' in inverted commas.

(3) It follows that even when we are dealing with literary or poetic meanings, or thoughts, this technical 'form' is something with which we have to reckon. The thoughts of literature are expressed by connotation, that is to say, by terms which are not merely denotative (denoting ordinary meanings) and therefore belong to the vocabulary of the language, but which produce particular unprecedented associations of meanings. Therewith we are confronted by an immense and inescapable difficulty: the case of those meanings, thoughts or values, or true forms, whose communication or expression belongs to a given linguistic system, yet at the same time transcends the *system as such*, transcends indeed any *system* of a linguistic type. Barthes side-steps the difficulty by referring to the work of literature as a 'system of signification'; then, having made the point that each of these 'systems' or works of literature is 'supported' by the 'body of information' of ordinary language, he assigns literature to the rubric of a 'metalanguage' of connotation, or 'connotative systems' [systems of connotative terms], which in turn constitute the 'ideology' of the society which uses them. From there he proceeds to the questions of a 'semiology of literature' . . .

It is around this difficulty, side-stepped by Barthes, that our disagreement with him (and others) begins. But before going into the reasons for our dissent, let us hear him through. Barthes's final conclusions are as follows: 'It is true that every structural analysis tends to create artificial synchronies. It therefore gives the impression of more or less wanting to immobilize history. But this is only the first stage of structuralism. A diachronic [i.e. evolutionary] structuralism is possible. . . . As far as literature is concerned, connotative meanings remained stable for more than a thousand years. They formed what was called *rhetoric*, whose perfectly codified "figures" regulated literary signification from antiquity to the 19th century (at least in France). However, it seems that towards the end of that century a notable change took place. Certain figures (elements of the code) disappeared,

others came into being. The rhetorical code [i.e. system] was trans-
formed and with it, obviously, the whole "ideology" of literature.
This is the sort of phenomenon that ought to be studied by a criticism
which is both historical and structural. . . . Marxism has on the whole
succeeded in showing the relation between social history and ideological [literary, or rhetorical] contents. In Lukács and in Brecht it has
even been closely involved with a certain idea of form, given [sic] in
the shape of "genre" (the novel, tragedy, epic). But the language of
literature is still a mystery to it.'

There are a number of objections to be made here. Firstly, there is
not much point in appealing to modern linguistics just to restore
rhetoric to its former glory (with its 'genres' and schemas of tropes),
indeed even to hand over the functions of literary criticism to it. Criticism, as an approach to the peculiar organism which is the work of
literature, is a good deal closer and more pertinent than anything
that can be filtered through the screens of rhetorical 'genre'-abstrac-
tion (even if they are Brecht's poetic of the tragic epos!).

Secondly, Saussurian linguistics and Hjelmslevian glossematics
provide us with a complete and scientific account of the instrumental
'form' which the linguistic sign is. Thereby they provide us with the
basic material out of which the literary or poetic work is actually
constructed, its technical framework. This enables first the epistemologist, and then the literary critic, to follow through in the poetic
text the process (which is of cognitive interest) of transformation
from language to style – using 'style' in the full epistemological and
not abstractly 'formal' sense of the term. That process is adumbrated
in the difficulty which arises from the fact that the literary expression
of meanings or thoughts, values or forms, both belongs to and at the
same time transcends the linguistic system. The so-called 'mystery'
of poetry lies here and nowhere else.

Thirdly, it follows that if criticism is to be rigorous and scientific,
rather than a matter of chance impressions, it can only be a comparison of the two elements: to start with, the ordinary thoughts and
ordinary meanings and the instrumental 'form' related to them (the
totality of their lexical–grammatical and phonetic elements), which
are the specific and technical basis of the poetic text; and then, the
un-ordinary thoughts and meanings which are *developed* in the poetic
text from the ordinary. The originally denotative lexical terms are

developed into connotative terms, while, running parallel, certain related phonic developments may also occur – the two resulting in what can be defined as stylemes. The comparison between ordinary and un-ordinary is to be executed through *paraphrases* of the un-ordinary meanings and the connotative terms in which they are expressed. Such paraphrase, however, being relational and dialectical, must be *discriminatory*. The object of its discrimination will be nothing less than the switch, the separation or progress, of meaning or thought or (poetic) cognitive value, realized (expressed) by the stylemes, with respect to the values realized (communicated) by the glossemes, or elements of the linguistic–instrumental 'form'. Critical paraphrase/ paraphrase as criticism in short. Paraphrase, which has always been a heresy for critics of a mysticizing bent indifferent to language, ceases to be one. The ingenuous conception these critics have of paraphrase has never extended beyond an unrelated, undialectical, *uncritical* para-phrase, which they see as an alien interference with aesthetic *raptus* or poetic 'ineffability'.

Finally, the poetic text or literary opus, which has been constructed in this way by the poet and can be re-constructed by the epistemologist and the critic, does not simply contain 'literary ideology', in other words the poetic and rhetoric of a given society. It contains much more. It contains at the same time, or rather it expresses, the whole range of moral, political, social class-ideology. This is precisely because the poetic meanings or thoughts of which it is woven together are, as particular modes of *thought*, the appropriate discursive reflection of the ideals of an epoch. The focal point of such reflection may be one of Brecht's plays, *The Caucasian Chalk Circle* for example, or a poem like *To Those Born Later*, rather than, and in preference to, the *Kleines Organon für das Theater* which sets out his poetic of the 'genre' of 'epic theatre'.

2. The conclusion implied by my argument is a negative one, indeed, if I may be allowed to say so, it amounts to a veto. As we shall see, this does not only apply to Barthes. But, as both glossemes and stylemes are instrumental in relation to the end which is the poetic idea to be expressed, so their respective disciplines, linguistics and poetics and rhetoric (or stylistics, if you prefer), can*not* be regarded by the literary critic as ends, for the end of literary criticism is the poetic idea or its recovery. Another way of putting it would be to borrow the very clear terms used by the well-known German critic Hugo Friedrich,

who strikes the one discordant note in the chorus of contributions to the *Inquiry*. 'Structuralism', he writes, 'aims at a knowledge of the combinations of phonemes and morphemes in a text in relation to both their possibilities and their limitations. The text is considered from a purely neutral, linguistic point of view. Its [expressive] quality is not of concern.'

We now come to the linguistician Samuel Levin. He too, on the basis of developments in Saussurian linguistics, resolves criticism (to the extent that it is scientific) into a sort of rhetoric. Discussing for example the process whereby metaphor is understood, he argues that we can give no credit to the illusions of intuition, the sudden penetrations, the imaginative leaps, of impressionistic criticism. The nature of metaphorical meaning rather obliges the critic to explain it on the basis of his understanding of the linguistic model (of a Saussurian type). Here Levin believes that the notion of [grammatical] paradigm can be of use; he thinks it can help the critic to uncover something of the nature of metaphor and so bring out what is implicit in the 'illuminations' and 'leaps'.

As a concrete example, he cites Dylan Thomas's metaphor 'a grief ago'.[2] Levin explains that here the syntagmatic frame (the frame of the phrase) 'a . . . ago' defines a paradigm (adverb of time) of which 'grief' is not normally a member. The paradigm, which includes forms like 'day', 'while', 'year', has a temporal meaning. Taking 'a grief ago' as a metaphor, the usual meaning of 'grief' and the temporal meaning related to it by the syntagmatic frame in which it is placed are fused together. The metaphor is a result of this fusion, which in its turn can only properly be understood on the basis of a prior knowledge of the linguistic model [i.e. the linguistic system] conceived by Saussure. He adds that the analysis of this metaphor, as of Aristotle's 'the evening of life', provides us with a basis on which to distinguish between two different types, substantive-metaphor and temporal adverb-metaphor.

Now this is all very well and all very true, but it still leaves us in the

2. The phrase can only be translated into Italian at the cost of losing its metaphorical character and hence its expressive status as a styleme, which English on the other hand allows. It is therefore untranslatable: a very simple example of how language conditions style (which yet transcends language!) not only from the (better-known) point of view of phonetic characteristics, but also from the point of view of grammar.

domain of the conditioning of style by language. We are still essentially within the purview of Hjelmslev's principle that a given semanteme can be used as hyperbole or metaphor, but its *grammatical* function 'does not change' as a result.[3] But it is pretty obvious that this is a long way short of critical judgement, the judgement of value, in any proper sense. The critic is not directly interested in whether a metaphor belongs to one type or another. He takes note of it, but does not argue about it; he makes use of this knowledge as a step towards reaching his goal with much greater certainty than his impressionist colleague. But what he is directly interested in is whether this or that metaphor 'works' or is 'beautiful', and why. Or, which comes to the same thing, whether it does not work or is ugly and why, a case in point being the celebrated Dr. Johnson's assessment of Shakespeare's image in *Antony and Cleopatra* (Act IV, sc. IX, ll. 15–16):

> Throw my heart
> Against the flint and hardness of my fault,

which he judges and dismisses as a precious and meaningless a conceit.

Levin concludes that whether we use notions like *langue*, code, rules, grammar or something else, what really interests us is what might be the *system* lying behind the production of [poetic] texts and making them possible. So he too confuses means with ends, in this case linguistics and rhetoric with the evaluation of the concrete literary work. The result in practice is still the same. Technical schemas are used to approach the living work, they are turned into ends and become screens. The critic remains light-years away from the work.

3. Cesare Segre seems to have suspected something was amiss in Rosiello's contribution, the most disconcerting of the linguistic-critical efforts of Italian provenance. Segre would have made his point more effectively if he had addressed himself to the illustrious example of Roman Jakobson, who is the real inspiration behind Rosiello.[4]

---

3. Cf. above, p. 102; and see Christine Brooke-Rose, *A Grammar of Metaphor* cit., p. 44, from whom the Thomas example is probably taken.

4. Avalle, who is certainly no enemy of Jakobson, introduces a critical essay by Jakobson on Baudelaire's *Les Chats* in the following way: 'From the outset our attention is focussed on the grammatical and metrical structures of the text, independently of its content, as if what really matters is not so much the kind of

Even so, he finds himself in new and instructive aesthetic difficulties.

Segre says he disagrees with Rosiello's insistence on the 'cognitive' interest of the poetic message, which, according to Rosiello, is directed 'not towards the world of objects, but towards the possibilities of communication that can be realized through the structures of a given language system'. He disagrees because 'this "cognitive interest" and man's "systematic repossession" [of the means of communition], are purely means, whereby the writer is able (better than anyone else) to convey thoughts, feelings, ideals, imaginings. We repeat: they are means. Indeed, it even seems to us curious that a structuralist should so insist on the poetic message as against the ordinary message. For it appears as though he is willing to sacrifice *langue* to *parole*, the collective structures of the language, the general features of which are unitary, to the extreme and intentionally or intuitively deformed structures of writers.'

So far as Rosiello, who is trying to renovate statistical-stylistic criticism, is concerned, Segre is absolutely right. But there seems to us something no less 'curious' in the celebration by a philologist and linguistician like Segre of the 'magic' of the 'uncommunicated'. 'Let us recall', he says in a doubly curious way, 'the suggestive application of the second principle of thermodynamics to human communication (Wiener). It is peculiarly appropriate to the poetic message. The critic may seem desperately bent on recovering the energy from the heat of the poetic message which the poet has imparted to it. The good critic can minimize the losses, but the energy recovered will never be equal to that expended. In the gap that remains lies the magic of the uncommunicated.' In short: who is this suddenly materialising from behind all the structuralism and technical rationalism? None other than the pallid but tenacious shade of Don Benedetto himself. Poetry, the shade proclaims, is 'ineffable'.

Now we can see just what Segre has in mind, and it is essentially *negative*, when he puts linguistics back in its proper place, as a 'means'. His motive is a Crocean, essentially romantic, intention. Technique in general is not involved organically or positively (but still as technique, i.e. means not end) in artistic expression. It takes us only to the

message conveyed by the composition as the presence within it of verbal structures which are rigorously co-ordinated and capable of making it a morphologically and metrically autonomous organism'.

threshold of poetry. True entry is for contemplation alone, the intuition which 'burns every dross away'. For still the intellect is poetry's greatest foe.[5]

Segre, like so many others, is a pupil of Gianfranco Contini, a scholar contested several times in these pages, but in his absence. At this point it is inevitable that we should confront him directly. The work that particularly concerns us is the 'Preliminari sulla lingua del Petrarca' which he has prefaced to his edition of Petrarch's *Canzoniere* (Torino, Einaudi 1964). Maria Corti has defined these 'Preliminaries' as 'the archetype in Italy of a critical mould fitted to structuralist demands'. It is archetypical because the stylistic, or neo-stylistic, criticism practised by Contini focusses on the history of language, its sources and institutions.

We have already had occasion to comment on the lacunae of this philological or historicist formalism, for all the partial success of its ambition to improve upon impressionist criticism. We have for example pointed out the danger of distinguishing, or overemphasizing in an abstract way the historicity of the language (i.e. that of the technical 'form') of poetic invention, against its overall organic historicity – its historicity *tout court*. Only the latter is of interest to an integrally functional, non-formalist, criticism of poetry, such as a modern sociological literary criticism can and ought to be. Contini, it will be recalled, goes so far as to suggest that the linguistic historicity of the poetic invention is something added to its 'functionality', though it is difficult to see what this functionality is or what it is worth if it is not to be understood as that of philology or history in its integrity. The upshot in the 'Preliminari' is that Contini sees Petrarch's religious ideology, no less, (his God who 'intervenes to placate tedium and comfort fatigue', as against the 'theocentrism necessary to Dante') as 'entering simply as a *psychological* theme'. It therefore 'lies outside the structures and systems which we are describing' – which is true once the critic has taken this path and erected such barriers between himself and the poetic work. But the ideology of the poem, whether it is religious or of some other kind, is both the nucleus which generates its particular moral 'atmosphere' and the point at which it intersects with history (all in the form of

5. See 'I Limiti del Gusto Crociano' and 'Problemi di un' Estetica Scientifica', in G. Della Volpe, *Il Verosimile Filmico e Altri Scritti di Estetica*, Rome 1962.

connotation). But let us turn our attention to the explicit aesthetic conclusion of the 'Preliminari'.

The 'linguistic initiative' taken by Petrarch is the establishment of a 'middle tone'. Contini gives an account of this, demonstrates the poet's moderate 'violations' (of the norm), and points to one of his characteristic stylemes, the 'procession of emblematic substances [read: substantives]': emblematic in part, 'as Leopardi perceived acutely in a famous page of his *Zibaldone*, because of the generic nature of the words, accompanied by an immaculate scoring of the sounds'. He ends by examining some of those ' "liquid" or "ineffable" lines' which are 'particularly resistant to the acids of the laboratory'.

In the first of these 'most celebrated clauses', the line,

Primavera per me pur non è mai

(Spring for me yet never is: *Canzoniere* IX, 1. 14),

it will be found that 'this unutterable utterance can yet to some extent be measured from without. Its semantic translation ("but I am ever unhappy") is totally irrelevant. What is important is its untranslatability, its non-semantic import. For the expressionist, on the other hand, the transference into ordinary language always figures ideally between the lines. Of equally little importance is the fact that the metaphor might be explained within the context of the poem's "conceit" (the signs of spring return for others). On the contrary, the conceit, and *agudeza*, exist in function of this last line. . . . The line then is characterized by litotes [statement of an idea by denial of its opposite] on a vast scale. . . . It is negative by images. It is therefore in keeping with Petrarch's constant evasiveness (the use of substances which are not actualized; see our other comments). The line is characterized further by its abundance of words and stresses, within a single rhythm: the most full-bodied and aggressive word stands at the beginning; it has every chance to spread itself and withdraw, which would not be the case – and I apologize for perpetrating this collage – if the line read:

*pure per me non è mai primavera

(*yet for me it is never spring).

The line then is characterized, to use a long-established metaphor, by

andante, itself in keeping with Petrarch's constant rhythmic dominant. Thus a line that is not ... one of the violent type, nor properly
speaking of the intermediate melodic type, nor properly speaking of
the epigrammatic type, a line then which would seem to lend itself
least to our exercise, has in fact shown us two constants [i.e., evasiveness and rhythmic dominant] of such general applicability as to enable
us to bring our remarks to a close at this point.'

There are a number of comments to be made on Contini's conclusions:

(1) The statement that a possible explanation of the metaphor within
the context of the poem's 'conceit' is 'of equally little importance' has
two very serious consequences from the aesthetic–epistemological
point of view. The first is a complete evacuation of the metaphor (even
though it concerns one of those 'emblematic substances' on which
'evasiveness' depends), in so far as its expressive dynamic as a metaphor, the relation between tenor and vehicle, is thereby devalued. All
that is left is the bare word, a *flatus vocis*. It follows, secondly, that the
attempt to justify this procedure by saying that it is the metaphor, the
'conceit' that is *in function* of the line is tantamount to saying (whether
Contini means it or not) that the line with its valueless metaphor is
to be reduced simply to its rhythm, its 'sound-score'.

(2) In that case there is no point in trying to characterize the line by
drawing on the rhetorical figure of 'litotes' (la pauvre!) or the formal-
stylistic constant of 'evasiveness'. The litotes would just be an empty
shell. What image is supposed to be expressed by this line which is
stated to be 'negative by images'? Or better, what *idea* is expressed?
Perhaps the opposite demanded by litotes (still a *logical* value!) of the
idea of 'Spring', itself devalued and expunged as metaphor, i.e. as
connoter? The constant of 'evasiveness' would then be a mere empty
shell as well. For evasiveness purports to be the module of extremely
subtle thought (not thought which does not exist as such!); but given
what has been said, here there would be no idea or thought at all.

(3) So then there is no point either in characterizing the line by 'its
abundance of words and stresses'. Obviously, if the words have lost
their thought-content (it cannot be otherwise, as far as one can see),
they have also lost their character as 'words' in 'ordinary language' –
as those denotative terms which are the *basis* of connotative trans-
valuation. Thereafter the stresses absorb whatever is left of the cele-

brated line, through the 'rhythmic dominant'. It can then be dubbed with the far from rare metaphor of 'andante', made-for-the-convenience-of-literary-critics.

(4) Contini falls into epistemological confusion and critical contradiction, by simultaneously claiming in the spirit of Croce and aestheticism that the line is 'unutterable utterance', and admitting what Contini the technician could not avoid, that it can have a 'semantic translation' or *paraphrase* ('but I am ever unhappy') – even if the latter is 'totally irrelevant'. Firstly, the assertion of poetic 'unutterability' or 'ineffability' or aesthetic *raptus*, which Contini the mystic will not renounce, is threatened by the subsequent admission (something has to be done with that semanticity!). Then the paraphrase, which is seen generically as 'transference into ordinary language', is accorded a sort of expressive status as 'an ideal between the lines' – but only, it should be noted, 'for the expressionist'.

(5) Contini is thus driven to make a distinction between expressionist poetry (presumably referring to poetry that is particularly rich in historical and social feeling or thought or ideals) and non-expressionist poetry. The distinction might have some appearance of sense in the empirical field of a *poetic*, but it has none whatsoever from the rigorous, unitary point of view of aesthetics and epistemology. That much should be clear from the presence of Petrarch's *thought* in the poem, represented by the metaphor-idea of spring, the force that generates the 'liquid' line in question.

(6) Contini repeats the same mistake of disputing the critical relevance of 'transference into ordinary language' later in his exposition, when he compares the line to a phrase made up of the same words but in a different order and therefore with a different rhythm ('*pure per me non è mai primavera'). He excuses himself to the reader for 'perpetrating this collage', but it is clearly not a *collage*, or the sticking-together of totally heterogeneous elements. Rather, it is a comparison of elements which are not and yet are the same. The words are phonetically the same as those in the line, even if their order and rhythm in the line is changed. But the change cannot be perceived or evaluated except by a comparison with the order and rhythm of the same words translated into ordinary language or ordinary phrasing – in other words a dialectical comparison, necessary and inevitable, between different word-orders and rhythms.

(7) But if a translation into ordinary language or paraphrase is (critically!) relevant in the case of the rhythm of the line – provided, we repeat, that it is a dialectical paraphrase – it will be no less, indeed all the more, critically relevant to the semantic dimension or the meaning of the line. The reason is that the dialectical power which eminently characterizes concrete thought dwells in the semantic side of literary language (to limit ourselves to literature); which in turn is made possible by *la langue* itself, ordinary language, whose signs, the words of our vocabulary, are essentially vehicles of meaning or thought.

(8) Finally, the foregoing leads us to the conclusion that only a dialectical paraphrase, articulated as paraphrase both of meaning and of rhythm, is an adequate criterion for an integrally functional evaluation of literature. Such evaluation will be distinct from any trace of aestheticist criticism, of a view of poetry as 'unutterable utterance' (a supremely contradictory notion when professed by philologists). But it will also be distinct from all so-called structuralist criticism which tends to turn the literary critic's job into that of a linguistician (albeit a super-linguistician), or at best a modern rhetorician.

A Note on Glossematics

Here, in the words of its founder, are the two 'particular features' of glossematics which concern our epistemological analysis of the linguistic fact, inasmuch as they provide us with a rigorously unitary concept of the linguistic sign. 'Glossematics insists on the [linguistic] form which hitherto has been neglected in favour of substance [whether that be thought, or meaning; or the material aspect of sound or writing, etc., or the material aspect of phonetic "expression", etc.]; ... [and] it seeks to include within linguistic form not only the [phonetic] form of expression, but also the [grammatical] form of content [=thought]'. See L. Hjelmslev, *Essais Linguistiques*, Copenhagen 1959, pp. 37–8. For the purely instrumental character, as *means*, of the comprehensive 'form' (grammatical+phonetic, etc.) that is the linguistic sign, see Section 14 above.

In conformity with the above, Hjelmslev himself describes the biplanar structure of the linguistic sign as follows: 'Language is a form organized between two substances, of which one [thought] serves as its *content* and the other [sound, writing, etc.] as its *expression*. The elements of this form, or *glossemes* [from the Greek γλῶσσα, tongue] are therefore, on the one hand, those elements which serve to form the content, or *plerematemes* (from πλήρης: that which can be filled with a content) and, on the other, those elements which serve to form expression, or *cenematemes* (from κενός: that which cannot be filled with a content). The two *planes* of language which are thus constituted, the plerematic plane and the cenematic plane, are perfectly analogous in their structure' (*op. cit.*, p. 152). In strict glossematic terms then the linguistic sign is made up of cenemes plus pleremes – elements which 'cannot be filled' and others which 'can be filled' by thought.

As regards the unmotivated or 'arbitrary' nature of the linguistic sign with respect to thought-meaning, which cannot be dissociated from its indispensability (arbitrary or not) to thought, Hjelmslev, again referring back to Saussure, makes the following points in the *Prolegomena*, ed. cit., p. 52: 'Each language lays down its own boundaries within the amorphous "thought-mass" and stresses different factors in it in different arrangements . . . Just as the same sand can be put into different moulds, . . . so also the same purport is formed or structured differently in different languages. What determines its form is solely the functions of the language, the sign function and the functions deducible therefrom. Purport remains, each time, substance for a new form, and has no possible existence except through being substance for one form or another. We thus recognize in the linguistic *content* [=thought or 'purport'], in its process, a specific *form*, the *content-form* [=grammatical form], which is independent of, and stands in arbitrary relation to, the *purport*, and forms it into a *content-substance*. No long reflexion is needed to see that the same is true for the *system* of the content. A paradigm in one language and a corresponding paradigm in another language can be said to cover one and the same zone of purport, which, abstracted from those languages, is an unanalysed, amorphous continuum'. See also Nils Ege, 'Le Signe Linguistique est Arbitraire', in *Travaux du Cercle Linguistique de Copenhague*, 1949, vol. V, pp. 11–19; and Siertsema, below.

As regards the technical importance of glossematics, as a scientific instrument of linguistic analysis, suffice it to recall the following points. (1) 'The object of the quest, then, still remains (to use Hjelmslev's words) "the phoneme behind the sounds, the grammatical and lexical form behind the significations" ' (Kristen Möller, in *Travaux* cit., p. 94). (2) 'The semiological function between the two planes allows us to draw up an *inventory* of the elements by means of the *commutation-test*. Within a paradigm [="a class within a linguistic system"] there is *commutation* between two terms, the exchange of which can bring about an exchange of two terms on the other plane. There is, on the other hand, *substitution* between two terms of a paradigm which do not fulfil this condition. If there is commutation, the two terms are "invariants"; if there is substitution, they are variants of the same invariant. The test is then carried out in the same way on both planes, and the description of content and that of expression mutually presuppose each other.' (Eli Fischer Jørgensen, in *Travaux* cit., p. 216).

To conclude our discussion of this rigorous, complete and unitary concept of the linguistic sign with which Hjelmslev, and no-one else, has provided the epistemologist, we may compare the confusing and empirical traditional terminology of the following passage from the recent *Elements of General Linguistics*, tr. E. Palmer, London 1964, p. 94, by a master of the stature of André Martinet (an authoritative representative of 'diachronic structuralism'): 'Another example is the English significatum "to cut" and the significatum "past tense"; the significans of the former is /kʌt/; that of the latter most frequently /d/. But when these signs are brought together in the utterance, they are manifested conjointly in the form /kʌt/ in "he cut", for instance'. Here we find a 'past tense' that is a grammatical or plerematic *element* of the linguistic sign, taken as a *signified* ('significatum') in just the same way as the signified 'cut'! This is the sort of confusion that has been resolved by Hjelmslev. For this reason linguistics – as a *general* theory of the linguistic sign – can and should concern the epistemologist. For it is developing the kind of synthesizing or truly general criteria which alone can serve the general theory of knowledge (as a scientific discipline).

For the benefit of the reader who may be interested, we give below the Hjelmslevian table of glossemes, and of the two correlated planes of the linguistic sign, as laid out by Siertsema (op. cit., pp. 208–9) with the warning that 'it is a very much simplified scheme'. But first, some general clarifications, again from Siertsema (pp. 16–18):

'The study of the elements of thought, directed to the plane of the content (Fr. contenu) is called *plerematics*, the units it deals with are pleremes (from Gr. πλήρης = full: these units "contain" a "lump" of meaning [or thought], so to say). The study of the elements of the other plane of language, the elements of expression [phonemes or their graphic equivalents, etc.], is called *cenematics*, the units it deals with are *cenemes* (from Gr. κενός = empty: these units "contain" no meaning). That this part of glossematics, which studies the same units as phonology does, is nevertheless given another name, has its reason in the other theorem introduced by de Saussure and interpreted by glossematicians as meaning that language is *form*, not substance, and that it does not matter, therefore, what substance is used to make the form visible or audible or tangible, as long as it manifests the form. . . . If the substance is sound, for instance, a ceneme may materialize in entirely different sounds at different times in the history of a language. . . . The "substance" has *nothing to do* [D.V.'s emphases] with the form as such; "la forme linguistique", says Hjelmslev, "ne recouvre aucune forme extra-linguistique" ['linguistic form does not overlie any extra-linguistic form']. That is why, for the units of expression, the term *"phonemes"* would not do as being too narrow, and why the term "cenemes" has been created. In the same way the units of the content (pleremes) may according to Hjelmslev materialize in different significations and in different "things" in the world around us. . . . Also *this* "substance" has nothing to do with the content-*form* as such . . . e.g., the phenomenon that two entirely different "content-substances" such as a black and a brown cow are in one language united in *one* content-form "cow" whereas in another language, which has no word for "cow" but only for either "black cow" or "brown cow", they are "formed" in *two* different forms. Also the content-forms are only defined *by their relations* [D.V.'s emphases].

'Thus we see that both cenemes and pleremes are exclusively defined by their *relations*, that is, what Hjelmslev calls their *functions*: ". . . the important thing is . . . the preparation of the analysis so that it conforms to the *mutual dependences* [D.V.'s emphases] between these parts . . ." Cf. de Saussure: "In a language-state everything is based on relations. How do they function?" [ed. cit., p. 122].'

CONTENT PLANE (Plerematic)

Constituents (Pleremes)		*Exponents* (Morphemes)	
Central const.	*Marginal const.*	*Intense exp.*	*Extense exp.*
(radical elements)	(derivational elements)	(noun morphemes): case comparison number gender article	(verb morphemes): person voice stress aspect mood tense

EXPRESSION PLANE (Cenematic)

Constituents (Cenemes)		*Exponents* (Prosodemes)	
Central const. (vowels)	*Marginal const.* (consonants)	*Intense exp.* (accents)	*Extense exp.* (modulations)

Siertsema observes of this table (op. cit., p. 210): 'It will be noted that such units as radical elements, derivational elements, morphemes are presented as units in the *content* plane. When seeing the content units referred to by terms which have always been used to denote units of the expression, the reader should remember that what is meant is actually: *the* [grammatical] *concepts expressed by* those units. In "he sings", for instance, the morpheme is not -*s*, but there is the *group of morphemes*: third-person-singular, present-tense, active, indicative. All these morphemes are *expressed by* -*s*. The concept "sing-" of "he sings" is not a morpheme in Hjelmslev's sense, it is called a "radical element", by which is meant again: *the* [grammatical] *concept expressed by* the radical element in the expression.' Compare Sapir, op. cit., pp. 92, 93.

Thus, using the example of the German *Nacht* : *Nächte*, Saussure indicates both the 'grammatical fact' – that is, in Hjelmslevian terms, the 'intense exponent' or 'morpheme' of the noun which is 'number', belonging with the other morphemes of the noun to the 'pleromatic plane', or the plane of grammatical elements 'which can be filled' with sense or meaning (or thought), or the 'content' (thought) plane – and the corresponding 'phonetic' fact, i.e. 'without umlaut or final -*e*' (the singular) and 'with umlaut and -*e*' (plural), to which the corresponding Hjelmslevian terms are the 'accents' of the noun, its 'intense exponent', and the implicit 'central constituents' (vowels) and 'marginal constituents' (consonants), all of them belonging to the 'cenematic plane', or the plane of those elements 'which cannot be filled' by sense or meaning (or thought), or the 'expression' plane (phonetic expression of the 'content' or thought).

Index of Names